THE ETHICS OF EVANGELISM

THE ETHICS OF EVANGELISM

A Philosophical Defence of Ethical Proselytizing and Persuasion

Elmer Thiessen

Paternoster:
thinking faith

17 16 15 14 13 12 11   7 6 5 4 3 2 1

This edition first published 2011 by Paternoster
Paternoster is an imprint of Authentic Media Limited
PO Box 6326, Bletchley, Milton Keynes, MK1 9GG
authenticmedia.co.uk

British Library Cataloguing in Publication Data

A catalogue record for this book is available from the
British Library

ISBN 978-1-84227-724-9

Cover design by David McNeill
Printed and bound by Lightning Source

Contents

Preface

This book has grown out of a sense that something important has been missing in discussions of evangelism or proselytizing, in religions that are committed to the same. Christians, and more specifically, evangelical Christians, rarely give serious consideration to the question of the ethics of evangelism. This work attempts to fill this gap.

My first serious exploration of the ethics of proselytizing occurred in 1985 when I wrote a paper in response to Jay Newman's treatment of the subject in a chapter of his book entitled, *Foundations of Religious Tolerance* (1982; see Thiessen, 1985). A subsequent bibliographical search on the topic, uncovered only a handful of relevant articles on the ethics of proselytizing. In 1999, I hired a student in the Library and Information Studies program at the University of Alberta to do an electronic search for me. I am thankful to Dan Mirau for his careful work. Despite every attempt to broaden the search using a variety of related descriptors, very few relevant articles and books were uncovered, although a few more than in my initial searches. Clearly, there was work to be done on the ethics of proselytizing. Hence, this first book-length philosophical treatment of the topic. (The reader is referred to Appendix 2, for a detailed review of the relevant literature.)

As should already be apparent, this book has had a long gestation period. I am grateful to Medicine Hat College for granting me a sabbatical leave in 2000–2001, when I began serious work on this project. My thanks also go to the administration and the Board of Medicine Hat College who provided some research funds for this project during my final years at the college.

My sabbatical in 2000–2001 was divided between two universities. I am thankful to the Centre for the Study of Religion at the University of Toronto for accepting me as a Research Reader for the fall semester of 2000. It was wonderful to have access to the wealth of research materials in the many libraries at the University of Toronto. I spent many a delightful day browsing through the ornate college libraries that make up this great university.

I am also very thankful to Harold Coward and his colleagues at the Centre for Studies in Religion and Society at the University of Victoria, for the Non-Stipendiary Visiting Research Fellowship that I was awarded for the winter semester of 2001. I thoroughly enjoyed being part of a genuine community of scholars, an all-too-rare phenomenon at our universities. I also appreciated the opportunity to try out earlier versions of the arguments of this book in lectures at both these universities.

My thanks also go to Tyndale University College in Toronto, for my appointment as "Research Professor" for a three-year period, beginning in May 2008. This appointment has given me the needed time and resources to work on the final revisions of this manuscript.

I am indebted to various Canadian and American friends and colleagues for their encouragement, advice, criticisms and suggestions as I worked on this project. In particular I would like to thank Perry Glanzer of Baylor University, for reading a first draft of the entire manuscript, and for giving me ongoing valuable feedback as the project continued. I am grateful to Jill Gatfield, Gary Colwell, Nathan Kowalsky, Henry Hubert, and Roger Martin for the feedback they gave upon reading portions of the manuscript. My thanks also to Harold Coward, Ron Neufeldt, Greg Pritchard, Geoff Wichert, Dallas Miller, and Rod Reynar for helpful conversations, regarding this project.

I have benefited greatly from the comments of several anonymous readers. My thanks also to Robin Parry at Paternoster, for his help and encouragement with this project. I would also like to thank Gregory Thiessen, for his technical help in producing the illustrations. Finally, thanks to my wife, Magdalene, without whose love, support, and ongoing encouragement this book would not have come to fruition. I dedicate this book to the estimated 4,587 students I have taught over the years, and who in turn have taught me so much, as we engaged in philosophical dialogue in what I hope was an atmosphere of trust and openness.

Portions of this book have appeared previously in somewhat different form and are here used with permission.

- "Proselytizing without Intolerance", in *Studies in Religion: A Canadian Journal*, 1985, 14(3): 333–45. (Permission granted by the Canadian Corporation for Studies in Religion).

- "Christians and Jews and Proselytizing: a Response to David Novak", in *Religious Studies and Theology*, 2003, 22(2): 55–63, © Equinox Publishing Ltd., 2003.
- "Religion, Proselytism, and the Air Force Academy", at www.globalengage.org
- "The Problems and Possibilities of Defining Precise Criteria to Distinguish between Ethical and Unethical Proselytizing/Evangelism", in *CulticStudies Review*, 2006, 5(3): 374–89. (Permission to reprint a substantial portion of this article has been granted by the International Cultic Studies Association.)

Quotations from the Bible are from the New International Version. Quotations from the Qur'an are based on a contemporary translation by Ahmed Ali, published by Princeton University Press, second revised edition, 1988.

The cartoon appearing in chapter 7 is reproduced with permission of Punch Ltd., www.punch.co.uk.

A brief overview of this work will hopefully entice the reader to continue reading. The first chapter addresses the question of defining the term "evangelism" showing how it is related to other terms like "proselytizing" and "mission". I also argue that the term should not be seen as restricted to a religious context. Evangelism or proselytizing occurs in a wide variety of contexts, including ordinary conversations, education, advertising, and public relations. Chapter 1 also cites examples, both popular and academic, of a variety of objections to proselytizing.

In chapter 2, I provide some further contexualization of my argument by examining the religious impulse to proselytize. Here I refer to three religions, Christianity, Islam, and Judaism, the latter being used as an example of a supposedly non-proselytizing religion. I illustrate my arguments throughout the book by referring to these three religions. I also refer to the cults or new religious movements (NRMs), though I avoid making the assumption that only they are guilty of unethical proselytizing.

This book has three central objectives: (a) to answer objections that are frequently raised against proselytizing and to defend the possibility of an ethical form of proselytizing (chapters 3–5); (b) to defend the practice of proselytizing generally (chapter 6); and (c) to develop criteria to distinguish between ethical and unethical proselytizing or evangelism (chapters 7 and 8). Various writers have called for a code of ethics for proselytizing, and I trust this work will make a contribution to that end. The book concludes with some suggestions on how to encourage and reinforce ethical proselytizing (chapter 9).

I want to stress at the outset that this work is not a blanket defence of all proselytizing. Indeed, while working on this project, there were times when I felt that with all the horrible things that religions have done throughout history, also with regard to winning converts, it was foolish, if not inappropriate, for me to write a defence of proselytizing. Proselytizing religions don't deserve to be defended, I would some-times think to myself. But then again, we need to be fair. We need to go where the argument carries us, as Plato said so long ago. And so I have tried to provide what I hope is a careful and fair philosophical defence of proselytizing, while at the same time, condemning immoral forms of proselytizing, which sadly have been all too frequent throughout the history of mankind.

Since my goal is to defend religious proselytizing against various objections, I would hope that both those making the objections, as well as those who often find themselves trying to answer these objections would benefit from reading this book. The intended readership includes both skeptic and religious believer. I would anticipate that various religious traditions would also welcome my attempt to pro-vide a clear and careful analysis of the distinction between what is and what is not morally acceptable in proselytizing. In a world that seems to be characterized increasingly by religious hostility and conflict, it is my hope that this book will make a small contribution to creating an environment of greater tolerance and harmony.

Elmer Thiessen,
January 2010

Part I:

Some Introductory Considerations

Chapter 1

Introduction

The topic of evangelism (or proselytizing, or the making of religious converts, or missions) tends to stir up a lot of controversy today. There is no better place to get honest opinions about just about any matter, than in discussion forums on the internet. Here, for instance are some comments on proselytizing made by "WindListener", prompting 99 additional responses in a religious newsletter, BeliefNet:

> I have nothing against the Christian religion itself. But I am tired of evangelical people going around the world forcing their religion on people. It's just not right! Most other religions don't have public sermons on TV every Sunday morning or have people going door-to-door trying to get people to convert. This just drives me crazy. Why can't they keep their belief to themselves? I know (about) freedom of speech and everything, but if I wanted to listen to a preacher I would go to a church or something like that.
>
> Also about missionaries, maybe they can lay off a bit about preaching their religion. I commend them for going into countries and helping the sick, but why do they have to put in their opinions on religion while doing so? Can't people just help for the damn sake of helping or is that too hard to ask without some other reason for doing so?[1]

In another dialogue on the same site, Tix makes this comment: "The call for this active, very aggressive proselytizing is what I find one of the most repulsive doctrines of Christianity." Astro5 is even more

---

[1] Retrieved on July 9, 2009, from http://www.beliefnet.com/boards/message_list.asp?pageID=1&discussionID=24208 (posted Sept 4, 2003). I have edited these comments slightly, correcting some obvious errors in spelling and grammar.

blunt: "Killing is wrong, but Christianizing the world is just as wrong."[2]

In the United Kingdom, the Department of Health recently published some guidelines defining how far public sector workers can go in communicating their faith in the workplace. The document entitled, "Religion or Belief: A Practical Guide for the NHS", is an attempt to give practical advice to all National Health Service organizations to help them comply with recent equality legislation. This document includes a section entitled "Proselytising", beginning with the recognition that some religions expect their members to preach and to try to convert other people. However, in a workplace environment, the document maintains, "this can cause many problems, as non-religious people and those from other religions or beliefs could feel harassed and intimidated by this behavior". Hence all organizations falling under the NHS are to make it clear from the first day of training or employment that such behavior will be dealt with "under the disciplinary and grievance procedures".[3]

These guidelines were the basis of the action taken by North Somerset Primary Care Trust in December of 2008 against a community supply nurse – an evangelical Christian – who engaged in a form of proselytizing on her job.[4] Caroline Petrie, after she had dressed her patient's legs, asked if she would like her to say a prayer. The patient politely declined the offer, and Caroline simply wished her well and left. Although Caroline thought no more about it, the patient mentioned the incident to another nurse the next day. Caroline was confronted that day by a nursing sister who told her the patient had been "taken aback" by the offer. The next day Caroline received a message on her home phone from her co-ordinator telling her that disciplinary action would be taken. She was summoned to an hour-long disciplinary hearing and formally suspended, based on the equality and diversity policies of the NHS.

---

[2] Retrieved on July 21, 2009 from http://www.beliefnet.com/boards/message_list.asp?boardID=426&discussionID=208381 (posted Dec 29 2002, and Jan 1, 2003). Again, I have corrected some spelling or typing errors.

[3] "Religion or Belief: A Practical Guide for the NHS", published by the Department of Health, UK (Jan 2009), p. 22.

[4] The description of this case draws on two articles, one by David Wilkes and Neil Sears, "Persecuted for praying: Nurse who faces the sack after offering to pray for sick patient", *The Daily Mail* (Feb 1, 2009), p. 1; and Nick Constable, "Exclusive: The nurse suspended for offering prayer gives her first interview" (Feb 7, 2009), retrieved on July 1, 2009, from http:/dailymail.co.uk/news/article-1138624/Exclusive.

During a later interview with a reporter, Caroline recalled part of the conversation with the disciplinary panel. "I explained the last thing I wanted was to cause patients distress. If they are very anxious then it might not be appropriate. I will never impose my beliefs on people, but I cannot divorce my faith from my job." The patient too told a reporter later, "It didn't worry me, it just struck me as a strange thing for a nurse to do . . . Personally I wouldn't want to see her sacked for something like that."

Caroline, convinced her suspension was unjustified, contacted the Christian Legal Centre, an organization that advises on potential conflicts between questions of faith and the law. After hearing the advice of one of its consultants, she decided to go public. The resulting publicity and the national outcry led to Caroline's reinstatement by the North Somerset Primary Care Trust.

Reports about several Christian organizations readying teams to enter Iraq soon on the heels of the completion of the "liberation" of Iraq by U.S. and British troops in March of 2003 created quite a stir in the media.[5] The Southern Baptist Convention, the largest Protestant denomination in the southern United States, and Franklin Graham's Samaritan's Purse had workers on the Iraqi-Jordanian borders ready to enter Iraq even before the war was over. While these organizations claimed their first priority would be to provide food, shelter, and other needs to war-ravaged Iraqis, they were quite forthright in admitting that when convenient they would also share their Christian faith with the Iraqis. Ibrahim Hooper of the Council on Islamic-American Relations expressed concern about the tendency of evangelical groups to obscure their proselytizing agenda with humanitarian aid: "They go after them when they're most vulnerable and hope that can get them to leave their faith. It's a very despicable practice."

In the spring of 2005, a story about proselytizing at the U.S. Air Force Academy in Colorado Springs, captured news headlines for quite some time. A task force was appointed to investigate accusations that "officers, staff members, and senior cadets inappropriately used their positions to push their evangelical Christian beliefs on cadets."[6] The task force eventually cleared the Academy of "overt religious discrimination", but the report went on to say that the Academy had failed to

---

[5] "Poised and Ready", by Deborah Caldwell – retrieved on July 11, 2009, from http://www.beliefnet.com/Faiths/2003/04/Poised-and-Ready.aspx; "Aid and Religion", by Doug Saunders, *The Globe and Mail* (Apr 9 2003), p. A7.

[6] My description of this case draws from Laurie Goodstein's article, "Air Force Chaplain Tells of Academy Proselytizing", *New York Times* (May 12, 2005), p. A16;

fully accommodate all members' religious needs, that there was a lack of awareness as to where the line is drawn between permissible and impermissible expression of religious beliefs, and that there were some cases where faculty members and officers were too aggressive in sharing their evangelical faith.[7]

The Dalai Lama stepped into one of the hottest religious controversies in South Asia in January 2001, when he joined a radical Hindu group in India in condemning the Muslim and Christian practice of actively seeking converts. "Whether Hindu or Muslim or Christian, whoever tries to convert, it's wrong, not good," the Dalai Lama said after a meeting with leaders of the World Hindu Council.[8] One of the objectives of this influential council is to make multi-religious India a Hindu state. "I always believe it's safer and reasonable to keep one's own tradition or belief," the Dalai Lama, winner of the Nobel peace prize, said.

Proselytizing on college and university campuses also frequently makes the news and is most often found to be very objectionable. Carolyn Kleiner, in an article entitled, "A Push Becomes a Shove: Colleges get Uneasy about Proselytizing", describes the phenomenon thus:

> Stroll across almost any college campus, and it's likely you'll spot a flurry of religious recruiting: colorful fliers touting Bible study and Sabbath dinners; tables staffed by bright-eyed young people offering pamphlets on everything from the Sikh faith to paganism.[9]

In 1999 the Maryland state legislature convened a controversial task force to study the effects of dangerous groups at its public colleges and

Melanie Hunter's article, "Air Force Academy Does Not Overtly Discriminate on Religious Grounds, Report Says", retrieved on June 26, 2005 from http://www.cnsnews.com//Page=\Culture\archive\200506\CUL2005; and Carolyn Bolls' article, "Group Fears Air Force is Discriminating Against Christians", retrieved on Nov 28, 2009, from http://www.crosswalk.com/news/religiontoday/1338588.html.

[7] A more recent controversy concerning U.S. soldiers surfaced following the release of a YouTube/Al Jazeera video showing soldiers being encouraged to spread the message of their Christian faith among Afghanistan's predominantly Muslim population. The footage also suggests that U.S. soldiers gave out Bibles in Iraq. See an article posted by Al Jazeera English – Central/S.Asia. http://english.aljazeera.net/nes/asia/2009/05/20095320131585432.html (accessed May 25, 2009).

[8] Retrieved on Jan 26, 2001, from CNN.com News - "Dalai Lama condemns Christian Muslim practice of converts". http://www.cnn.com/20...south/01/25/india.lama/index.html.

[9] *U.S. News & World Report* (Mar 13, 2000), p. 49.

universities. The task force was started after the parents of a University of Maryland student lodged a complaint about their daughter being a victim of a cult recruiter on campus. The girl had gone to a dorm adviser for advice, but the dispensed wisdom came complete with an invitation to join the advisor's religion.[10] Concerns about this sort of proselytizing prompted the university police at the University of Toronto to carry an article in the student manual warning about aggressive religious recruiting, encouraging them to contact the police if they were having any difficulties with such groups.[11]

Proselytizing has also become an issue in schools in the U.S., sometimes even leading to court action. An Indiana public school teacher, who was fired after he ignored warnings to stop proselytizing in the classroom, lost his final appeal before the U.S. Supreme Court. Helland, a substitute teacher in South Bend, was removed from the substitute list in 1993 after fifth graders complained he was interjecting religious topics into instruction. School officials noted they had repeatedly warned Helland to stop proselytizing and carrying a Bible into class. Helland refused, insisting his religious freedom was being violated.[12] Several cases involving students delivering overtly religious messages during graduation ceremonies have also made their way to court.[13] In the United Kingdom, a five-year-old girl in a Devon primary school was scolded for talking to a classmate about Jesus.[14]

As a final illustration of public controversies regarding proselytizing, I want to mention the many countries in which proselytizing is prohibited. Laws are often simply a means to reinforce what is seen to be highly objectionable or even immoral. Thus most Islamic states prohibit or severely restrict foreign missionary activity within their borders. In countries where the Orthodox Church is dominant, foreign

---

[10] *U.S. News & World Report* (Mar 13, 2000), p. 49.

[11] Retrieved on July 14, 2003, from http://www.utm.toronto.edu/~police/religious.html. This warning seems to have been removed (checked July, 2009). See also essays in Rudin (1996) for suggestions on policing cult recruitment on university campuses.

[12] Reported in *Church & State* (Mar, 1997) p. 3. (*Helland v. South Bend Community School Corporation*, 1997).

[13] See *School Law News* 31.3 (Mar 2003), pp. 1–3.

[14] The incident made headlines after the girl's mother, a receptionist at the same school, was reprimanded after the principal got a hold of an email the mother had sent to some of her church friends, asking for prayer. Caroline Gammel, "Primary school receptionist 'facing sack' after daughter talks about Jesus to classmate" (Feb 11, 2009). Retrieved on July 25, 2009 from http://www.telegraph.co.uk/news/newstopics/religion/4590870/Primary-school-receptioni...

proselytizing is seen as an intrusion or even a subversion of state/church identity. Lest it be thought this phenomenon is restricted to communist and Islamic countries, it needs to be pointed out that legal constraints on proselytizing also exist in Western liberal democracies.[15] Even in North America, there has been much controversy surrounding attempts to introduce laws to curtail the proselytizing activities of various new religious movements, cults, and more recently anti-abortion groups (Sawatsky 1986).[16]

Many more examples of controversies concerning proselytizing could be provided. Indeed, more will be provided as my argument proceeds. My intent here is simply to illustrate that proselytizing is often in the news, that it is most often seen as a very controversial topic, and that most often it is described in pejorative terms, even as an immoral activity. This book is an exploration of the ethics of proselytizing. Is it ever morally right to engage in proselytizing? If so, what criteria can we use to distinguish between ethical and unethical forms of proselytizing? These are the central questions to be addressed in this monograph.

Definitions

Proselytizing. I have discovered, when I have tried it out in the classroom, that this word is not familiar to many students. However, Lawrence Uzzell describes the term as having become "the world's most overused religious term", and growing "less and less precise the more often the word is used" (16, 14). The term has also acquired a widespread pejorative connotation.[17] Indeed, because of its overuse and because it has acquired a strongly negative connotation by those

---

[15] For some examples, see Aagaard (1998, 467–68) and Kerr (1999, 11).

[16] Achal Mehra (1984), in a review of some of the 150 court cases which the International Society of Krishna Consciousness now is, or has been, involved in, as it seeks to protect its members' rights to perform sankirtan which it sees as an extension of the First Amendment protection for speech activities in public places, concludes that these court decisions are leading to an erosion of proselytizing rights in America. Mehra also draws attention to the battle the Jehovah's Witnesses have had in U.S. courts in the 1930s and 1940s in order to retain the right to proselytize (109). This battle would seem to be continuing worldwide as the Jehovah's Witnesses face opposition to their persistent evangelism (How and Brumley 1999). See Appendix 2, #E for further references.

[17] Garnet has noted that in "sophisticated circles" the connotations of the term "are almost always more negative, even sinister" (2005, 465).

opposed to all forms of Christian evangelism, Uzzell recommends that we retire the term "to the linguistic museum where it belongs" (2004, 16). However, I still want to use the term, and shall argue for a neutral definition.

As I have already indicated, I am using *evangelism*, or *missions*, or *the making of religious converts*, as synonyms for *religious proselytizing*. Other words and phrases describe the same phenomenon. *Religious recruitment* is often used when talking about the proselytizing activities of cults or new religious movements. Evangelical Christians prefer the use of terms like *evangelism, witnessing, sharing one's faith, saving souls,* or *proclaiming the gospel. Pushing* or *peddling the faith* is how many critics would describe proselytizing.[18]

Clearly the words or phrases introduced in the previous paragraph do not all mean exactly the same thing. But, there is a core meaning. I want to focus on the core meaning of these terms – seeking to bring about a religious conversion in another. The *Oxford English Dictionary*, defines proselytize as "To make proselytes". Proselyte is defined as "One who has come over from one opinion, belief, creed, or party to another; a convert."[19]

But what exactly is involved in conversion? Again, the OED includes the following as definitions of convert:

> 1. To turn in mind, feeling, or conduct. 2. To cause to turn to a religion, belief, or opinion. 3. To cause to turn from a sinful to a religious life. 4. To turn into something different; to transform; to change in character or function.

I want to test this definition and see if we can tighten it somewhat. There is obviously some arbitrariness in doing so, since the understanding of religious conversion varies across religious traditions and over time. But I believe there are still some essential commonalities. Each of the four dictionary meanings just considered begins with "to turn" or "to cause to turn". Everybody, I'm sure, would agree that change is at the heart of conversion. Most people will also agree that a religious conversion involves, amongst other things, a change of beliefs. Jay Newman, for example, restricts the meaning of proselytizing to

---

[18] See title of the anthology by Marty and Greenspahn (1988).

[19] The English term proselyte comes from the Greek word meaning "one who has come to a place", or "one who has arrived". Philo of Alexandria used the term to refer to someone who had left polytheism to join Judaism (Hill 1997, 323). For a biblical and historical overview of proselytism, see Stalnaker (2002, 339–47).

bringing about a change of beliefs (1982, 88–9). This would seem to be the primary focus in our understanding of conversion, but surely changes in behavior are normally assumed to follow from a change of belief. Thus the *OED* refers to a change from a sinful to a religious life, or a change in character or function. Implicit in such a change of belief and behavior there is also a change of identity, of who you are. Finally there is a corporate dimension to conversion – a re-socialization into an alternative community. Hence, a change of belonging. Thus Alan Kreider has described a genuine religious conversion as involving a change of belief, behavior, and belonging (1999, 1–2).[20] Proselytizing or evangelism therefore involves any activity in which a person or an organization is trying to convert another person or group of people in the four senses just described.

Here some further distinctions might be in order. Conversion can be brought about in a variety of ways. Sometimes the lifestyle of a person can lead another to inquire about that person's religious faith, eventually leading to a conversion. Does proselytizing occur in this case? Well, in some sense, yes. Surely covert proselytizing is still an instance of proselytizing. Proselytizing can be intentional or unintentional, direct or indirect, and overt or covert. These qualifiers can be attached to proselytizing, but interestingly the word proselytizing is still being used in all these expressions.

However, most often what we are thinking of when we use the word proselytizing is the intentional, direct, and overt communication that results in someone's conversion. Even in the examples of covert proselytizing in the previous paragraphs, it is most often the communication resulting from inquiries regarding an attractive life-style that will finally lead to conversion. So proselytizing in the full sense must involve

---

[20] Lofland and Skonovd (1981) provide a careful analysis of various conversion motifs that have emerged in the burgeoning research on conversion. They refer to the oft-quoted definition of conversion as given by Richard Travisano: "a radical reorganization of identity, meaning, life" (Lofland and Skonovd 1981, 375). For a more recent discussion of conversion, see the essays in Lamb and Bryant (1999). In their introduction, Lamb and Bryant suggest that conversion be understood in terms of a sliding scale, "from the dramatic personal and inward experience of being turned around, to a very external institutional and formal process of induction into a religious community" (12). Although the focus here seems to be more on the process of conversion, both extremes on this sliding scale still would seem to include Kreider's description of conversion as a change of belief, behavior, identity, and belonging. Janja Lalich prefers the term worldview shift, and similar to Kreider includes the adopting of a new perspective and becoming a practicing adherent as essential elements of conversion (2004, 15).

some explicit verbal communication. Consider another example. Sometimes people are converted as a result of humanitarian aid. Mission agencies are often engaged in educational, agricultural, and medical activities as part of their missionary activities. These activities and acts of charity can lead to people being converted.[21] Is this proselytizing? Again, this can be classified as indirect proselytizing. But, typically, these activities will be accompanied by some form of verbal communication, and it is only here where we would begin to talk of proselytizing. While we will need to explore the connection between humanitarian aid and proselytizing, the focus in this book will be on proselytizing in the form of explicit verbal communication that is intended to lead someone to convert.

We are now in a position to provide a formal definition of the central meaning of proselytizing which will be the focus of this study.

> Proselytizing = (def.) The deliberate attempt of a person or organization, through communication, to bring about the conversion of another person or a group of persons, where conversion is understood to involve a change of a person's belief, behavior, identity, and belonging.

I would now like to compare this understanding of proselytizing with words often associated with or used instead of the word proselytizing. First of all, it should be noted that proselytizing is only one facet of the mission of various religions. Judaism, while it tends to de-emphasize proselytizing, nevertheless sees itself as having a mission. Israel's vocation is to be "a light to the nations".[22] This broader sense of mission is also shared by other religions. Closely related to this mission of upholding the good and calling the nations to return to what is just and moral is the social mission of the various religions. The Torah, for example, commands the children of God "to be openhanded toward your brothers and toward the poor and the needy in your land" (Deut 15:11). Again, the question arises as to the relation between this kind of a social mission and proselytizing. Clearly they are different, and yet humanitarian aid as an expression of social mission can lead to proselytizing and conversion. There is also a political dimension to the

---

[21] For example, in a *Time* essay on "The New Missionary" (27 Dec, 1982, pp. 42–48), the work of Jesuit missionary Father John Dahlheimer and 366 other Christian workers in Nepal are described. Though proselytizing is forbidden in this officially Hindu land, and although these missionaries obey this law, yet their example has inspired more than 3,000 Nepalese to convert since 1954.

[22] See Isa 42:5–7; 60:3; Novak (1995, 158).

Islamic understanding of mission, which again has its parallels in other religions. This brief review of other dimensions of religious mission must suffice to help us better understand the central focus of this book, which is on proselytizing. *Proselytizing is only one part of the mission of most religions.* Other aspects of the broader mission of religions will be dealt with only insofar as they relate in some way to proselytizing.

As already suggested, many Christians prefer to use the word "evangelism" instead of "proselytizing". Evangelism too has a variety of connotations. These vary from "evangelism is social action", to evangelism is "announcing the gospel to non-Christians with a view to faith and conversion and their eventual incorporation into the Church by baptism."[23] We see in the latter connotation the core meaning of my definition of proselytizing. Proselytizing, for Christians, includes the task of proclaiming the gospel. In the Middle Ages, the word propaganda was even used to describe the mission of the Roman Catholic church (Marlin 2002, 15). Given the pejorative overtones associated with propaganda today, this term is no longer viewed by the church as a suitable synonym for evangelism, though critics would no doubt disagree. It should be noted, however, that in Latin countries "propaganda" simply means advertising, with no negative associations attached, although with time, the term will no doubt be affected by one's perceptions of what is being propagated (Marlin 2002, 16).

Another very important use of the term "proselytizing" merits some comment. As already noted, the term is often used as having a strongly pejorative, even sinister, connotation by those opposed to all forms of Christian evangelism.[24] Even in Christian circles the term is used in a pejorative sense to denote evangelistic *malpractice* (Anderson 1996, 1). A Catholic study of the problem of the defection of new immigrants from Catholicism contrasts Christian witness and proselytism. Proselytism is a corrupted form of witness according to this study (King 1991, 14). Now clearly one can choose to introduce different words to describe the positive and negative forms of the same phenomenon. But this seems rather arbitrary. Surely it is better to use the same word to describe the same phenomenon, and then distinguish between moral and immoral expressions of this phenomenon. To introduce two different words to

---

[23] Cited in Thangaraj (1999, 335).

[24] John Graz, in his opening remarks to a conference on proselytizing, held in Spain in 1999, suggests the term is used mainly in a negative manner. "Proselytism and Religious Freedom", *FIDES LIBERTAS: The Journal of the International Religious Liberty Association* (1999), p. 7. See also Gruen (1985, 301), Langone (1985, 374–75), Uzzell (2004), and Garnett (2005, 465–66).

describe efforts to convert another encourages a tendency to skirt issues needing to be faced. This in turn leads to charges and counter-charges being made, with issues seldom being resolved. As has been noted by several writers, what is evangelization to one person or group is prose-lytizing to another.[25] I have therefore chosen to define the word prose-lytizing in a neutral way, which then allows for the possibility of ethical and unethical ways to proselytize.

Another special and narrower sense of proselytizing needs to be brought to the fore. For the last four decades the problem of proselytiz-ing in this narrower sense has been the special concern of ecumenically minded Protestant, Orthodox, and Roman Catholic leaders.[26] Here pros-elytizing refers to the attempt to attract Christians from a particular church tradition to another church. Opponents to this kind of evangel-istic malpractice sometimes refer to it as sheep-stealing, i.e. stealing members (sheep) from someone else's church. Criticisms of this "war for souls" have been raised recently and most vehemently by the Orthodox Church since the break-up of the former Soviet Union (Witte/Bourdeaux 1999). For example, in August 1992 the heads of the two most venerated Episcopal sees in Armenian Christianity issued a joint encyclical entitled "Fatherly Advice". The two patriarchs objected to the notion that Armenia was a field ripe for proselytism. "Armenia is not a mission-field for Christian evangelism," they insisted. They spoke of proselytizing as soul stealing, the illicit conversion of Christians from one confession to another within an already Christianized nation. This activity is "a threat to Christian unity . . . and to national unity" (Guroian 1999, 231).[27]

One of the problems with the repeated condemnations of prosely-tizing in this narrow sense is that this pejorative and narrow notion of

---

[25] See, for example, Robeck (1996, 2) and Haughey (1998, 257).

[26] For some important essays on this narrower sense of proselytizing, see Appendix 2, #D2.

[27] Another region where the issue of proselytizing in this narrower sense has been, and still is festering, is in Latin America. According to the Latin American Catholic Bishops Conference, some 8,000 Roman Catholics a day convert to other Christian bodies, most of them Pentecostal. It is this phenomenon that prompted Pope John Paul II to caricature the charismatic and neo-Pentecostal churches in Latin America as "rapacious wolves" in his opening address to the 1992 Conference of Latin American Bishops (Kerr 1999, 12). Robeck questions this interpretation of what the Pope said, but admits others have said as much (1996, 4). Again in 1996, during Pope John Paul II's visit to Latin America, he highlighted the Catholic resentment towards evangelical "prosperity" (Lerner 1998, 479). For another statement of Catholic resistance to proselytizing, see Roland Minnerath (2000).

proselytizing is invariably loaded with other nuances, which then make it easy to condemn proselytizing or sheep-stealing. For example, in a case study of a major ecumenical effort at evangelism in Russia, Nicastro concludes a discussion of definitions of proselytizing with a synthetic definition: "aggressive targeting and winning of converts from their (recognized) church to one's own, especially through improper means" (1994, 226). In a study document of a Joint Working Group of the World Council of Churches and the Roman Catholic Church, the term "proselytism" is applied to "activities of Christians to win adherents from other Christian communities," based on "unworthy motives" or done by "unjust means that violate the conscience of the human person" (1996, 216).

Definitions such as these simply confuse the matter. We need to separate the issue of trying to convert someone already belonging to a church, from the issue of using unjust or improper means in doing so. Obviously the use of unjust or improper means such as coercion or distortion of other churches' beliefs and practices is immoral. But is the attempt to convert someone when he or she already belongs to a church – is this in itself immoral? This question needs to be treated separately. Most Christians, including evangelical Christians who are frequently the target of charges of proselytizing in this narrow sense, acknowledge the wrongness of unjust means of evangelism that violate the conscience of the human person (Robeck 1996, 7). But is winning adherents from other Christian communities in itself immoral?

It is beyond the scope of this book to address this question in detail. To do so would involve a consideration of some theological issues having to do with the nature of the church and the nature of conversion. Briefly, regarding the theology of the church, virtually all the churches in formerly Soviet and Communist countries think of themselves as national churches and therefore assume a kind of ownership over the cultures and societies whose names are most often affixed as adjectives to the church, e.g. the Russian Orthodox Church (Guroian 1999, 242). Evangelical groups engaged in evangelism in such contexts belong to what is sometimes referred to as the free-church tradition, having its origins in the radical Reformation. Here conversion is understood in individualistic terms, directly challenging the emphasis on group identity in the pre-Reformation *landeskirche mentalität* that still pervades some branches of Christianity (Nicastro 1994, 241).

Debate concerning proselytizing in the narrow sense also hinges on the nature of what it means to be a Christian. For example, an evangelical trying to convert someone who is a lapsed Catholic does not consider the latter to be a genuine Christian. Catholics may not like such categorizations, but there are some theological differences here that need to be understood and perhaps even respected.

As already suggested, it is not possible here to do justice to the theological issues underlying the controversy surrounding the narrow sense of proselytizing. Nor is it necessary to do so. I want to bracket these issues and focus on what this narrow sense of proselytizing and poroselytizing in general have in common. Again, I use the term proselytizing in its broad and neutral sense, referring to any attempt to convert another person, whatever his or her religious or irreligious affiliations. Many people today maintain proselytizing in this broad and neutral sense is most often, if not always wrong. This is the position to be evaluated in the following chapters.

A final and very important point needs to be made with regard to the definition of proselytizing. This study will focus on religious proselytizing. But proselytizing is not limited to the area of religion. We have seen that the *OED* defines proselyte in terms of a person who has been brought over to any opinion, belief, creed, or party, though the term applies especially to a change from one religious belief to another. Similarly, the word "convert" is not limited to religion. Again, the *OED* defines "convert" in terms of a turning "in mind, feeling, or conduct", or causing "to turn to a religion, belief, or opinion", or even more generally – "To turn into something different; to transform; to change in character or function." So proselytizing, understood as trying to bring about a conversion, in terms of a change of belief, behavior, identity, and belonging can be applied to other areas.

Take for example the area of commercial advertising or marketing. What is really being attempted in advertising is to bring about a conversion. Think of the commercial success of Amway, which, it should be noted, is short for the American Way. Amway is all about selling a certain lifestyle. Randal Marlin, in his recent treatment of propaganda, includes the massive promotion of the McDonald's fast-food chain in North America as an example of propaganda, and I would add that it also falls under the category of proselytizing. Marlin describes an advertising executive who boasted some years ago that in America, McDonald (the clown) had "a recognition factor among children second only to Santa Claus" (2002, 23). Of significance here is also Naomi Klein's study showing how many items are marketed through a "branding" process, which tries to associate the product, through its logo, with a lifestyle or worldview, so that the consumer is buying not only a product, but also an identity (Klein 2000). There you have it – marketing as bringing about not only a change of behavior (buying a product), but also a change of identity (belonging) and of course also a change of beliefs (this product is better than its competition).[28] A colleague of mine who recently spent some time in Russia had this to say about a specific form of capitalist marketing/proselytizing in Russia: "I found Coke more aggressive than Christians in trying to gain converts." Hence also talk about "proselytizing about Prozac", or expressions of concern about commercial interests barging into public school classrooms and libraries in the United States in order to cultivate new markets and "to proselytize for industry positions on issues such as environmental protection and taxes."[29]

Indeed, in ordinary language the term proselytizing is used to talk about everything from picnics as a means of proselytizing about a flamboyant life-style, to the proselytizing of political opinions via literature.[30] In the United Kingdom, variants of the term evangelism are used to describe Kellogg's UK chief as a "cereal evangelist", and Sarah Beeny as engaged in "no-nonsense evangelism" for the housing industry.[31] So the term proselytizing must not be thought of as limited to the religious context. Any attempt to convert someone or to change someone's belief, behavior, identity, and sense of belonging in any area of

---

[28] Some time ago, I saw an advertisement, a 10 page insert in *Maclean's*, a Canadian weekly newsmagazine, which made this statement about Seiko watches and personal identity: "It's not your hair. It's not your income. It's not your music. It's your watch that tells most about who you are."

[29] Taken from abstracts of an article and an editorial: Sara Rimer, "With Millions Taking Prozac, a Legal Drug Culture Arises", *New York Times* 143.49544 (Dec 14, 1993), p. A1; Lillian N. Gerhardt, "Tending to Business II", *School Library Journal* 41.7 (July 1995), p. 4. See also an article abstract, critical of Martha Stewart and "her proselytizing ventures" (J. Adler, "Attention, K Mart Shoppers!" *Newsweek* 116.21 [Nov 19, 1990], p. 74).

[30] Digby Anderson, in an article entitled, "Picnics for Evangelists", suggests that the point of a great picnic is "to proselytize and teach the ignorant and lazy by example and contrast" (*National Review* 44.18 [Sept 14 1992], pp. 66–7). Ruth Jacknow Markowitz reviews a fictionalized diary dramatizing the strike staged by 20,000 New York City shirtwaist makers in April 1910. Markowitz suggests that the author's dual agenda was that of recounting the event and "proselytizing the workers about socialism" (*Journal of American Ethnic History* 12.4 [Summer 1993], pp. 80–83).

[31] See Andrew Cave's business profile: "Early start for breakfast evangelist", *Daily Telegraph* (June 12, 2006), p. 6; and Angela Pertusini, "Sarah Beeny: 'It's simple. If you really want to sell, you have to drop the price'". *Daily Telegraph* (Sept 13, 2008), p. 2.

human endeavor is a case of proselytizing. Although the focus of this study is on evaluating religious proselytizing, I will from time to time draw attention to parallels with other forms of proselytizing.

It should be noted, however, that these other forms of proselytizing might not be that far removed from religious proselytizing, in any case. David Loy, in an essay provocatively entitled, "The Religion of the Market", draws attention to "the aggressive proselytizing of market capitalism, which has already become the most successful religion of all time, winning more converts more quickly than any previous belief system or value-system in human history" (Loy 1997, 276).[32] So perhaps with a broader definition of religion this study can be seen as having a broader focus. However, I will limit myself in the main to a narrower definition of religion, and to the phenomenon of religious proselytizing.

Academic objections to proselytizing

Now that we have settled on a definition of proselytizing, I would like to return to the topic of contemporary attitudes towards religious proselytizing. At the beginning of this chapter we looked at some of the controversy surrounding the issue of proselytizing. Much opposition to proselytizing occurs in the media, on the internet, and in ordinary conversations on this topic. I would now like to examine whether such opposition is also reflected in the world of scholarship.

Jay Newman, in an important study entitled *Foundations of Religious Tolerance* (1982), introduces a chapter on "Proselytizing and Intolerance", by calling attention to the popular image of the proselytzer. "We usually do not like the people who come to convert us. We often find them arrogant, ignorant, hypocritical, meddlesome" (88–89). Newman goes on to give his own academic assessment: "[M]any forms of missionary activity and overassertive 'witnessing' accompany, foreshadow, and promote more radical forms of religious harassment. There is something essentially intolerant about the missionary, the proselytizer" (88). He concludes the chapter: "Most religious proselytizing tends to promote resentment. Resentment promotes intolerance, which in turn promotes barbarism" (110). Newman's position, though commonly held, is not entirely clear. At times he is making the more

---

[32] For other writers who have argued that our market-driven economy is itself religious in nature, see Cox (1999) and Nelson (2001). Another writer very explicitly describes advertising as "the new religion of modern life" (Jhally 1990, 200).

modest claim that much or most proselytizing is immoral. However, at times he seems to call into question the very act of proselytizing – there is something essentially intolerant about the proselytizer, i.e., proselytizing is *by its very nature* immoral.[33]

Margaret Battin, in *Ethics in the Sanctuary* (1990), explores some of the practices of organized religion, both from the point of view of ordinary morality and professional ethics. In a chapter devoted to the ethics of proselytizing, she develops "an overall, composite scale of aggressiveness in religious convert seeking" (140). Battin's scale of aggressiveness in proselytizing also serves as "a scale of ethical repugnance" (147). What is significant about this scale is that all proselytizing activities are located somewhere along the scale of aggressiveness and ethical repugnance. In other words, no proselytizing is morally acceptable.[34] This is further confirmed by the fact that religious groups not at all involved in convert seeking, are described as not even being on the lower end of the scale (146). At one point Battin also identifies making "a deliberate attempt to disrupt a person's previously held framework of belief" as morally problematic (137). In other words, trying to convert someone is by its very nature morally problematic.

Sometimes the objections to proselytizing come from religious adherents themselves, particularly from those who belong to supposedly non-proselytizing religions. For example, David Novak, Professor of Jewish Studies at the University of Toronto, while conceding that some proselytizing has occurred within Judaism, nevertheless tends to downplay the same, in part because of "the aversion most Jews have to Christian efforts to proselytize them" (1999, 43). Towards the end of this essay, Novak raises some specific objections to proselytizing, and it is important to note that he twice describes these as moral objections. He describes most Jews as being "deeply resentful of the arrogance of

---

[33] Newman, at one point sums up by suggesting "that proselytizing is not necessarily immoral" (1982, 103). But this claim is not easy to reconcile with his earlier claim that there "is something essentially intolerant about the missionary" (88). Given that intolerance is immoral, it would seem that Newman is saying that missionary proselytizing is "essentially" immoral.

[34] Battin is not entirely clear on this. Sometimes she describes her ideal of invitational evangelism as "wholly non-aggressive", i.e. off the scale (1990, 142). But at other times, she seems to locate it at the lower end of her scale, as being "barely aggressive at all", or as violating ordinary moral norms "only in a very slight way" (141). It is precisely the "deliberate attempt to disrupt a person's previously held framework of belief" that is implicit even in invitational evangelism that would seem to be the problem for Battin and that would make it still mildly aggressive and immoral (137).

those who proselytize" (43). Why? Because proselytizers "inevitably come across as men and women who are so self-righteous that they feel no moral compunction in denigrating other faiths and their cultures for the sake of cajoling their adherents to cease being what they have been and change their identity by becoming what the missionaries are" (43).

Novak also draws attention to the fact that "missionary efforts have often proved quite useful for various forms of political imperialism" (1999, 43).[35] Earlier in this essay, Novak considers modern Judaism and its adjustments to today's secular political and cultural climate.

> Proselytizing efforts seemed to violate the new atmosphere where religion in general could no longer claim to be the foundation of anything of public significance. That is why, to this very day, Jewish resistance to Christian proselytizing efforts usually takes the form of protesting that such efforts violate the spirit of democratic cultural diversity (Novak 1999, 42).

Novak's position too is not entirely clear. Sometimes he seems to be suggesting that the bad attitudes and the negative consequences of proselytizing are contingently related to proselytizing. But, sometimes he would seem to be saying that proselytizing "by its very nature" is immoral.

I have already referred to the Dalai Lama's wholesale condemnation of proselytizing, early in 2001. "Whether Hindu or Muslim or Christian, whoever tries to convert, it's wrong, not good," the Dalai Lama said after a meeting with leaders of the World Hindu Council. These comments spawned a vigorous debate among a group of Hindu-Christian academics on an email discussion list.[36] Some wondered whether the Dalai Lama had been misquoted, given his general support for freedom of religion. One participant, however, pointed out that the Dalai Lama "has consistently and in many places" opposed religious proselytizing, despite his opposition also to the persecution of religious minorities. Others asked whether his real concern was not "aggressive religious marketing", or seeking to bring about conversions by material inducements, about which most agreed – this was wrong. But, as was pointed out by some participants in the dialogue, there are difficulties in defining "aggressive proselytizing", as well as

---

[35] Elsewhere Novak highlights the connection between arrogance and imperialism. "[P]roselytizing is a supreme form of human pride, and something which more often than not in human history has gone in tandem with conquest and domination of others" (Novak 1995, 161).

[36] hcs-l@lists.acusd.edu. My references to this debate are taken from comments made on the list serve between Jan 26 – Feb 2, 2001.

in evaluating the motives behind providing material care for the poor and the needy.

There was also debate as to whether or not proselytizing occurs in Buddhism – some expressing bewilderment at the Dalai Lama's comments in light of the fact that Buddhism is very much a missionary religion, with monks of the Dalai Lama very active in Europe, winning a large number of converts. Some scholars pointed to the consequences of proselytizing, which has a long history of creating tension and conflicts between religious communities, and which continues to impair goodwill, tolerance, and harmony between differing faith-traditions. One participant went further: "Conversion efforts which explicitly or implicitly are based on notions of the superiority of one tradition vis-à-vis the inferiority and/or inadequacy of another can fuel resentment, misunderstanding, hatred and eventually perhaps even violence." He therefore supported the Dalai Lama's call for an end to conversion efforts in India and elsewhere.

Still others in this Hindu-Christian dialogue rejected this extreme position, calling instead for scholars to draft an "Ethics of Proselytizing" that would be debated and eventually endorsed by religious leaders and scholars. What is further significant about this debate is its tone. It would seem even a group of scholars cannot avoid the rhetoric, unsupported generalizations, and even misrepresentations, that often accompany popular discussions on the issue of proselytizing. The degenerating tone of the debate prompted one of the members of the listserve to express his concerns about the discussion, even to the point of wondering whether his piece might be censored. He went on to remind the participants that the increasingly negative climate of the debate was undermining the basic objective of the HCS listserve – to further the understanding and relationship among academics, activists, and practitioners of various religions.

Objectives and approach

How then does one respond to this opposition to proselytizing and evangelism? Here we need keep in mind two quite different expressions of such opposition. The radical position is to object to *all* proselytizing, to suggest that proselytizing *by its very nature* is immoral. Then there is the more modest claim, namely that *much*, if not most proselytizing is immoral, that although it might be possible to engage in a moral form of proselytizing, it is very difficult to do so, and in fact most often proselytizers fall short of the ideal. I want to respond primarily to the radical rejection of all proselytizing as immoral, though what I have to say in the following chapters will at the same time provide an indirect response to the more modest expressions of opposition to proselytizing.

Let me clarify the objectives of this monograph in outline format.

- To clarify the charges often made against religious proselytizing.
- To attempt to answer these charges.
- To defend the possibility of ethical proselytizing.
- To define some criteria that can be used to distinguish between moral and immoral forms of proselytizing.
- To apply these criteria to some forms of proselytizing.

It should be obvious from this list of objectives, and from what has been said so far, that I have a thesis to defend. My overall aim is to provide a philosophical defence of proselytizing, showing that an ethical form of proselytizing is indeed possible. However, it is not at all my intent to provide a blanket defence of all proselytizing. Indeed, another central thrust of this book is to clarify the distinction between ethical and unethical proselytizing. All this will at the same time serve to weaken the more modest claims against proselytizing, to the effect that much if not most proselytizing is immoral.

I want to stress that this book is not just a review of the pros and cons of proselytizing, leaving it up to the reader to be the final judge. I consider such an approach to writing dishonest and uninteresting. I believe in writing (and teaching) from and for commitment.[37] Thus, while the approach might be seen by some to be polemical, I want to avoid mere polemics and the rhetoric often accompanying polemical writing. Here I would remind the reader that polemics and rhetoric are all too often found in statements of opposition to proselytizing. Sadly, argument can undergo such degeneration, even among academics, as I have already illustrated. I want to avoid this in my defence of proselytizing. I want to take great care in providing a careful analysis of the charges made against proselytizing. I want to ensure that they are being fairly represented. And then I want to answer these charges in a careful, rational manner. This is to be a work in patient philosophical analysis and argument. Having said this, however, it needs to be underscored that my presentation is an exercise of advocacy, not of disinterested neutrality.

---

[37] See my *Teaching for Commitment* (Thiessen 1993).

A few words about my own background might be in place here. In terms of religious commitment, I am a Christian of a fairly orthodox variety – Mennonite and evangelical. Evangelicals are by self-definition very much committed to evangelism. I share this commitment, though I would hasten to add I have some concerns about the evangelical understanding and emphasis on evangelism. My primary worry has to do with the lack of concern on the part of evangelicals to ensure that evangelism is done in an ethical manner. Indeed, evangelism is often carried out in immoral ways. Evangelicals sometimes seem to be so preoccupied with the end of "winning souls for Christ", that they have little concern about the means to achieve this end, and even succumb to the Machiavellian principle that the end justifies the means.[38] So the argument of this book is as much addressed to those who are strongly committed to evangelism as it is addressed to those who are opposed to the same.

I am also a philosopher. Philosophers specialize in subjecting established opinions to critical scrutiny. In relation to proselytizing this means that I, as a philosopher, must be willing to critique both established opinion within the evangelical church and other religious traditions committed to proselytizing, as well as established popular and academic opinion that rejects all or most proselytizing as immoral. I must be fair in evaluating arguments, always being willing to go where the argument carries me. Philosophers are also concerned about language and about clarifying the confusions often surrounding controversial issues. Here it is important to move beyond conceptual clarification, to substantive argumentation. Although the primary orientation of this work is philosophical, it should be noted that the subject matter is such that it cannot help but be interdisciplinary in nature. A treatment of the ethics of proselytizing will also draw on the insights of missiology, history, and even politics. Considerations in psychology, sociology, epistemology, and linguistics will also be touched on. The central focus however will be philosophical, and more narrowly philosophical ethics.

---

[38] Other concerns about evangelicals and evangelism include the following. Some evangelicals have too narrow an understanding of what evangelism means – i.e. saving souls. Sometimes an emphasis on evangelism results in the neglect of other important areas of the Christian life, such as ethical living, or being salt and light in the world. Some evangelicals tend to define the church primarily in terms of evangelism, with the result that church growth is seen as the primary aim of the church. I am planning a sequel to this book to deal with these concerns and to consider the ethics of evangelism from a specifically Christian theological framework.

Significance of this study

Clearly a consideration of the ethics of proselytizing is of immense practical importance. Mark Juergensmeyer has documented the rise of global religious violence today (2000, 6). For many people, there is a connection between the proselytizing tendency of religions and violence. If this is indeed so, and if other reasons can be given as to why proselytizing is an immoral activity, then we need to face these charges squarely. And if it is true that proselytizing is by its very nature immoral, then of course there might be some justification for the laws against proselytizing in many countries and for the seeming tendency of some Western democracies to be moving in this same direction. This conclusion would further require of the proselytizing religions that they do some serious theological revisions concerning the underpinnings of their proselytizing tendencies. On the other hand, this extreme position might just be mistaken.

But if so, there still remains the possibility of proselytizing *sometimes* leading to religious violence, of it being immoral *some* of the time. This possibility also needs to be taken seriously because here again the consequences of immorality and violence are serious, as Juergensmeyer so graphically portrays. So we are still left with the important task of distinguishing between moral and immoral forms of proselytizing. In a world that seems to be increasingly characterized by religious hostility and even violence, it is my hope that this work might provide some necessary background to creating an environment of greater tolerance and harmony.

Is there a need for this specific book? I have already drawn attention to some considerations suggesting an affirmative answer to this question. Within religious traditions committed to proselytizing and evangelism, far too little attention is paid to the ethics of proselytizing. For example, within the evangelical Christian tradition with which I am more familiar, one will hear countless exhortations in sermons, articles, and books, challenging the faithful to do evangelism. There are perhaps even more things said and written in the "how to do" genre – manuals and training seminars abound, and there are any number of tools available to help with the actual task of evangelism. At the theoretical level there are also careful theological treatments of the subject of evangelism. But the question of the *ethics* of evangelism tends to be skirted by evangelicals (see my review of the literature in the Appendix 2, #D5). I believe this dearth of materials on the ethics of proselytizing is also found in other branches of the Christian faith and in other religious traditions committed to proselytizing.

A few exceptions to this generalization should be noted. First, there are some ecumenical discussions surrounding proselytizing understood in the narrow sense of one branch of the Christian church seeking converts in another branch (see Appendix 2, #D2). Though these discussions touch on ethical considerations, the central issues are theological in nature, as I have already pointed out, and hence will not be given separate treatment in this book. Discussions on the ethics of proselytizing can also be found in a number of conferences and books devoted to Jewish/Christian relations and the particularly contentious issue of evangelical Christian mission to Jews (see Appendix 2, #D3). These concerns will be entertained in chapters 3 to 5, as part of a larger discussion of arguments attempting to show that all proselytizing is immoral.

If one looks beyond religious traditions themselves, there are of course many critiques of evangelism, proselytizing, and missions. Often these are nothing more than passing polemical flourishes, lacking critical and scholarly rigor. There are also some careful critiques. However, little is found by way of a careful philosophical response to these critiques of proselytizing, or a positive defence of proselytizing (see Appendix 2, #D6). This book is meant to fill this gap in the scholarly literature.

The legal dimensions of proselytizing and its relation to human rights has received a fair amount of attention, but only seldom do these treatments deal with the ethical dimensions of the problem (see Appendix 2, #E).

Further, extensive literature exists on the so-called cults or new religious movements (NRMs), some of which is very critical of their recruitment activities (see Appendix 2, #D4). These critical studies have themselves come under increasing critical scrutiny more recently. While I will obviously need to draw on this literature in the chapters that follow, I want to avoid getting preoccupied with the proselytizing activities of cults or NRMs. As I explain in Appendix 2, in part this is because much of this literature is not that useful for my purposes. Another important reason has to do with the danger of making cults a scapegoat, thereby hindering critical scrutiny of proselytizing in other religions. Various writers have drawn attention to the existence of cult-like behavior in conventional religious groups.[39] I want to avoid making any assumptions as to where unethical

---

[39] See, for example, Young and Griffith (1992, 91–93). Sawatsky (1986) points to similarities between the recruitment activities of cults and the evangelistic activities of evangelical Christians.

proselytizing is occurring. I want to examine religious proselytizing wherever it might occur.

As we have already seen, proselytizing is not limited to the area of religion. Advertising and marketing also attempt changes of belief, behavior, identity, and belonging. But, as a literature review in these areas will show, a consideration of the ethics of persuasion in these other areas is also decidedly underdeveloped (see Appendix 2, #B). The same can be said for the more general area of the ethics of communications (see Appendix 2, #A). Here a cautionary note is perhaps in order. While I will occasionally be making some comparisons between religious proselytizing and the proselytizing going on in other areas like advertising and marketing, it is not at all my intent to argue that because we accept advertising and marketing, therefore we should also declare religious proselytizing to be morally acceptable. This would obviously involve a *tu quoque* fallacy. Unethical proselytizing needs to be condemned wherever it occurs. Of course, to provide a careful analysis of proselytizing in all areas where it occurs would be a vast undertaking. So, the focus of this book will be on religious proselytizing, though some comparisons to the broader field will be made from time to time. Obviously, my treatment of the ethics of proselytizing should have some relevance to these other fields as well, but it is beyond the scope of this book to extrapolate to these other fields.

The need for a more careful treatment of the subject can be highlighted finally by the frequently made call for scholars and religious leaders to draft a collection of principles governing ethical proselytizing that would be debated and eventually endorsed by religious leaders and academics.[40] I agree, and trust that this book will begin to address this need for a careful constructive philosophical treatment of the ethics of proselytizing.

---

[40] Lawrence Uzzell, president of International Religious Freedom Watch, has repeatedly argued that there is a need for Christian missionaries to develop their own specialized code of ethics (2004, 16; 1999, 323). For other calls for religious leaders to get together and write a document outlining ethical means of proselytizing, see Hassan (2000, 342) and Boothby (1999, 46). See Appendix 2, #D5 for a review of a few attempts to develop a code of ethics for proselytizing.

Chapter 2

Foundational Issues

She was a good student – bright, conscientious, and genuinely interested in the philosophical questions that were being raised in the religious studies course that I was teaching. Then one day she surprised me. It happened on a Sunday, at noon. My wife and I had just returned from church and we were enjoying our lunch at home. I saw a car full of strangers pull up on our driveway. I then recognized my student coming up the front steps of our house. Trying desperately to remember her name, I greeted her at the door. She smiled, and said she had a little gift for me. Holding out a Book of Mormon, she offered it to me expressing her hope that this would help me in my search for truth. I hesitated a moment, but quickly realized that I had no choice but to graciously accept her gift, obviously offered with sincerity and good will.

Why the momentary hesitation? Because I was finding this somewhat embarrassing. But, why my embarrassment? Perhaps it was because I don't like receiving gifts from students – there have been cases where the gift seemed to be a bribe for a better mark! But this case was clearly different. Was my embarrassment, perhaps, due to the role-reversal involved in this incident – a student trying to enlighten the teacher? This probably was a partial explanation of my feelings, though hardly justifiable. Many times students have taught me something. Besides, academics could probably benefit from the occasional lesson in humility. Had this student done something morally wrong in giving me a Book of Mormon, sincerely hoping that it would help me to come to the truth? Again, surely not! There is nothing unethical about a student engaging in a little bit of proselytizing, especially if it takes the form of simply giving her unenlightened philosophy professor a copy of the Book of Mormon.

This book attempts to address more carefully the embarrassment that I felt and that many of us feel when someone is engaged in proselytizing us. Is our embarrassment rooted in ethical concerns? If so, is proselytizing always morally wrong? If only sometimes wrong, how can we distinguish between ethical and unethical forms of proselytizing? Before I address these central questions, three additional introductory and foundational issues must be dealt with. First, what prompts people to engage in religious proselytizing? Second, why are concerns about proselytizing coming to the fore in our day? Third, what are the ethical foundations from which proselytizing can be evaluated?

Religious impulse to proselytize

I am using the term proselytizing in a neutral sense to describe any activity that attempts to bring about a conversion. Conversion is understood as involving a change of belief, behavior, identity, and a sense of belonging. While conversion can be applied to any number of areas of life, the central focus of this study is an evaluation of attempts to bring about religious conversions. So far I have simply been assuming that people of various religious persuasions do engage in proselytizing. But why? What prompts people to engage in proselytizing activities? Here it will be necessary to become more specific, looking at some particular religious traditions that proselytize.

It will be helpful to contrast religious traditions that do promote proselytizing with those that allegedly discourage it. I will limit my discussion here to three religious traditions that are somewhat representative of the various approaches that religions take. I am most familiar with the Christian tradition and so I will have more to say about this tradition by way of illustration here and in later chapters of this book. I have already referred to Judaism in chapter 1, as an example of a religion that seems not to engage in proselytizing. I also want to look at Islam as another proselytizing religion. As mentioned in chapter 1, I will also refer to the so-called cults or new religious movements (NRMs), occasionally throughout the book, but here I focus on just three historically important religious traditions.

All three traditions belong to what is sometimes referred to as the Abrahamic religions. All three have an authoritative written scripture at the core of their identity, and this will help us to understand the doctrinal foundations that lie behind their particular approaches to proselytizing. My intent here is merely to provide some background to the proselytizing impulse in a few major religious traditions.[1] Within each of these religious traditions, there are of course differing schools of thought, which approach the issue of proselytizing in different ways. I will focus primarily on the more traditional stance on proselytizing taken by each of these religions.

Christianity

Evangelism and mission is at the heart of Christianity. Emil Brunner's aphorism, "The church exists by mission as a fire exists by burning", captures the drive and the dynamic of the New Testament.[2] Nowhere is this better summarized than in the Great Commission of Jesus to his disciples: "All authority in heaven and on earth has been given to me. Therefore go and make disciples of all nations, baptizing them in the name of the Father and of the Son and of the Holy Spirit, and teaching them to obey everything I have commanded you" (Matt 28:18–20).[3] For many Christians, this is all that needs to be said about the importance of evangelism – it is mandated by Jesus. The early disciples clearly acted in obedience to this mandate. Thus we find Peter preaching in Jerusalem on the day of Pentecost, calling to repentance an audience representing many nations (Acts 2:38–39). Later Paul, after his own dramatic conversion, tirelessly traveled the then known world pleading with Jews and Gentiles to find salvation in Jesus Christ. At the end of his life he explains his motive and mission to the church at Rome: "I am obligated both to Greeks and non-Greeks, both to the wise and the foolish. That is why I am so eager to preach the gospel also to you who are at Rome. I am not ashamed of the gospel, because it is the power of God for the salvation of everyone who believes: first for the Jew, then for the Gentile" (Rom 1:14–16).

Other motifs help to explain the missionary impulse of Christianity – the belief in one God, the Father over all humankind, who knows no

---

[1] For a more detailed treatment of the theology of proselytizing in each of these traditions, I would refer the reader to an anthology edited by John Witte and Richard C. Martin (1999).

[2] Quoted in Grounds (1984, 202). Or, as Max Muller puts it, Christianity "would cease to exist if it ceased to be missionary" (quoted in Burridge 1991, 58).

[3] In the gospel of Mark, the language of the commission changes to that of proclamation: "Go into all the world and preach the good news to all creation. Whoever believes and is baptized will be saved, but whoever does not believe will be condemned" (Mk 16:15–16). This mandate is repeated at the ascension of Jesus: "But you will receive power when the Holy Spirit comes on you; and you will be my witnesses in Jerusalem, and in all Judea and Samaria, and to the ends of the earth" (Acts 1:8).

cultural barriers, and who is therefore the source of light and life for all
(Jn 1:1–5); the central doctrine of the incarnation, God becoming flesh,
God becoming an evangelist as it were, so that humankind could witness the grace and truth that is available in Jesus (Jn 1:14); Jesus' exclusive claims, "I am the way and the truth and the life. No one comes to
the Father except through me" (Jn 14:6; cf. Acts 4:12). All this assumes
that there is something fundamentally wrong with humankind – it is
because human beings are in the dark that they need light; it is because
they have sinned that they need salvation (Rom 3:23–24). And finally
there is the doctrine behind appeals like Jonathan Edwards' famous
sermon, "Sinners in the Hands of an Angry God," the doctrine concerning the final day of judgment, when the books will be opened, and
anyone whose name is not found written in the book of life will be
thrown into the lake of fire (Rev 21:11–19). Hence, the importance of
proclaiming the good news of the gospel of Jesus Christ.

Texts like these, and many more could be cited, have inspired
Christians to become tireless evangelists and missionaries, carrying
their message, literally, to the ends of the earth. These efforts, as well as
those of current Christian missionaries, estimated to be 210,000 in
number, have been chronicled in any number of histories and biogra-
phies of Christian missionary endeavor.[4] The evangelistic and missionary impulse of these texts has also been captured in a countless
number of Catholic encyclical letters, Protestant statements, and
evangelical calls to evangelism.[5]

Of course, not all would agree that evangelism and mission are as
central to Christianity as I have been suggesting. Liberal theological
responses to pluralism reject the exclusive claims to truth within
classic Christianity, thereby challenging the underlying basis of the

---

[4] See, for example, the classic studies by Stephen Neill (1964) and Latourette
(1937–45). The estimate on the number of today's Christian missionaries is taken
from an anthropological study of missionaries by Burridge (1991, 10).

[5] Pope John Paul II, for example, put the Great Commission at the heart of his
thought, teaching, and ministry calling time and again for "a new evangelization
and mission to all" (Pope John Paul II, *Redemptoris Missio*, No. 3 [Dec 7, 1990], also
found in Donders [1996, 145]). The Lausanne Covenant, an enduring legacy of The
International Congress for World Evangelization (1974), remains the benchmark
statement for evangelical mission theology. A more recent statement on evangelism
was the result of another major gathering in 2000: "The Amsterdam Declaration: A
Charter for Evangelism in the Twenty-first Century" (summarized in *First Things*
[Jan 2001]: 64–66. See Scherer and Bevans (1992) and Nichols (1998) for a collection
and a review of important statements on evangelism and mission in Roman
Catholic and Protestant Christianity.

missionary impulse (e.g. Hick and Knitter 1987). But these attempts to reinterpret and even challenge the centrality of the missionary impulse of the Christian church need not concern us here. The church's traditional posture is one in which evangelism, and proselytizing is seen as at least one central component of the mission of the church.

Judaism

Judaism provides a quite different perspective on proselytizing, and is used here as an example of religions that do not seem to emphasize proselytizing.[6] There is considerable debate within Judaic scholarship regarding proselytizing. Some scholars maintain that the Jewish tradition does not seek to convert individuals to the Jewish faith, or even that it prohibits proselytizing.[7] Other scholars maintain that proselytizing activities are part of the history of the Jewish faith.[8] David Novak takes a more moderate position (1999). Clearly Judaism does not prohibit proselytism, according to Novak (17). He further concedes that within Judaism there has always been a place for the Gentile convert, and he explores this notion and the regulations associated with conversion. He also explores the historical evidence for proselytizing in Judaism, but cautions against interpreting this evidence as providing conclusive evidence of overt proselytizing in Jewish history.[9]

I agree that historically there is less emphasis and less involvement in proselytizing within the Jewish tradition than within the Christian tradition. But this is more a matter of historical circumstance than of

---

[6] Hinduism and Buddhism are often cited as examples of non-proselytizing religions. However, this is disputed by some scholars. Lamb and Bryant, in the introduction to their anthology, suggest that there is "a strong missionary mentality within Buddhism" (1999, 8). James Richardson points out that even religions from the Hindu tradition have become more oriented toward proselytizing within the context of American society (1988, 143).

[7] See, for example, Broyde (1999, 45–60), Goodman (1994), and Polish (1982).

[8] See, for example, Epstein (1991), Feldman (1993), and Stalnaker (2002, 343–47).

[9] For example, Novak does make a passing reference to the evidence of the far-reaching missionary activity of the Jews in Graeco-Roman era as found in Matt 23:15: "Woe to you, teachers of the law and Pharisees, you hypocrites! You travel over land and sea to win a single convert, and when he becomes one, you make him twice as much a son of hell as you are" (Novak 1999, 25; n.49). See also Ben Zion Bokser who cites the "gibe at the Pharisees" as evidence of Jewish proselytizing (quoted in Grounds 1984, 201). However, Novak suggests that this passage is better interpreted as Gentiles being attracted to the Jewish faith rather then overt proselytizing. See also Bird (2004) for a review of the literature on this question, as well as a contrary interpretation of the Matt 23:15 text.

intent or doctrine (Prager and Telushkin 1983, 185). Clearly, a covenant theology and the doctrine of election lead to less emphasis on proselytizing (Novak 1995). However, I suggest that there is perhaps more proselytizing occurring within Judaism than even Novak is prepared to admit. Indeed, there have been some recent calls for more active proselytizing within Judaism.[10]

Some other issues underlie the seeming hesitancy of Jewish scholars like Novak to acknowledge the level of proselytizing that does exist within Judaism. For one, this tendency is a response to the aversion most Jews have to Christian efforts to proselytize them, a point that Novak himself concedes (1999, 43). Then there is a question as to how one defines proselytization. As noted in chapter 1, Novak distinguishes between overt and covert proselytizing. But is covert proselytizing not proselytizing in some sense?

Here a distinguishing feature of the Jewish approach to proselytizing emerges. The emphasis seems to be more on *covert* proselytizing, on silently bearing witness to the light. Israel is described as being chosen by God: "You are my witnesses", declares the Lord, "and my servant whom I have chosen" (Isa 43:10). True, the Jewish understanding of such witness might best be described as a passive kind of witness, but as Daniel Polish is forced to concede, even passive witness might conceivably have the effect of converting someone, in which case the effects of active and passive witness are indistinguishable (1982, 166–68).

More generally, Jewish scholars acknowledge that there is a Jewish mission, though they prefer to see it in terms of being a moral light to the nations. This raises a key philosophical question. Does not the very presence of Jews and the attractiveness of their lives based on God's law, involve a kind of proselytizing? Novak admits that in the first and second centuries C.E., "Jews and Christians were in competition for

---

[10] American Rabbi Alexander Schindler, for example, in his presidential address to the Board of Trustees of the Union of American Hebrew Congregations said: "I believe that it is time for our movement to launch a carefully conceived Outreach Program aimed at all Americans who are unchurched and who are seeking roots in religion . . . My friends, we Jews possess the water that can slake the thirst, the bread that can sate the great hunger. Let us offer it freely, proudly – for our well-being and for the sake of those who earnestly seek what it is ours to give" (quoted in Berger 1979, 35, and in Grounds 1984, 202). See also Dennis Prager and Joseph Telushkin who very explicitly call for Jews "to increase the number of Jews through converting many non-Jews to Judaism", in part as a way of combating anti-semitism (1983, 184). Then there are also the current on-going efforts of ultra-orthodox Jews to convert less observant Jews or even secular Jews.

which community would attract more of these former pagans" (1999, 23). But attracting converts is a kind of proselytizing. The recent DABRU EMET statement also affirms proselytizing, when it speaks of the emphasis on the inalienable sanctity and dignity of every human being inherent in the moral principles of the Torah, as providing "a powerful witness to all humanity for improving the lives of our fellow human beings and for standing against the immoralities and idolatries that harm and degrade us."[11] The words "powerful witness" are surely somewhat akin to proselytizing. Clearly, though, there is still an important difference between being an attractive *but silent* witness to a way of life, and proselytizing that involves communication and persuasion about this way of life. My focus is on proselytizing that involves communication.

I conclude that there is perhaps more proselytizing occurring within Judaism than Novak and other Jewish scholars are prepared to admit. The same can be said about other so-called non-proselytizing religions.[12] Indeed, as is pointed out by Doudou Diene, it is in the very nature of religions that they proselytize, given the interactions, exchanges, and mutual influences that are generated through the movements of peoples and ideas, especially in a world that has become a global village (1999, 29). I would add though, that a religion like Judaism, with its emphasis on covert proselytizing, attracting converts, and being a witness, may have something to teach us about the nature of ethical proselytizing.

Islam

There are some difficulties in treating the Islamic understanding of proselytizing. Donna Arzt (1999, 79) alerts us to the problems of Western ignorance and misunderstandings about Islam's basic principles and obligations, particularly concerning *jihad*. It is also more difficult to separate descriptive and normative analyses of proselytizing in

---

[11] The "DABRU EMET: a Jewish Statement on Christians and Christianity," was first published as a full page ad in *The New York Times* (Sept 10, 2000), p. 37. It has also been printed in *First Things* 107 (Nov 2000), pp. 39–41.

[12] After a journey to the United States and Europe in the 1890's, the Hindu Swami Vivekananda asked, "Where are the men ready to go out to every country in the world with the message of the great sages of India? . . . Such heroic souls are wanted to help spread the truth. Such heroic workers are wanted to go abroad and help to disseminate the great truths of the Vedanta" (quoted in Sell 1990, 111). See also Sharma (2005, 427).

the Islamic tradition. A final difficulty concerns translation. Arzt, for example, suggests that the Qur'an does not adopt the use of the term proselyte even though Islam accepts both the Jewish and Christian Testaments as books of revelation, though inferior to the Qur'an. Muslims also don't use the term missionary which they associate with Western colonialism. Indeed, professional missionaries do not exist in Islam, according to Arzt. But these claims can be disputed, and Arzt herself is not entirely consistent on these points.[13]

Arzt points out, for example, that there are terms used in the Qur'an that roughly translate as proselytizing or the call to preaching (1999, 83). These terms are used in the Qur'an, though much less often than *jihad*, which unfortunately is most often misunderstood by non-Muslims when translated as holy war, according to Arzt. *Jihad* is perhaps best translated into English as the duty to struggle or to sacrifice in the path of God. The Qur'anic use of the term refers to making Allah's cause succeed. This struggle can be personal and internal, or communal and external, the latter expressing itself in various ways – combating evil, establishing a just political order, and spreading the cause of Allah among unbelievers. "Come to believe in God and His Apostle, and struggle in the cause of God (*jihad*), wealth and soul" (Q. 61:11). Clearly *jihad* also refers to military struggle – fighting for Allah when Muslims are attacked or wronged (Q. 2:190; 22:39). A link is also made between fighting and spreading the faith when the Qur'an advises that unbelievers are not to be attacked outright without first receiving a summons (*da'wa*) either to convert or to submit to a tax that Islamic law (*shari'a*) imposes on non-Muslims (Q. 17:15).

Another phrase related to missionary activity occurs several times in the Qur'an and was more fundamental to early theological discourse, and connoted a potentially less political notion of *da'wa*, a term that means commanding the good and prohibiting evil (Q. 22:41). Like *jihad*, commanding the good and prohibiting evil expresses a duty that applies to all Muslims. They should also be witnessing to non-Muslims concerning the Qur'anic commands and prohibitions. This kind of missionary calling is very similar to the call to be the light of nations in Judaism.

The Islamic religion sees itself as a universal religion, which began with Adam and Eve, the first humans, developed through Abraham and his son Ishmael, was modified by Jesus, and finally came to its

---

[13] Contrary to Arzt, Arnold, in his classic study of proselytizing in Islam, argues that Islamic missionary societies do appear in the twentieth century (1913, 408, 438–39).

fullest expression in Mohammed (Q. 42:13). Thus there is considerable overlap in the motifs that inspire Christian and Muslim proselytiza-tion. In addition, there is Islamic law and doctrine (*shari'a*), the primary sources of which consist of the Qur'an and the Sunna, which are addressed to all humankind, and give us "the path", or the "road to follow" (Arzt 1999, 81–83). "We have sent you only as a bearer of good tidings and admonisher for all mankind" (Q. 34:28).

Muslims, therefore, have a duty to propagate the message of the Qur'an to the rest of humanity, in order to establish a universal civi-lization. "Call them [non-Muslims] to the path of your Lord with wis-dom and words of good advice; and reason with them in the best way possible. Your Lord surely knows who strays from His path, and He knows those who are guided the right way" (Q. 16:125; cf. 42:15).[14] In fact one aspect of the meaning of the Arabic term *islam* is to seek to bring converts to Islam, which literally means "to submit" (Martin 1999, 97). Hence this explanation of a recent Muslim writer that the people of his faith "are . . . charged with the noble mission of bringing the whole world to its Supreme Sovereign, and of freeing it from servi-tude to any false god. The propagation of Islam to all people is a reli-gious duty which must be undertaken by all true Muslims . . ."[15]

Proselytizing, therefore, has always been a significant component of Islamic history, as is well documented in the classic study by T.W. Arnold, *The Preaching of Islam: A History of the Propagation of the Muslim Faith* (1913). In a more recent essay, Martin explores the differing approaches to proselytizing within Islamic history (1999). Whatever the approach used, converting humankind to Islam, is a mandate that is at the heart of the Islamic religion.[16]

Why the growing controversy over proselytizing?

There are additional psychological, sociological, historical, and politi-cal factors that might provide further explanations of the impulse to

---

[14] For a list of other passages from the Qur'an and the Medinite Surahs that exhort Muslims to proselytize, see Arnold (1913, 3–6).

[15] Badru D. Kateregga, quoted in Sell (1990, 111).

[16] Contemporary Muslims are quite active in Western universities where a more open and dialogical approach to proselytizing is being used. I attended an excellent evangelistic apologetic for the Muslim faith put on by the local Muslim association at the Catholic University of Leuven, Belgium (Winter semester, 2005). See also Mumisa (2002) for a description of ongoing Islamic proselytizing occurring in South Africa and Malawi.

proselytize. However, I do not want to provide a separate treatment of these additional explanations, in part because to do so might detract from the doctrinal explanations for the impulse to proselytize considered in the previous section. I will also be touching on these further explanations of the impulse to proselytize in the chapters that follow. Indeed, already in this section, I make reference to some of these factors which, I believe, help to explain why there is a growing controversy today concerning proselytizing.

For example, we are faced today with the fact of a growing pluralism within societies. It is this growing pluralism that helps to explain why there seems to be more emphasis on proselytizing in our day. The changing situation is well described by Peter Berger:

> The religious tradition, which previously could be authoritatively imposed, now has to be marketed. It must be "sold" to a clientele that is no longer constrained to "buy." The pluralist situation is, above all, a market situation. In it, the religious institutions become marketing agencies and the religious traditions become consumer commodities (Berger 1967, 138).[17]

While such competition can be friendly, it can also lead to a "war for souls" (Witte and Martin 1999, xii), and also to more and more people being irritated by this war. Hence, the growing concern about proselytizing today.

The fact of religious pluralism has had other consequences in some parts of the globe – the separation of church and state, or the disestablishment of the church in the U.S.A. and Canada. This ended the religious monopoly of any one Christian denomination, resulting in various denominations – religious or even pseudo-religious – being treated as equals. Hence, the need for active recruitment of members, and hence also the growing concern about such proselytization.

But many countries still have an established religion or a state church. We therefore see controversies concerning proselytizing erupting in countries which have been dominated by one religion, and which for various reasons are experiencing some opening up to secularizing, democratic, or pluralizing forces (e.g. countries dominated by the Orthodox church, Hinduism, Buddhism, or Islam). Proselytizing is

---

[17] See also Berger (1979) where the proselytizing impulse is again explained in terms of a response to pluralism, though here the focus is on maintaining religious identity for individuals or a religious community.

seen as an intrusion or even subversion of state/church or religious identity. Nowhere has this been exemplified more clearly than in the pressures to end the short-lived experiment with religious freedom in the former Soviet Union. The surprisingly liberal 1990 "Law on Freedom of Worship", opened the door to an avalanche of foreign missionary activity, predominantly by North American evangelical groups and new religious movements. This led to a clash with the Orthodox Church, which, in concert with Communist and nationalist groupings, pressed for a new law on religion.[18]

Controversy concerning proselytizing is not restricted to communist, Hindu, and Islamic countries. It is also found in Western liberal democracies. In North America there has been much controversy surrounding attempts to introduce laws to curtail the proselytizing activities of various new religious movements or cults. Among the sociological forces challenging the impulse to proselytize, Sawatsky cites increasing pluralism of our societies, the relativizing influence of pluralism, and the dominance of the religion of civility and tolerance (1986).[19] There are also psychological trends, which have made us very suspicious of authority. A dislike of proselytizing also seems to stem from the fact that liberalism has become less of a political theory and more of a worldview. John Rawls has described this as the difference between political liberalism and comprehensive liberalism (1993). As a result, freedom of conscience has been transformed into a moral imperative not to influence anyone's conscience on worldview matters.[20]

Another important and more recent contributing factor to the rising controversy over proselytizing, is the association of any kind of religious activity with extremism and fanaticism. We are living post-September 11, 2001 – a date which for many will serve as the inauguration of the new millennium. Some scholars would interpret the events of that day as a forecast of the religious conflict that we might

---

[18] Despite much internal controversy and international pressure, the Russian Duma passed the "Law of Freedom of Conscience and Religious Organizations", in Sept 1997. The law acknowledges "the special contribution of Orthodoxy to the history of Russia and the development of Russia's spirituality and culture", and imposes the legal requirement of registration on all religious organizations as well as a gradation of restrictions on religious groups who have come to Russia more recently. While the law makes no explicit reference to proselytizing, its catalog of forbidden activities effectively proscribes any form of religious propaganda that would impinge on the Orthodox Church (Kerr 1999, 11).

[19] The religion of civility has been highlighted in John Murray Cuddihy's book, *No Offense: Civil Religion and Protestant Taste* (1978).

[20] This point was suggested to me by Perry Glanzer.

expect in the third millennium. For example, even prior to September 11, political scientist Samuel Huntington argued that we may be entering a momentous and dangerous phase of history as we face the coming "clash of civilizations" based on collective cultural and religious identities. So severe will this clash be, according to Huntington, that it will dwarf the controversies of the past (1996). Again, prior to September 11, sociologist Mark Juergensmeyer explored "the global rise of religious violence", to use the subtitle of his book, *Terror in the Mind of God* (2000). In searching for an explanation, he suggested that religious terrorists see the world in terms of a cosmic struggle between the forces of good and evil. Master terrorist Osama bin Laden liked to say, "The world is at war." Such a worldview, it would seem, leads inevitably to violence. No wonder then that there is increasing suspicion about religious proselytizing which is based on the same worldview, the same war metaphor, and the same polarizing between "us" versus "them", right versus wrong, and good versus evil.

Whatever the causes of controversy concerning proselytizing, we need to take an honest look at the underlying arguments surrounding it. But first, we need to set forth the ethical foundation from which we want to evaluate these arguments. We also need to provide a framework for the later development of criteria to distinguish between ethical and unethical proselytizing in chapters 7 and 8.

Some examples of immoral proselytizing

On what basis do we make an ethical assessment of proselytizing? Which philosophical voice will be appealed to? Whose ethics will we use? In today's postmodern environment it might be tempting simply to treat the subject of this book from multiple ethical perspectives.[21] While this approach is certainly conceivable and perhaps even interesting, it is not the approach I want to take. I want to dare to take an exclusive and universalist approach, hence the book's title, *The Ethics of Evangelism*. I seem to have an incurable faith in an objective and universal morality. I believe there are a few broad and basic ethical principles, or ideals of virtue, that are shared by all rational human beings concerned about the good life. I am not talking about *actual* behavior

---

[21] This is the approach that tends to be taken in the literature on communication ethics (See Appendix 2, #A1).

or about what *is* the case. I am talking about what *ought* to be the case. Deep down inside, all of us (or at least most of us – those of us who are rational and interested in living the moral life) know when we do fail in the moral realm.

In order to help the reader to understand the moral framework that is being assumed in this book, I would like to begin with some concrete examples of unethical proselytizing. I begin with this approach because it is easier to come to agreement on ethical issues when dealing with concrete situations and actual violations of moral norms. I promise to get to the problem of the theoretical foundations of ethics eventually, but for now, I want the focus to be more practical.

Sadly history is littered with stories of moral failure in the area of proselytizing. In the history of Christianity the phenomenon of forced conversion recurs with embarrassing frequency. Alan Kreider, in his study of the evolution of conversion in the first five centuries of Christianity, describes the effects of Constantine's initial protection and then establishment of Christianity as the official religion of the Roman Empire. By the end of the fourth century patterns of pressure – Sir Herbert Butterfield called them "inducement and compulsion" – were developed and these contributed much to the rapid growth of the churches (Kreider 1999, 38–39). The inducements included imperially conferred benefits for church leaders and the advancement of the careers of civil servants who had become Christian. Compulsion developed more slowly, from the labeling of pagan worship as "superstitious", to the banning of pagan public worship, to preferential hiring policies for Christians in the civil service, to the edict of Justinian in 529, making conversion, including the baptism of all infants, compulsory (39).[22]

In the eighth century Charlemagne forced the Saxons to be baptized. After they revolted, he issued a "Saxon Capitulary", one of whose articles read, "If any man among the Saxons, being not yet baptized, shall hide himself and refuse to come to baptism, let him die the death" (Daves 1972, 122–27). In the ninth century King Olaf of Norway forced Christianity on the bulk of his subjects using every kind of violence. In

---

[22] This interpretation of early Christian history has been challenged in two recent books by Drake (2000) and Digeser (2000). See a review of these books by Robert Louis Wilken, "In Defense of Constantine", *First Things* (April 2001), pp. 36–40. Drake and Digeser point out that Constantinianism was simply a consequence of the Church's success, and that Constantine himself had a very clear doctrine of freedom in religion inspired by Lactantius' *Institutes*.

the twelfth century the Swedes conquered and forced the Catholic faith on the Finns.[23]

Then there are the abuses of the Christian Crusades of the eleventh, twelfth, and thirteenth centuries. Here we must be careful to avoid the all too common characterization of the Crusades as a series of holy wars against Islam, where Christians attacked Muslims without provocation to seize their land and to forcibly convert them.[24] While the crusades were primarily about recapturing Christian territory from the Muslims, like all wars, the violence was brutal and forced conversions sometimes did become part of the mandate. This distortion of the crusade mandate is perhaps most clearly made and defended by Pope Innocent III who came to the papal throne in 1198 and who was surely the most important figure in the crusading movement after Pope Urban II. The language used by Innocent III in a letter to the king of Denmark, encouraging him to take part in the Baltic Crusade is most suggestive.[25]

The letter refers to Satan as one who "has blinded certain people, who ought to be compared to the senseless asses they resemble". The king is praised as having "often undergone many labours and expenses in fighting the war of the Lord against the barbarian nations of this sort which border on your kingdom". These efforts have been blessed with "a recent shower of divine grace, . . . so that, set on fire with the love of divine law, you are planning once more to take up your arms and shield to compel, just as in the parable in the gospel, the *feeble* and infirm, *the blind and the lame* to *come in* to the wedding feast of the highest king." Finally, the king is commended for his resolution in the Lord. "[We] advise your royal devotion most carefully and encourage and enjoin you for the remission of your sins that, out of love for [Christ], . . . you gird yourself manfully to root out the error of paganism and spread the bounds of the Christian faith."

A curious feature of this discourse is Innocent's use of the parable of the wedding feast, where Jesus describes a king as instructing his servants to *compel* the guests to come to his banquet (Matt 22:1–14). Although the theologians of the time had always held that the heathen

---

[23] Here I am drawing on an historical catalogue of Christian failures in proselytizing as given by Megivern (1976, 67). See also Arnold (1913, 7–8) who compares Christian and Muslim failures in order to correct a bias in the reading of Islam with regard to coercion in proselytizing.

[24] See Riley-Smith (2008) and Madden (2008) for recent challenges to these common misconceptions of the Crusades.

[25] All the quotations in the next paragraph are from Riley-Smith (1981, 77–78).

should be converted by reason, and although canon law forbade forcing the faith on the infidel, these principles were eventually disregarded in the passionate climate surrounding the crusades. Such a subversion of principle was in part inspired and justified by Augustine's earlier and strange reconciliation of the use of force with the demands of Christian love. Augustine employed this same parable to justify force against heretics. Interestingly, the word "compel" is translated as "invite" in more recent translations of the gospel accounts.[26] Mistranslations do have consequences! Augustine, the crusaders, and Pope Innocent III, should have known better. Compulsion in proselytizing is always wrong. To talk about having "dragged the barbarian nations into the net of the orthodox faith", is a violation of the principle of freedom, so essential to the dignity of persons. It is wrong also to refer to idolaters as "senseless asses". And the motivation appealed to can also be questioned. There seems to be something problematic about encouraging royal devotion by promising "the remission of your sins".[27]

This same kind of questionable motivation sadly also appears in the later Spanish conquest of the Americas, ably documented by Luis Rivera (1992). Las Casas, a prophetic Dominican critic, wrote that the conquistadors make war against the Indians and enslave them "to reach the goal that is their god: gold" (259). In the entire process of conquest and evangelization of the Americas, the cross and the sword were inextricably linked. Sadly, this was sanctioned by the highest religious authority of the time. Pope Clement VII, in a letter to Carlos V, dated May 8, 1529, very explicitly advocated the use of "force and arms if necessary", to bring souls to God (220).

Examples of what I see as obviously unethical proselytizing can also be found in Islam. From the earliest missionary activities by Mohammed's generals and closest companions, "we sense the strong but troubled link between spreading the faith and the use of physical force to do so." This frank assessment comes, interestingly, from a writer anxious to correct Western perceptions of Islam as a religion of the sword (Martin 1999, 100). Typical of the stories recorded by Ibn Ishaq and his editor of the next generation, Ibn Hisham, is the following, in which

---

[26] Augustine's interpretation of this parable was already disputed in the seventeenth century by Bayle (2005).

[27] In a treatise on crusade preaching, written at the request of Pope Gregory X, Humbert of Romans is rather blatant in his appeal to self-interest: "[T]he faithful amass for themselves the merits of good works and acquire indulgences for themselves through which they are absolved from their sins" (Riley-Smith 1981, 113).

Mohammed sent his redoubtable general, Khalid ibn al-Walid, to a tribe in Najran, Arabia, ordering him to invite them to Islam three days before he attacked them. If they accepted then he was to accept it from them; and if they declined he was to fight them. So Khalid set out and came to them, and sent out riders in all directions inviting the people to Islam, saying, "if you accept Islam you will be safe," so the men accepted Islam as they were invited. Khalid stayed with them teaching them Islam and the book of God and the Sunna of His prophet, for that was what the apostle of God had ordered him to do if they accepted Islam and did not fight.[28]

Such conversions to Islam can hardly be described as being freely made. Indeed, they are a betrayal of the Qur'anic injunction not to use coercion in religion. As such they are wrong and immoral. Sadly, "instances of forced conversions . . . may be found scattered up and down the pages of Muhammadan histories," as is conceded by Sir Thomas Arnold in his famous history of proselytism and conversion in Islam, and this despite his inclinations to political correctness, which "led him to dismiss the exaggerated claims made against Islam as a religion of the sword and of forced conversions" (Arnold 1913, 7).

Even in Judaism where there is less of an emphasis on proselytizing, there are troubling stories of failure to respect the freedom and dignity of persons. Josephus recorded what is admittedly an unusual case in Jewish history when there was a forced conversion of the Itreans and the Idumeans by the Maccabean king in the second century B.C.E. (Novak 1999, 22).

Stories of more recent moral failures in the area of proselytizing also abound. I will cite only one example of a Christian failure. In 1992, three officials from the Russian Ministry of Education, in response to the perceived moral vacuum in post-communist Russian education, invited representatives of the CoMission, a group of sixty (eventually over eighty) evangelical Christian organizations to spearhead a program to instruct Russian public school teachers on how to teach Christian ethics (Glanzer 1999, 2002). Throughout the implementation of this program there was a tension between offering education *about* Christian morals, and leading teachers and students towards conversion to Christianity. One CoMission leader had this to say about the curriculum: "In my opinion, it is not a curriculum of ethics. It is more

---

[28] Cited in Martin (1999, 99). A passage in the Qur'an supports the action taken by this general. "We never punish till We have sent a messenger" (Q.17:15). This is supported further by a hadith: "the invitation to Islam is essential before declaring war" (cited in Arzt 2000, 84).

an introduction to Christianity . . . To be honest, I think it is a little unethical" (Glanzer 2002, 42).

Although there was some awareness of the problems inherent in a program of state-imposed Christianity, some of the leaders of the CoMission had no moral qualms about using a state-run education system to accomplish the aims of evangelism and church planting. Moreover, there was some obvious dishonesty in representing the aims of the CoMission. In marketing this project to American churches, para-church organizations and fund-raisers were very explicit about their evangelistic intentions. However, the emphasis was quite different when communicating with Russian education officials and the Orthodox Church of Russia. Glanzer also points to the duplicity in recruiting missionaries/educators. In the main, the 1,500 people recruited to help train teachers in Russia, were not educators, and were not trained to teach Christian ethics, but were in fact evangelists and missionaries, this deficiency leading Glanzer to conclude that the enterprise was "ethically problematic" (Glanzer 2002, 196).

In the end it was the Orthodox Church that brought to a close not only the CoMission's government partnerships at the national level, but also the short-lived experiment with religious freedom in Russia. Glanzer, in reviewing this experiment in mission and education sums up: "The Orthodox Church had good reason to distrust Western missionaries who were using government schools to further their evangelistic and church planting aims without revealing this agenda" (1999, 305). Several moral failures come to the fore here – dishonesty and duplicity about evangelistic intentions, the use of state power and institutions to further evangelistic ends, and again, a lack of sensitivity regarding a coercive environment for proselytizing. Of course, the Russian Orthodox Church was also not without moral fault, what with seeking state-supported favoritism in order to recover their religious monopoly (Glanzer 2002, 197).

My intent in reviewing these historical and contemporary moral failures in the area of proselytizing has been fourfold. I wanted to show that immoral proselytizing does occur, quite frequently, in fact. But, as I will argue in the chapters that follow, proselytizing is not immoral by its very nature. Secondly, this review was meant to preempt an anticipated counter-argument to my overall thesis. There would seem to be a tendency to reject any defence of the possibility of moral proselytizing by citing failures in this area. I admit that there are moral failures in the area of proselytizing, indeed, many failures. But the fact of moral failure does not entail that there are no morally exemplary ways to

proselytize. Thirdly, this review was meant to bring us closer to clarifying the ethical starting point of this study. Finally, by starting with
the concrete and the practical, I trust that I will have moved the skeptical reader closer to acknowledging the possibility of a shared moral
framework, thus also preparing the way for an articulation of the
moral foundations from which I will be evaluating proselytizing.

Ethical foundations

It is my hope that the reader will agree with my negative moral assessments of the proselytizing occurring in the stories reviewed in the previous section. Proselytizing that dehumanizes the person is simply
wrong. Using force and violence to convert someone is wrong.
Proselytizing that expresses itself in hostility and malice is morally
wrong. Dishonesty and duplicity about evangelistic intentions is
wrong. Selfishness as a primary motivation to proselytize is wrong.

These negative moral assessments can be converted into positive
moral norms, and here again I hope readers will be in general agreement about these norms. Human beings ought to be treated as having
dignity and worth. We ought to care for others. The freedom of individuals must be respected. Decisions of individuals should be made on
the basis of free and informed consent. We have a moral obligation to be
tolerant, allowing others to disagree with us, and treating people who
disagree with us with respect. There ought to be integrity in what we
say and do. We ought to speak the truth, and we should be honest in
describing our intentions. Actions motivated by concern for another's
well being are good. I am assuming that there is little need to defend
these moral values. Surely these are values that all decent, caring, and
reasonable human beings accept.

But what is the basis of these moral values? It is far beyond the scope
of this study to provide a careful outline of the theoretical foundations
of ethics. Nor do I believe that it is necessary to do so here. A brief treatment of this topic might, however, be of interest to some readers. Those
who are satisfied with the above analysis of case studies as a preface to
the ethical foundations of this book may simply want to move on to the
next chapter. My appeal thus far has been to the reader's moral intuition, and there are philosophers who believe that this is an adequate
foundation of ethics.

It should be apparent that there is a basic assumption underlying my
historical and contemporary analysis of proselytizing, as well as the

negative moral assessments and the positive moral norms that I deduced from this analysis. I am assuming the dignity of persons. It is the dignity and worth of the human being that I believe is the foundation of any adequate ethical theory. Historically, this emphasis on the dignity and worth of human beings has led to an ethics formulated in terms of certain rights and duties. But defining ethics in terms of rights and duties is not enough. Human beings are also characterized by a need for love and care. Thus feminist ethicists such as Carol Gilligan (1982) and Joan Tronto (1993) have argued for an ethics of care. I think these two approaches need to be seen as complementary. We need to emphasize both the dignity and worth of persons and their need for love and care.

It was Immanuel Kant, in the eighteenth century, who gave us the modern and secular version of an ethical theory based on the dignity of persons. Kant repeatedly appeals to the absolute worth of human beings who are rational and free. This leads to the second formulation of his categorical imperative: "Act in such a way that you treat humanity, whether in your own person or in the person of another, always at the same time as an end and never simply as a means" (1981, 36). And why should persons be treated as ends in themselves? Because, a person "is not a thing and hence is not something to be used merely as a means", says Kant. Because, persons are free, autonomous, and rational creatures. Kant goes right on to give some applications of this principle of human dignity. "Therefore I cannot dispose of man in my own person by mutilating, damaging, or killing him" (36). Making a false promise also involves using another person because this other person cannot possibly concur with my way of acting towards him or her. The principle of dignity also precludes attacking the freedom and property of another person. Kant has little to say about love and care for persons, but these virtues can certainly be extrapolated from his emphasis on the worth of persons.

Another approach can be taken to defending the dignity and worth of persons – an appeal to religion. Indeed, it can be argued that Kant's secular defence of human dignity ultimately draws on a Judeo-Christian framework. Here I will only refer to one recent expression of a Christian foundation for defending the dignity of persons. Similar defences can also be found within Jewish and Muslim religions, as is to be expected given the historical connections between these three religions. In his biography of Pope John Paul II, George Weigel suggests that the dignity of the human being was one of the central themes of John Paul II's twenty-five year pontificate (Weigel 1999, 289, 348). Even before his election as Pope, Karol Wojtyla was developing his understanding of the dignity of the human person in his philosophical and theological writings.[29] In a recent essay entitled "Pope John Paul II and the Dignity of the Human Being", John Coughlin identifies two ancient truths that provide the philosophical foundation of John Paul II's defence of the dignity of the human being (2003, 66–71). First, it posits the universality of our shared human nature that transcends the limits of history and culture. Second, like Immanuel Kant, John Paul II accepts the classical metaphysical view that understands the human person as characterized by intellect and free will.

From a theological perspective the most fundamental reason for respecting the dignity of the human being is that each person is created in the image of God. This, together with the theme of redemption, provide the key theological foundations of John Paul II's defence of human dignity according to Coughlin (2003, 71–74). In the first encyclical letter of his pontificate, *Redemptor Hominis*, John Paul II focused on the theological principle that the redemption of Christ fulfills and enhances the dignity of the human being.

The Great Commandment, which appears in all three of the religious traditions being used for illustrative purposes in this monograph, assumes the dignity and worth of human beings. We are to love our neighbor as ourselves (Lev 19:18; Lk 10:27). Love of one's neighbor, however, is ultimately rooted in love of God who created the neighbor in his own image (Deut 6:5). That is why the second part of the Great Commandment is seen as related to the first (Matt 22:39). We can only claim to love God if we treat people with love and respect and dignity.

The dignity and worth of persons, respect for persons, and love for persons – these are the foundations on which my treatment of the ethics of proselytizing rests. My later analysis of criteria to distinguish between ethical and unethical proselytizing will also be built on these same foundations. The reader may prefer a religious or a secular interpretation of these foundations. Here it needs to be kept in mind that my treatment of the ethics of proselytizing is meant to bridge the divide that sometimes separates believers and nonbelievers. This book is addressed to both sets of readers. Hence the need to try and find an ethical foundation that believers and non-believers share. The practical question remains as to whether a consensus on these values is possible.

---

[29] See, for example, Wojtyla (1981, 1979).

Consensus and relativism

In addressing this practical question I again want to approach this from both a secular and a religious perspective. I begin with a strand of philosophical ethics that has been referred to as pragmatic liberalism.[30] The methodological heart of liberalism is to try to overcome the conflict that exists because of differences in the deeply held beliefs of people. The original goal of liberalism was very practical – to find a way of resolving differences and thus avoid the conflicts that used to divide societies. This goal of liberalism, as Jeffrey Stout notes, is surely a good thing (1988, 238). However, it is difficult to achieve this goal, because we cannot begin reasoning from a neutral foundation.

> None of us start from scratch in moral reasoning. Nor can we ever start over again, accepting only beliefs that have been deduced from certitudes or demonstrable facts. We begin already immersed in the assumptions and precedents of a tradition, whether religious or secular, and we revise these assumptions and set new precedents as we learn more about ourselves and our world (Stout 1988, 120).

Our ethics is therefore always a work in progress, and in a global village, it will of necessity grow out of contacts with all people in the world, however different their beliefs. Though somewhat flexible, traditions do eventually emerge, though they are always changing, argues Stout (1988, 288). "Our task . . . is to take the many parts of a complicated social and conceptual inheritance and stitch them together into a pattern that meets the needs of the moment" (292).

Does this lead to moral relativism? No, says Stout, because as we engage in dialogue with others, we will find common ground, particularly with regard to practices, which are obviously wrong (1988, 287). John Rawls introduces the idea of an overlapping consensus to describe this common ground (1987). Here a picture might be useful (see Figure #1: Overlapping Ellipses).[31] Imagine a series of ellipses, each representing a different worldview or belief system, but all overlapping to some degree. Each ellipse is unique, and yet there is some common ground. The common ground represented by the overlap will be interpreted and justified in different ways in each particular belief

---

[30] See Rorty (1982) and Rawls (1971; 1987; 1993).

[31] I have borrowed this diagram from a presentation made by Trevor Cooling at the International Seminar on Religious Education and Values, held at Banff in 1992.

system. But there is still some common ground based on the need for a pragmatic consensus in a pluralistic world.

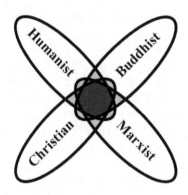

Figure #1: Overlapping Ellipses

This notion of an overlapping consensus also has a religious counterpart. For example, Hans Küng has argued for the possibility and necessity of a global ethics shared by all major world religions. In 1989, a major UNESCO symposium in Paris explored the possibility of support for common ethical values and human rights in the religions of the world. A core paper given by Hans Küng, "No World Peace without Religious Peace", argued that only a religion, which promotes true humanity, *humanitas*, is a true and good religion. This paper eventually led to a consensus amongst the representatives of the various religions present, where each was able to support the ideal of the truly human, leading to some basic common moral values, though such support would be expressed in different ways in each religion (Kuschel 1990).[32]

In another essay, "Towards a World Ethic of World Religions", Küng identifies basic ethical imperatives that he sees as common in all the major world religions (1990). He also finds strong convergence on the Golden Rule, either in its positive or negative form: "Do not do to

---

[32] Hans Küng's later book, *Global Responsibility: In Search of a New World Ethic* (1993), again argues that the religions of the world can make a contribution to the peace of humankind only if they develop a consensus with regard to ethical norms. This book prompted a Parliament of the World's Religions in Chicago in 1993, which in turn led to a "Declaration towards a Global Ethic" (see Küng and Kuschel 1993). See also Hans Küng's "Inauguration of the Exhibition: World Religions – Universal Peace – Global Ethic", 19 September 2002 http://www.global-ethic.org/dat-english/00-washington-2002-kueng.htm (retrieved July 16, 2009).

anyone else what you would not like done to you," or "Do to others as you would be done by." Küng sees Kant's categorical imperative as basically a modernization and secularization of the golden rule (1990, 117). Küng is careful to allow for different theoretical and conceptual approaches to these common moral principles. But for him, what is important is agreement in practice. "An ethic is concerned in the last analysis not with a variety of theoretical frames of reference but rather with what should or should not be done, quite practically, in life as it is lived" (Küng 1990, 118). We see here a pragmatic emphasis very similar to that found among pragmatic liberals.

J. Vernon Jensen applies the seeming ethical convergence of world religions to the area of communication ethics (1992).[33] He examines both Eastern and Western religions, and finds that despite significant differences in religious beliefs, the seven religions that he reviews share some common principles in relation to communication ethics. Included in the core ethical standards for communication are such principles as telling the truth, avoiding slander, avoiding blasphemy against sacred persons, symbols or rituals of other religions, avoiding communication that demeans other persons, cultivating character that leads to trustworthiness, and in general, aiming to edify others in your communication. This list of principles surely goes a long way in providing some common ground for an ethics of proselytizing.

Why is there such an overlap? My answer is that we live in the same world. Regardless of our worldviews, we have a common source of data, which imposes constraints on the extent to which we can interpret reality. Human nature is roughly the same. Humans share "moral powers" and "certain fundamental intuitive ideas".[34] We are trying to understand the same reality. We are striving for the same truth. This is what makes an objective and universal ethics possible. Of course, many religious adherents will add that an overlapping consensus is made possible because God established a moral order.

In explaining the reasons for this overlap and the reasons why decent and caring human beings of all religious (or irreligious) persuasions

---

[33] Jensen's paper is summarized in Johannesen (1996, 107).

[34] Interestingly, these terms come from John Rawls, who repeatedly makes reference to "fundamental intuitive ideas regarded as latent in the public political culture" (1987, 6, 8, 20). Here we see a connection between pragmatic liberalism and the appeal to intuition with which I started my treatment. For a contemporary defense of human beings as having a peculiar set of capacities and proclivities, relating to an inescapable moral and spiritual dimension that distinguishes them from animals, see Smith (2003).

agree with regard to basic moral convictions, we seem to be driven to the notion of natural law. This interpretation of the foundations of ethics has both secular and religious defenders. Admittedly, the term natural law has not been understood in the same way in every age. The ancient Stoics saw the whole universe as governed by laws that exhibit rationality. Human beings have within them a divine spark that enables them to discover the essential eternal laws necessary for individual happiness and social harmony. Thomas Aquinas combined the sense of cosmic natural law with Aristotle's view that human beings, like every other natural object, have a specific nature, purpose, and function. "To the natural law belong those things to which a man is inclined naturally; and among these it is proper to man to be inclined to act according to reason."[35]

Pope John Paul II's affirmation of the universality of one human nature includes the idea of a permanent natural law contained within the human person and known by reason (Coughlin 2003, 67). The early Church Fathers and the Protestant Reformers too presumed natural law as a realm of common grace that is accessible to all people by virtue of creation – hence in Paul's terms, all are "without excuse" (Rom 1:20). Today there would seem to be a renewed interest in natural law among Catholic and Protestant thinkers.[36]

In both the secular and religious versions of natural law, two questions are closely linked: What is right? How do we discover what is right? It is because the universe is a rational whole that human beings, who are also rational, can discover natural law by reason. Yes, difficulties do emerge as to how to interpret reason. While we cannot be entirely objective, we must try to observe and describe nature as accurately as possible. Further, clearly not all of nature can be followed, because nature itself is rather ambiguous. Hence some principle of selectivity is required, and thus natural law theory tends to appeal to nature in some ideal, original, or primeval sense. Rational observation of nature can also involve a study of the broader consequences of human actions. Why do human codes and conventions seem eventually to converge? Because, "natural law . . . tests itself in the laboratory of history," argues Gonsalves (1985, 136). Individuals, tribes, and nations, if they adopt a form of life contrary to the natural law, will

---

[35] Quotation from Thomas Aquinas, *Summa Theologica*, Question 94, Second Article (1945).

[36] Budziszewski (2006), Charles (2006), and Cromartie (1997) review Catholic, Protestant, Jewish and Secular advocates of natural law.

eventually suffer the consequences. History has a way of punishing the folly of such living because it violates our very nature.

At other times reason in natural law theory has been equated with intuition, the notion that deep down inside, all of us (or at least most of us – those of us who are rational and care about morality) know when we do fail in the moral realm.[37] Even philosophers who would otherwise espouse some other ethical theory often find it necessary to resort to an appeal to self-evidence. Everybody knows that we ought to be kind and caring in our relationships; everybody knows that we ought generally to tell the truth. Everyone knows that we ought to be just in our dealings with others. Particularly with regard to extreme abuses of the human person, there is remarkable convergence. Everyone knows that indiscriminate torture is wrong, that it is generally wrong to coerce someone to do something against his or her will. How do we know? Well, human beings just know certain basic moral truths. There are certain things that "we can't not know" (Budziszewski 2003).

I hope the reader will agree with my outline of ethical foundations. But if there should be disagreement about the theoretical foundations of ethics, then I hope there will at least be agreement on my analysis of the cases studies of proselytizing that I gave as a preface to my treatment of ethical foundations. It is sometimes easier, and certainly more important, to reach consensus about practical ethics than about theoretical ethics. But if the reader should disagree with either approach, then he/she will simply have to grant me my assumptions so that we can proceed to a consideration of the ethics of proselytizing.

---

[37] For a classic statement of an appeal to intuition as a basis for ethics see Sir William David Ross, *The Right and the Good* (1930). Ross sees the basic *prima facie* duties as self-evident. "The moral order expressed in these propositions is . . . part of the fundamental nature of the universe." "We have no more direct way of access to the facts about rightness and goodness and about what things are right or good, than by thinking about them; the moral convictions of thoughtful and well-educated people are the data of ethics just as sense-perceptions are the data of a natural science" (Ross 1930, ch. 2, "What Makes Right Acts Right?").

Part II:

Objections to Proselytizing

Chapter 3

Epistemological/Ethical Objections to Proselytizing

Criticizing proselytizers seems to be rather popular. Such criticisms are to be found in any number of dialogues on the internet, newspaper editorials, letters to editors, student newspapers on university campuses, and the media generally. Academics too have joined in the fray. These critics hold that much, if not most, proselytizing is immoral. Others make the stronger claim that proselytizing is essentially immoral, that it is, by its very nature, immoral. In this, and the next few chapters, I want to focus mainly on the sweeping generalization that proselytizing is *inherently* wrong. This claim is, I believe, mistaken. In trying to respond to this very negative assessment that all proselytizing is immoral, I will at the same time be weakening the more modest claims often made to the effect that most proselytizing is immoral.

In attempting to defend proselytizing I am of course assuming that the question as to whether proselytizing is moral or not is an open question. Unfortunately, it would seem that for some critics, proselytizing is immoral *by definition*. For example, Astro5, in an internet dialogue I referred to in chapter 1, maintains: "Killing is wrong, but Christianizing the world is just as wrong." No reasons are given for this comparison. It is just assumed that Christianizing the world is obviously and inherently wrong. Richard Perloff, in a book on persuasion, points to another expression of such a question-begging association. Proselytizing obviously involves persuasion, and Perloff points out that in the popular mind, persuasion is associated with a wide variety of phenomena, including brainwashing, mind control, hypnotic suggestion, mass conformity, coercion, and propaganda (1993, 11).

Unfortunately, this kind of arbitrariness also seems to be found among more serious critics of proselytizing, particularly with regard to the association of proselytizing with coercion. I want to postpone treatment of some examples of such association until the next chapter where I will deal with the issue of coercion in proselytizing.

For now, I want to point to the danger of simply assuming that proselytizing is coercive or that it is inherently wrong. My concern here is that we don't beg the question by arbitrarily making this assumption. To argue with those who appeal to such stipulative definitions is pointless. In the chapters that follow, I am assuming that the question as to whether proselytizing is necessarily immoral is an open question. Hence, we need to examine carefully whether or not the features often associated with proselytizing, such as irrationality, intolerance, cajoling, aggressiveness, deception and brainwashing, are in fact necessary, or even probable accompaniments of proselytizing.

A further problem with the frequently stated objections to proselytizing needs to be dealt with before we go on to consider some specific objections. The problem is this – objections to proselytizing most often come as a package – a whole series of objections are lumped together, the collective force of which is to make proselytizing sound as an irredeemable evil. Jay Newman, for example, alerts us to the fact that we often find proselytizers "arrogant, ignorant, hypocritical, meddlesome" (1982, 89). In the concluding paragraph of this same essay he sums up with another catalogue of proselytizing sins: "Most religious proselytizing tends to promote resentment. Resentment promotes intolerance, which in turn promotes barbarism" (110). There is some justification for such groupings of objections, as often one objection is in fact related to the other. But there is also a danger in such collective cataloguing of the evils of proselytizing. It discourages careful and critical analysis. In the interests of clarity, I therefore believe it is important to treat each objection to proselytizing individually. At the same time, an attempt will be made to show how one objection is related to another.

In this chapter, I examine those objections to proselytizing that are in some way related to epistemological/ethical concerns. In chapter 4, I will examine objections that relate to the integrity of individuals and societies. Chapter 5 will be devoted to objections that have their roots in liberal assumptions. There is some arbitrariness in any classification. I trust the reader will see some merit in the way in which I have grouped the various objections to proselytizing, as well as in my attempt to deal with specific objections one at a time.

Persuasion

I begin with a suggestion that our negative attitudes towards proselytizing are in fact more generally rooted in a negative attitude towards persuasion. Genevieve McBride points out that there would seem to be "a great deal of public unease about persuasion" (1989, 14). A book on communication ethics points to a widespread defensive attitude towards persuaders (Jaksa and Pritchard 1994, 76).[1] Indeed, this negative evaluation of persuasion is very widespread, and has had a long history, extending from ancient attitudes towards the sophists, to modern critics of advertising such as Vance Packard (1957). This suspicion carries over to various practitioners of persuasion, for example, people involved in public relations, merchandizing, and of course, proselytizing.

It will be helpful here to examine more carefully the language that is used in describing persuasion or the persuasive component of proselytizing in particular. For example, a key concern for Margaret Battin is the element of persuasion in proselytizing. She uses terms like "accosting", "buttonholing", and "haranguing" to describe proselytizing/persuasion, and finds these strategies to be morally problematic because "they invade privacy and characteristically involve a deliberate attempt to disrupt a person's previously held framework of belief" (Battin 1990, 137).

Sonja Foss and Cindy Griffin, in an article revealingly entitled, "Beyond Persuasion: A Proposal for an Invitational Rhetoric", provide us with a feminist expression of opposition to persuasion (1995). As might be expected, Foss and Griffin object to the patriarchal bias that undergirds most theories of rhetoric, one manifestation of which is defining of rhetoric as persuasion. "As far back as the Western discipline of rhetoric has been explored, rhetoric has been defined as the conscious intent to change others" (2). In rhetoric, self-worth is "derived from and measured by the power exerted over others" (4). It also involves "a devaluation of the life worlds of others" (4). In summary, Foss and Griffin argue that the traditional conception of rhetoric "is a rhetoric of patriarchy, reflecting its values of change, competition, and domination" (4).

In my introduction to chapter 1, I referred to a dialogue on the internet where one critic of Christian missionaries raises a suggestive

---

[1] In a similar vein, Richard Johannesen, in discussing Martin Buber's distinction between monologue and dialogue, suggests that some writers equate monologue and persuasion, and hence "contend that all attempts at persuasion are unethical" (1996, 71).

question: "Why can't they keep their belief to themselves?" Martin
Marty and Frederick Greenspahn, in the dust-jacket of their anthology
of essays based on a symposium on the subject, *Pushing the Faith* (1988),
suggest that the essayists are all trying to answer comedian Jimmy
Durante's celebrated question: "Why doesn't everybody leave everybody else the hell alone?" Marty, in a concluding essay, suggests this
question was probably voiced by Durante as a signal of impatience,
"perhaps after having been approached too often by proselytizers for
too many causes" (1988, 155). I believe the question posed by Durante
highlights the main reason for the widespread suspicions about persuasion – we like to think of ourselves as autonomous.[2] We see
ourselves as independent thinkers and we believe that we don't need
anyone meddling around with our beliefs. Leave us alone! After all, we
can make up our own minds, thank you very much!

There is a problem with this attitude, however. None of us are quite
as independent as we like to think we are. The human condition is characterized fundamentally by inter-dependence, and this also applies to
the way in which we acquire our beliefs. Indeed, most (maybe even 95%)
of the beliefs that we hold are a result of persuasion. Just think of all the
beliefs that we've inherited from our parents. Here we need to keep in
mind that persuasion can be both, explicit or implicit. Some time ago
Vance Packard, a noted critic of the advertising industry, correctly drew
our attention to hidden persuaders. The phenomenon of hidden persuasion applies especially to the beliefs, attitudes and prejudices that we
absorb in childhood. This is similarly true for many of the beliefs that we
absorb via our immediate environment – the media and our culture.
These are powerful persuaders, and we can't avoid them.

Then there are our teachers. Much of what we believe is accepted on
authority. Children believe what their teachers say. Even at universities,
professors exert a powerful persuasive influence on students. Indeed,
university professors themselves are not quite as independent as they
would like to think. They too submit to the latest academic fads and to
pressures of political correctness. The late Richard John Neuhaus, a
prominent churchman and writer, liked to characterize the intellectual
elite and the chattering class as a herd of independent minds!

What is interesting here is that modern suspicions about persuasion
can be traced to the Enlightenment. Stephen Toulmin traces Western

---

[2] Foss and Griffin are very explicit in identifying self-determination as a key third
principle that typically comprises a feminist worldview, and that underlies their
critique of rhetoric as persuasion (1995, 4).

culture's disinterest in oral rhetoric to the seventeenth century and the rise of modern science and philosophy. Given the conception of rationality that evolved during this time, "formal logic was in, rhetoric was out" (Toulmin 1990, 31). But this notion of being persuaded by pure and objective reason alone is increasingly coming under attack given recent developments in philosophy and the emergence of a new epistemology since the 1960s. Thus various hermeneutical philosophers today, following Nietzsche, recognize the rhetorical dimensions of language generally, and therefore maintain that we can no longer sharply separate logic from rhetoric. At the same time, these philosophers reject the idea of a sovereign rational subject – atomistic and autonomous, disengaged and disembodied.

What is needed here is a realistic view of human nature and autonomy. With Lawrence Haworth (1986), I argue for an ideal of normal autonomy, which balances individual worth and independence with our social nature and an inescapable degree of human interdependence.[3] We also need to be more realistic about belief and knowledge acquisition, and acknowledge our dependence on others and our need to have others persuade us about many things. Indeed, as has been noted by Henry Johnstone, a human being is, among other things, "a persuading and persuaded animal" (1981, 306).

More generally, I want to suggest that we are not consistent in our evaluation of persuasion. Our suspicions about persuasion do not always accord with common usage and practice. All of us spend a good deal of time persuading others. A mother persuades a child to tie her shoelaces. A father persuades his teenage daughter to consider attending college. A professor tries to persuade her students to do their homework and not to plagiarize on their essays. A liberal politician tries to persuade the public to vote for him. A NASA scientist tries to persuade his colleagues about the dangers of proceeding immediately with the next space launch. I am trying, in this book, to persuade the reader that ethical proselytizing is indeed possible. Is there anything inherently wrong with these attempts at persuasion? I hope all my readers will concur with my assumed negative answer to this rhetorical question. Of course, the attempts at persuasion in each of these cases could become immoral if they included the abuse of children or students, for example. But, there is nothing wrong with

---

[3] For a more detailed analysis of this argument, see Thiessen (1993, ch. 5). Charles Taylor similarly stresses the cultural and social aspects of individual identity (1989).

persuasion *in and of itself*. Persuasion is a natural part of being human.

Here let me add a note addressed particularly to academics who are suspicious about persuasion. If academics like Newman, Battin, or Foss and Griffin, wish to hold that all attempts to alter the beliefs of others are suspect, then they should extend their suspicions also to the areas of education and scholarship, since the purpose of argumentation, scholarship, and indeed the educational enterprise generally, is precisely to persuade and alter beliefs. However, as Baber correctly notes, it is unlikely that these scholars hold this view about practices in which they themselves engage (2000, 338). I would suggest that it is because of this practical inconsistency that there is an ambiguity in the positions held by each of these critics of persuasion and proselytizing. For example, Foss and Griffin, after their sharp critique of the patriarchal bias that undergirds most theories of rhetoric and persuasion, are forced to concede that they are in fact trying to persuade others by the very fact of having written their article (1995, 8). Of course, they try to downplay the persuasion involved by describing it as an offering of an alternative viewpoint, or as "invitational rhetoric" (5). But, a rose by any other name is still a rose! Indeed, in seeming contradiction to their entire position, they at several points admit that "persuasion is often necessary" (5, 17). I would go further and argue that persuasion in inescapable.

A further problem with any interpretation of persuasion in terms of power and control over others, is that such charges are ultimately self-defeating. Foss and Griffin, in their attempts at persuading us to adopt a model of invitational rhetoric are themselves exerting power over their readers. If all that is involved in persuasion is a wielding of power, why should we listen to them? Indeed, why should we pay attention to anybody? Let's fight it out instead. Perhaps a shared, honest, and humble search for truth might help us to avoid the blood-letting that is all too characteristic of our university campuses today. Perhaps truth does matter, after all! More on this in a later chapter.

Of course, persuasion can be conducted in such a way as to be invasive and a violation of another person's dignity. For example, if in the course of a normal conversation, I begin to try to persuade you about something, and you decide that you don't like what I am doing, and you tell me so, it would be immoral for me to continue to try to persuade you. Thus there is something right about a suggestion that is sometimes made to the effect that we do not have the authority or entitlement to persuade others unless they specifically invite us to do so.

But, the requirement that there needs to be an invitation to persuade is too strong. It would be better to talk about giving permission to persuade, realizing that permission can be given implicitly or explicitly. It is when permission to persuade is denied, in whatever way such a denial might be expressed, that it is immoral to continue to try to persuade. There are of course other ways in which persuasion can become immoral. But persuasion is not in and of itself immoral. So, rather than condemning persuasion outright, what we need to do is to identify criteria to make the distinction between acceptable and unacceptable means of persuasion.

Arrogance

The second objection to proselytizing that I want to consider has to do with the seeming arrogance of proselytizers. This is a frequently made charge as we have already seen in the previous two chapters. Take, for example, a letter to the editor, written in response to a report that the Southern Baptist Convention was sending missionaries into post-war Iraq. LeMaitre objects to this project: "The Southern Baptist Convention, in suggesting the Iraqi people need deliverance, displays an arrogance that is astonishing in its scale."[4] Jay Newman too identifies arrogance as one of the problems we often have with proselytizers (1982, 89). David Novak, after highlighting the fact that he is raising some moral objections to proselytizing, describes most Jews as being "deeply resentful of the arrogance of those who proselytize"(1999, 43). Novak is very clear in suggesting that proselytizers are by their very nature arrogant because he goes right on to say that they "inevitably come across as men and women who are so self-righteous that they feel no moral compunction in denigrating other faiths" (43). We have here also an explanation as to why the charge of arrogance is made against proselytizing. Proselytizers assume that they have the truth. They further proclaim their truth as something that everyone should believe.

In the previous chapter we have already seen how such a conviction about possessing the truth is a basic motivation for proselytizing.

---

[4] *The Globe and Mail* (10 April 2003), p. A20. The Southern Baptist Convention came under similar scrutiny a few years earlier when it issued a prayer for the conversion of Jews. The Anti-Defamation League called it "an act of theological arrogance" (Michael Kinsley, "Don't Want to Convert? Just Say No", *Time* [19 Feb 2001], p. 35).

Those who proselytize assume that they have the truth and that everyone needs to hear their truth. Of course, this assumption itself needs to be evaluated, and I will deal with it later in this chapter. Here we see how one objection to proselytizing is closely related to another. For now I want to focus more narrowly on the attitudinal charge of arrogance.

Clearly, there is a kind of arrogance that colors proselytizing, but I do not believe it is of the morally culpable sort. Most human communication, by its very nature, is arrogant to some degree. I write a letter because I arrogantly believe that I have something to say to someone. I disagree with you, and argue my case. Again, this involves a degree of arrogance. Who am I to dare to defend my position against yours? A physician tries to persuade a patient to stop smoking because she, though a fallible expert, believes this will help to alleviate some of the health problems faced by this patient. Again, this cannot help but seem somewhat paternalistic and arrogant. Both disagreement with another, and trying to persuade another, presume that I am right and that the other is mistaken or misguided. But, surely there is nothing wrong with this kind of arrogance. Further, as Alvin Plantinga has argued, if contradicting others is arrogant and egotistical, so is dissenting. "These charges of arrogance are a philosophical tar baby: Get close enough to them to use them against the exclusivist and you are likely to find them stuck fast to yourself" (2000, 177).

Of course, I can disagree with you *in a haughty manner*, and *then* you would be able to charge me with failing to display a proper humility. But disagreeing with you, or trying to persuade you of my position, is not in and of itself arrogant in a morally culpable sense. Neither is proselytizing. This distinction, between persuading someone, and doing so in an arrogant and haughty manner is a subtle one, so let me illustrate. Right now I am trying to convert some of my readers who disagree with me about the morality of proselytizing. Some of you belong to the anti-proselytizing camp, and I am trying to get you to belong to my camp. Some of you believe proselytizing is always wrong, and I am trying to change your beliefs. Ultimately, I may even be trying to change your behavior. So three of the elements of conversion, as outlined in chapter 2, are present. But surely there is nothing morally wrong with this little enterprise of mine. Nor should my trying to convert you be seen as a display of arrogance.

Now you might find that I am doing so in a haughty manner – this would be even more apparent if I were giving a speech. I sincerely hope that an audience would not find me arrogant and haughty. But if

I were very dogmatic in what I said, and sounded cocky, and strutted around putting on airs, then I could legitimately be accused of being arrogant. In actual fact, I admit that I might be wrong – I am, after all, a fallible human being. That is why there will no doubt be critical reviews of this book, and I look forward to receiving them. My own Christian commitment demands humility in the pronouncements that I make, because human knowledge is imperfect, we only know in part, and we see but a poor reflection of the full truth.[5] At the same time, I do have a position that I hold, and I do think that those who disagree with me are wrong, and when given a chance I will even try to convert opponents to my position. That in itself should not be seen as an expression of arrogance.

One further point needs to be made about the relation between arrogance and humility, and their relation to truth and falsity.[6] Pronouncements and attempts to persuade often seem to be arrogant only because there has been a prejudgment as to the falsity of what is being said. Consider, for example, a centuries-old debate concerning the shape of the earth. Round-earth believers were challenging the established beliefs of flat-earthers. The latter clearly thought the round-earth believers were mistaken, and it is precisely because of this that the pronouncements of the round-earth believers will have seemed to be arrogant. In fact, those holding to the round-earth theory may have been very humble men, doubting their own position from time to time, and only tentatively putting forth their theory. Similarly, Christians who believe that Jesus was the Son of God in the flesh, the Messiah promised in the Old Testament, and God's ultimate revelation, may seem to be making arrogant pronouncements to Jews and Muslims and atheists, but this may simply be due to the fact that Christian claims are believed to be obviously false. Clearly, at some point we need to address the question of the truth or falsity of the message being proclaimed. But we need to separate this question from the question of attitudes or character-traits of arrogance and humility.

I therefore believe that it is a mistake to characterize proselytizing as immoral because it is arrogant, or because it involves implicit and explicit negative judgments about the worldviews and religious positions held by those who are the object of proselytism. However, I would

---

[5] See 1 Cor 13:9–12, and Gooch (1987).

[6] I was alerted to this point by an article, "Must the Truth Offend?" by Jerry L. Walls, in *First Things* (June/July 1998), pp. 34–37.

hasten to add that sometimes proselytizing is done in an offensively arrogant manner. Sometimes missionaries have approached the "heathen" with a condescending air (Thangaraj 1999, 339). Many European Christian missionaries adopted hopelessly paternalistic attitudes towards the Indians of North America. They assumed, with the colonialists, that their European society was inherently superior to that of Native peoples, and therefore they took it upon themselves to transform the entire culture of the Native peoples into an image more acceptable to European sensibilities (Furniss 1995, 15–16). But here again we need to be careful. Not all Christian missionaries adopted an arrogant and paternalistic attitude.[7] And might it be that the Christian missionaries were in fact right at some points?

What I have been arguing in this section is that proselytizing isn't inherently arrogant and condescending in a morally culpable sense. Therefore, rather than condemning proselytizing as immoral by its very nature, Novak and others should focus instead on defining the distinction between arrogant proselytizing and acceptable proselytizing that is done in a humble way.

Truth and religious pluralism

As already noted, the charge of arrogance against proselytizing grows out of the assumption that the one doing the proselytizing has the truth. Proselytizers also invariably proclaim their truth as something that everyone should believe. The assumption of truth is what inspires religious adherents to propagate the faith. But suppose that these assumptions are wrong. Suppose a particular religious position cannot be seen as being the "Truth", or even as being better or "truer" than another. Does this not then make any sort of proselytizing seem arrogant? Indeed, would not proselytizing as a whole be unwarranted and even immoral if there is no such a thing as truth in the area of religion, or, if there is no such a thing as truth, period?

There are a variety of ways in which the notion of truth has been called into question. For example, postmodernism has been a significant contributing factor, as has been highlighted by Middleton/Walsh in their intriguingly titled book: *Truth Is Stranger Than It Used to Be* (1995). Some writers go so far as to suggest that truth is just an artificial construction, a product of particular circumstances. Another

---

[7] William Penn and Roger Williams might be cited as humble proselytizers.

contributing factor has been the growing awareness of pluralism. Competing claims to truth would seem to undermine the idea that there is such a thing as truth with a capital "T". Then there are various forms of relativism and skepticism.

These kinds of arguments are also found within discussions of religion. A greater awareness of religious pluralism has brought to the fore a tension between exclusive and inclusive approaches to religion. Following current practice, I will define the religious exclusivist as one who holds that the tenets of one religion, say Christianity, are in fact true; and hence any other religious beliefs that are incompatible with those tenets are false (Plantinga 2000, 174). Inclusivist approaches to religion attempt to be more accommodating to the fact of religious pluralism and are essentially relativistic in orientation. For example, Hinduism tends to be inclusivistic and maintains that differing religions represent various manifestations of the divine. Interestingly, there is little of the proselytizing impulse within Hinduism.[8]

This same inclusivist approach is also found within liberal Protestantism. For example, liberal Christian theologians like John Hick and Paul Knitter (1987) have tried to eliminate the absolute claims to truth within Christianity in order to be more accommodating to other religions. I want to look more carefully at an expression of this position as found in an oft-reprinted introduction to pluralism and world religions by Harold Coward (2000). In the conclusion to his study, Coward objects to "the simplistic pattern of the past in which the problem of pluralism was overcome by application of the principle of non-contradiction", where, when two religious positions were seen to be contradictory, it was assumed that "both could not be correct at the same time", and an attempt was made to overcome the contradiction by making a decision "as to which of the positions was correct" (147–48). He specifically objects to Hans Küng's Christocentric theology in which "all religions are recognized (in varying degrees) to be particular manifestations of God", but where Christianity is still "seen as the only religion that fully (or most fully) manifests God and therefore must serve as the criterion for all others" (151).

This leads Coward to object to "missionary activity that occurs when the superimposition of one's own criteria upon the other is followed by efforts to convert the other" (2000 143–44). He advocates instead respectful dialogue and sharing of religious perspectives, which can result in spiritual growth and enrichment for all, and even the possibility of conversion (144, 152–58). It would seem, however, that active

---

[8] This claim can be disputed, as I have noted in chapter 2, n.#12.

proselytizing based on the acceptance of universal and exclusive truth is unacceptable.

In fairness to Coward it needs to be pointed out that in places he seems to be more sympathetic with conservative religious traditions and their notion of exclusive truth. He recognizes the need that all human beings have for sharing their deepest convictions with others.

He acknowledges that such sharing is based on a feeling of absolute commitment, "that deep religious commitment is necessarily absolute", in terms of one's own personal experience (Coward 2000, 154). He describes "ego-attachment to one's own position", as a "universal human characteristic" (150). But in the interests of tolerance and respect for other religious positions, Coward does not want us to impose our absolutist feelings onto others. This would again seem to suggest that he is opposed to proselytizing based on the making of exclusive and absolute truth claims. Indeed, he suggests that even with his favored approach of religious dialogue, the introduction of absolutism would cause such dialogue to "self-destruct" (159).

But is Coward right in linking the making of exclusive claims to truth in a religion with immoral proselytizing? Here it should be noted that we will not, nor do we have to, settle the theological differences between liberal and conservative interpretations of Christianity. Nor do we have to assess the epistemic legitimacy of making exclusive truth claims. Alvin Plantinga (2000) has tried to answer various epistemic objections to exclusivism, but this issue is not our concern here. Rather, I want to argue against any claim that proselytizing in the name of exclusive truth is immoral. I am focusing on Coward's argument as a representative of this position.

There is first of all a problem with Coward's alternative to proselytizing – respectful dialogue. I fail to see how respectful inter-religious dialogue, which is open to the possibility of conversion is so very different from ethical proselytizing. Coward further seems to acknowledge a kind of absolute truth when he expresses the hope that such dialogue will lead to spiritual growth and enrichment for all. Surely growth and enrichment point to some goal that functions at least as an heuristic absolute. Coward further falls prey to either-or thinking when he suggests that the only alternative to religious dialogue (i.e. proselytizing) involves an attempt "to attack or degrade other religious" (2000, 144). Proselytizing can surely be done in such a way that it is respectful of other religions. Coward is not alone in proposing dialogue as an alternative to proselytizing, and so I will come back to this important alternative later in this book.

We have seen that while Coward wants to acknowledge the fact of absolutist feelings, he does not want to impose absolutist feelings onto others. But is the language of imposition even appropriate here? Having absolutist feelings, and even expressing these feelings has nothing to do with imposition. Indeed, the language of coercion is introduced all too often and too quickly in Coward's analysis. For example he uses the term militant exclusivism, to describe conservative religious positions (2000, 147). But surely exclusivism is not necessarily militant. And I want more evidence than the history of modern Iran to back up the claim that exclusivism "usually" breeds "religious violence". I quite agree that religious exclusivism *can* lead to violence, but it is rather arbitrary to claim that it is the doctrine of exclusivism itself that is the cause of religious violence, or that proselytizing based on the assumption of truth will necessarily or even usually lead to religious violence. To hold to a doctrine of religious exclusivism simply does not automatically make one imperialistic or oppressive (Plantinga 2000, 176).

Another more general theoretical problem inherent in liberal and relativistic approaches to religion needs to be brought to the fore. Liberal Christian theologians who adopt a more accommodating and inclusivist approach to other religions are forced to say that their approach is the right way, and that those who don't adopt such an approach are wrong. Thus, Coward assumes he has got it right and Hans Küng has got it wrong. He himself is overcoming the pluralism of religious positions by appealing to the principle of non-contradiction, which he calls simplistic and no longer acceptable (2000, 147–48). Similarly, the Hindu approach of saying that there are many manifestations of the divine seems to be more open, and less arrogant, but again we need to be careful. To say that there are many different manifestations of the divine is still to adopt an exclusive position. It suggests that those who deny this pluralist approach to religion are wrong. Interestingly, Coward acknowledges this very point earlier in his study on pluralism: "The Hindu approach to other religions is to absolutize the relativism implied in the viewpoint that the various religions are simply different manifestations of the one Divine" (Coward 2000, 125). Yes, indeed! But Coward seems to forget all this when discussing Hans Küng.

What seems to be particularly worrisome about the making of universal and absolute truth claims is that they implicitly or explicitly entail criticism of other positions. This is clearly part of Coward's concern when he criticizes the principle of non-contradiction which forces us to identify certain positions as correct and other as incorrect. This is also David Novak's concern when he worries about "denigrating other faiths" when proselytizing (1999, 43). I would argue, however, that judgment and criticism of other positions is inescapable. When we affirm something as true, we are at the same time saying that the opposite is not true. Thus, if "ego-attachment to one's own position" is a "universal human characteristic", as Coward maintains, then by implication he should also acknowledge that criticism of others is inherent in human nature. Coward himself identifies one position as correct and another as incorrect. He specifically criticizes Hans Küng and other militant exclusivists. *Criticism is simply inescapable.* Coward tries to take the edge off criticism when he encourages us "to constructively criticize and learn from one another" (2000, 155). But there is a contradiction inherent in the very notion of constructive criticism. Criticism is by its very nature critical, and even destructive in a certain sense.

Of course, what Coward no doubt has in mind here are the harmful attitudes that sometimes accompany criticism – self-righteousness, destructive negativism, and criticism for the sake of criticism. I agree that these are wrong. But, we must not shy away from honest, truthful, and caring criticism. And we must not make the mistake of thinking that respect for differing religious convictions precludes making critical judgments about them. It seems that we are unable to avoid making denigrating statements about other religions. Even David Novak, who criticizes the denigration inherent in Christian proselytizing of Jews is forced to defend Judaism as "the highest truth and the greatest good" in order to counter the supersessionist claims of Christianity (1999, 35–36, 44). To say that Judaism is the highest truth and the greatest good is to suggest at the same time that Christianity does not have this elevated status. I have no problem with the making of such an exclusivist claim with its implicit denigration of Christianity. Let's just admit that we are doing it. And when we do, we will no longer have problems with the exclusive truth-making claims inherent in proselytizing.

Coward goes further than most liberals in acknowledging the importance of making exclusive claims in religion. He recognizes that "deep religious commitment is necessarily absolute", though it needs to be underscored that he is only talking about one's personal experience here (2000, 154). Coward draws on Paul Knitter's distinction between one's commitment to truth and one's grasp of truth, suggesting "that while there are no absolute expressions of truth, there are absolute commitments" (154). Here I disagree, first of all, with the claim that deep religious commitment is necessarily absolute. I, for one, consider myself deeply committed to the Christian faith, and yet have doubts about my commitment from time to time. Some degree of tentativeness would seem to be inescapable with any religious commitment that is held by honest and rational individuals. Another problem is that both of the polarities introduced by Knitter still are only dealing with human experience – human expressions of truth, and human commitments to truth. In the end Coward and Knitter refuse to allow for an ideal of absolute truth in the area of religion. All religions are ultimately treated as equally valid. Hence, his rejection of an appeal to the principle of non-contradiction, which necessitates evaluating which of two contradictory positions is correct. Hence also, Coward's rejection of Hans Küng's Christocentric exclusivism. And therefore also Coward's hesitancy with regard to proselytizing based on the assumption that one really has the truth about religion.

I want to go further than Coward in allowing for an ideal of absolute truth even in the area of religion. At the same time, I want to acknowledge the limitations inherent in the human search for absolute truth. Only such a balanced approach to truth will do justice to conservative religious traditions and at the same time answer the objection to proselytizing which we are now considering. Let me expand on this briefly.

The notion of absolute truth is needed as a goal or as a regulative or heuristic principle. William James captures this regulative function of absolute truth well when he describes the absolutely true as "that ideal vanishing point towards which we imagine that all our temporary truths will someday converge" (1968, 170). Thomas Nagel describes absolute truth as "a view from nowhere" (1986). Although we cannot get a view from nowhere, according to Nagel, there is within each of us an impulse to transcend our particular personal point of view. This occurs because we recognize that it *is* merely a point of view, a perspective, and not simply an account of the way things really are. "The recognition that this is so", he writes, "creates pressure on the imagination to recast our picture of the world so that it is no longer the view from here" (Nagel 1986, 70). In other words, each of us is aware of the possibility that our particular perspective might be wrong, and so we aspire to "the view from nowhere", to a view uncontaminated by any perspectival factors.[9] This

---

[9] Or, as Nagel puts it in his more recent work, the last word is not that this is justified "for me" or "for us". Instead, it is an affirmation of objective truth that any reasoner is obliged to recognize. The last word does not belong to human nature. "The idea of reason, by contrast, refers to nonlocal and nonrelative methods of justification – methods that distinguish universally legitimate from illegitimate inferences and that aim at reaching the truth in a nonrelative manner" (1997, 5).

view from nowhere can alternately be described as an all-encompassing perspective that only God could have (James 1968, 160).

The notion of absolute truth, or a view from nowhere, or an all-encompassing perspective of God is required for an adequate epistemology. Only if we assume such an ideal can we make sense of the human tendency to absolutize, which Coward and Knitter acknowledge. Heidegger reminded us that the essential meaning of truth is *disclosure (Erschlossenheit)*, and thus ultimately truth always seems like a gift. In a way, it forces itself on us. Once convinced, we have no choice but to acknowledge it as absolute truth.[10] At the same time we are always aware of the fact that we might be wrong. Such an admission again requires an ideal of truth, which serves as a standard of comparison by which we come to recognize our mistaken convictions. I quite agree that we can never presume to have arrived at absolute truth. As fallible human beings we are stuck with having a limited perspective. We only see through a glass darkly, as is stated in the Christian scriptures (1 Cor 13:12). The human search for truth is finite and fallible. But this search only makes sense if we presuppose an ideal of absolute truth.

Yes, there are limitations inherent in our search for truth and we need to be honest about these limitations. However, I in no way want to do away with the notion that human beings must, and invariably do, attempt to transcend these limitations in their search for universal and absolute truth. Without balancing the emphasis on limitations with an equal emphasis on the need to try to transcend these limitations, we end up with epistemological relativism. While the human search for truth may be relative, we still need a notion of Truth with a capital "T" as an ideal towards which we are striving (see Figure #1: Ladder of Truth).

I believe this approach to truth can also be applied to the area of religion. We must allow for both, the particularity of religions, and an ideal of religious truth, which is universal and absolute. This approach does justice to Hans Küng's bold claim that one should be a Christian because Jesus of Nazareth is "ultimate, decisive, definitive, and archetypal for man's relations with God, with his fellow man, with society", which is the phrase that Coward finds so offensive and wrong (Coward 2000, 151). At the same time, this approach acknowledges the

---

[10] William James quite correctly suggests that we may not be as free as we think we are in choosing the beliefs that we consider to be true ("The Will to Believe", Section II, in James 1968, 90–93)

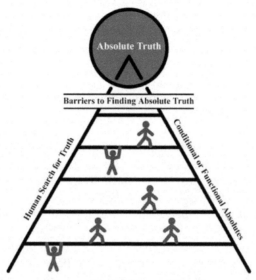

Figure #1: Ladder of Truth

finite limits of the human mind in grasping this truth. Indeed, upon careful reflection, the Christian (including Hans Küng) must confess that he might have it wrong, because there are other religious adherents who feel similarly about their own commitments.[11] In the meantime, religious adherents can proselytize in the name of such claims to absolute truth without moral impunity. And such proselytizing will bring with it implicit and explicit criticisms of other religious traditions.

Two recent Christian and evangelical statements on truth and evangelism provide a good illustration of the balance I am arguing for. Trevor Hart tries to balance sharing religious truth with others and learning from other religious stories. We do the latter not because we are uncertain of the truth of our own tradition, says Hart.

> Rather, it is precisely because we are confident of its truth that we wish to share our story with others, to expose them to its truth, and to

---

[11] Küng, in fact, admits that "while claiming absolute validity", Christianity must be "ready to revise its own standpoint wherever this turns out to be in need of revision" (1977, 114). Christianity must be open to "self-criticism" (114). Küng also admits that Christians have much to learn from other religions (113). Coward is therefore wrong in suggesting that Küng fails to do justice to the finite limits of the human mind (2000, 104).

integrate it into a fruitful synthesis with whatever purchase upon truth their stories may have to offer. Once again, the point is that while we are committed to our tradition, we are more committed still to the truth, and we refuse to mistake the contents of the one for the other in any simple and arrogant sense (Hart 1995, 228).

Then there is the recent "Amsterdam Declaration: A Charter for Evangelism in the Twenty-first Century":

> Because God's general revelation extends to all points of His creation, there may well be traces of truth, beauty, and goodness in many non-Christian belief systems. But we have no warrant for regarding any of these as alternative gospels or separate roads to salvation. The only way to know God in peace, love, and joy is through the reconciling death of Jesus Christ, the risen Lord. As we share this message with others, we must do so with love and humility, shunning all arrogance, hostility, and disrespect. As we enter into dialogue with adherents of other religions, we must be courteous and kind. But such dialogue must not be a substitute for proclamation. Yet because all persons are made in the image of God, we must advocate religious liberty and human rights for all. We pledge ourselves to treat those of other faiths with respect, and faithfully and humbly serve the nation in which God has placed us, while affirming that Christ is the one and only Savior of the world.[12]

Sadly, the history of Christian evangelism includes all too many cases in which the belief in universal and absolute truth has led to proselytizing that is arrogant, and disrespectful of persons holding contrary beliefs. And sometimes, even more sadly, such proselytizing expresses itself in hostility and even militancy. And this is obviously part of Coward's concerns with regard to militant exclusivism and his encouragement of constructive criticism. This may also be what Novak has in mind when he objects to proselytizing which denigrates other religions. In a conversation I had with Novak, he specifically objected to *hostile* denigration, and to the misrepresentation of a religious position when trying to proselytize. I agree entirely – this is wrong, as is self-righteous criticism and blatantly militant exclusivism which breeds religious violence. But this doesn't make all proselytizing wrong.

---

[12] "The Amsterdam Declaration: A Charter for Evangelism in the Twenty-first Century", quoted in *First Things* (Jan 2001), p. 65.

Rather than condemning proselytizing outright because it invariably involves an element of disagreement with the person being proselytized, based on the assumption of universal and absolute truth, what we need to do is to clarify the distinction between moral and immoral ways of expressing our disagreement with other religious or world-view commitments.

Rationality and certainty

There is a softer version of the previous argument that needs to be considered. It might be argued that we cannot be certain about the claims that we make in religion or that religious beliefs are not verifiable or entirely rational. And is it not immoral to try to persuade another person about religious claims that we make when we cannot be certain of them, cannot verify them, or cannot give good reasons to support them?

Jay Newman, for example, in reflecting on his own experience with proselytizers argues that

> it would appear that (1)proselytizers do not generally have compelling (or even good) reasons for believing x; (2)proselytizers do not generally have a clear idea of what distinguishes good reasons for believing from bad ones; and (3)the theories that proselytizers want men to believe are usually highly speculative, and I am not sure myself what would be the proper method for going about verifying or falsifying them (1982, 101–2).

It is only in a later summary that Newman draws out the implications of these epistemologico-ethical (and deontological) considerations – "none of them suggest that proselytizing in general is morally right, and some of them suggest that it is actually morally wrong" (103). In other words, proselytizing would seem to be inherently immoral according to Newman. This is a radical conclusion and it is difficult to see how Newman can go on to maintain that he is only opposed to some proselytizing.[13] In part this is due to Newman's introduction of some factual considerations at the same time that he is treating epistemological considerations.

Newman's first two objections to proselytizing are in fact empirical in nature. I agree with Newman that not all missionaries and proselytizers pay sufficient attention to the problem of providing rational

---

[13] For a detailed description of the ambiguity in Newman's position, see ch. 1, n. 33.

evidence for the religious beliefs they are propagating. But how many missionaries do this? Many? Most? When making such sweeping generalizations, we must make sure that these are backed up with sufficient empirical evidence. We must also be careful not to demand too much of missionaries. After all, they are not, and probably do not claim to be, theological experts. Nor should we expect missionaries to be experts in philosophy, and thus be able to make the subtle distinction between good and bad reasons in religious belief. Missionaries are supposedly experts in spreading the "good news", but that is quite different from being a specialist in theology or philosophy. The missionary is like the expert in advertising, and we do not demand of the latter that she also be capable of "extended rational discussion" on the intricacies of the product she is advertising. Nor do we conclude that a Mazda salesman is immoral because he does not inform us of Ford products. Politicians too most often only have scanty understanding of certain fields, but this does not stop them from trying to persuade people when on the campaign trail. And while we might adopt cynical attitudes towards politicians because of this, we certainly don't describe them as immoral because they speak of that which they do not fully understand.

Further, how many ordinary people, or even teachers for that matter, proclaim scientific, historical, or political truth without being able to back them up with sufficient reasons? And how many lay-people can make a distinction between good and bad reasons in the area of history, for example? Although we would hope that lay-people are able to provide some reasoning to support the claims they make, we do not demand the sophistication of the specialist. For most people the beliefs they hold in any area is based on some appeal to authority, and we generally have no problem with this. Nor should be when it comes to proselytizing.

Proselytizers, Newman argues, are rarely committed to making known the whole truth. I agree that proselytizers are often hesitant in acknowledging the fact that there are competing claims to religious truth. And I also agree that there is a tendency to conceal some of the more unpleasant aspects of the history of their particular religion. However, here again we must not make impossible demands on the proselytizers. Given the fallibility and finiteness of human beings it is simply impossible for anyone, including teachers, to make known the whole truth about anything. To charge that "most missionaries methodically conceal truths" not only borders on *ad hominem* argument, but requires empirical verification, an assignment which will be difficult to carry out especially because it will need to establish that most missionaries *intentionally* conceal truths. In fact, Paul Grice (1989), noted philosopher of language, has argued that people generally obey the "cooperative principle" in their use of language, and so will generally give the necessary information, avoid falsehoods or claims for which there is no evidence, and try to be relevant. Perhaps proselytizers too generally follow the cooperative principle.

So far I have been focusing on some empirical claims made by Newman relating to epistemology. Implicit in these factual concerns there is however a deeper concern. The more significant epistemologico-ethical problem for Newman is whether it is even possible to give good reasons in the area of religion where speculation and disagreement seem to be standard fare. This becomes explicit in the third concern Newman raises about religious proselytizing, namely that religious theories being propagated are usually highly speculative and unjustifiable. Here it should be noted that there is an ambiguity in Newman's position concerning the status of religious beliefs. At times Newman is careful not to base his negative conclusion concerning the ethics of proselytizing on a quick dismissal of religious claims as unjustifiable or unverifiable (1982, 100–1). But the fact remains that he does also say that "the theories that proselytizers want men to believe are usually highly speculative, and I am not sure myself what would be the proper method for going about verifying or falsifying them" (102). And it is this uncertainty surrounding religious beliefs that would seem to lead Newman and others to conclude that proselytizing is morally wrong.

Clearly there would seem to be some justification for believing religious theories to be somewhat speculative given the plurality of religions. The fact that many religions make contradictory claims would further seem to suggest that proselytizers not only generally do not, but simply cannot have compelling (or even good) reasons for believing a certain religion. But here we need to step back and ask if there are not some epistemological assumptions being made here that can be called into question. What is it that makes a belief highly speculative? And what does it mean to have a compelling or even a good reason for any belief? Typically it is science that is seen as providing us with a standard of non-speculative and compelling argumentation. But this standard is increasingly being called into question today, as I have argued at length elsewhere.[14] Since the ground-breaking work of Thomas Kuhn there is a growing recognition that there is a significant

---

[14] See Thiessen (1993, chs. 3 and 4).

degree of subjectivity that colours observation and theory-making in science. Then there are various post-modernist emphases in epistemology which have suggested that rationality, knowledge, and the justification of our beliefs are, to some degree, shaped by historical, social, and even psychological conditions. All this would suggest that science too is somewhat speculative, a point that is easily seen when one looks at the frontiers of scientific thought today. And the idea of a compelling or a good reason for holding a belief can no longer be glibly defined in terms of an Enlightenment model of scientific reasoning.

Of course, there is a danger here of making reasoning too subjective and I believe this is in fact what has occurred in the post-modern reaction to the Enlightenment. What is needed is a reconciliation of the epistemological insights of modernism and postmodernism.[15] This will result in what William J. Abraham has called a soft rationalism, a humbler rationalism which recognizes its limits (1985, ch. 9). Richard Rorty (1987) too calls for a weaker sense of rationality that has the effect of equalizing the epistemological status of claims in the sciences and the humanities. But this revised and more defensible view of rationality entails that religion is not as highly speculative as many sceptics hold. Religious believers do have *good* reasons for holding the beliefs that they do – perhaps not *compelling* reasons, but these are not possible even in many areas of science. Therefore, if we accept as moral, attempts to persuade others of scientific beliefs that are somewhat speculative, then surely we should do the same with regard to religious beliefs.

Closely related to having compelling or good reasons for religious beliefs is the question of their verifiability. Here again, we need to be careful not to draw a sharp divide between science as the domain of verifiable beliefs, and religion as the domain of unverifiable beliefs. Logical positivism foundered precisely in its attempt to draw a sharp divide between science and metaphysics.[16] Science includes unverifiable first principles, and there are aspects of religion that are verifiable. The new epistemology that I have already referred to, calls into question the dominant view of science from the seventeenth century until the mid-twentieth century, which assumed that science was strictly empirical, objective and rational. It is now generally recognized that observation is theory-laden, and that the scientist brings a host of commitments, assumptions and values to his or her task. Science, like

---

[15] See Toulmin (1990) for an outline of such an attempted reconciliation.
[16] I have argued this point at length in Thiessen (1993, ch. 3).

religion, is trying to explain reality, and in both domains, attempts are made to interpret our experience by constructing belief systems. And how do we assess competing interpretations or claims to have found the best explanation? The following criteria have been proposed: simplicity, explanatory comprehensiveness, aesthetic elegance, internal consistency, and empirical accuracy.[17] These criteria of good reasons can be applied equally to the areas of science and religion. So given the new epistemology that is emerging today, it is becoming increasingly difficult to draw a sharp distinction between science and religion with regard to the status of statements in each domain. And so again it would seem to be rather inconsistent to accept persuasion and proselytizing in the one area and rule it out as unethical in the other.

A final point that grows out of the above considerations concerning the status of religious beliefs has to do with the question of certainty. Here again I believe we are suffering from an illusory goal of absolute certainty that we have inherited from the Enlightenment (Toulmin 1990). I would suggest that complete certainty is impossible. Further, there are many instances where we try to convince others of matters of which we are not entirely certain, and where the suggestion that this might be immoral does not even cross our minds. Indeed, there are situations where all of us would admit that it would be our moral obligation to engage in persuasion over matters that are uncertain. For example, I might feel obligated to persuade you to see a physician about a lump in your chest even though I am not at all certain that it is malignant. Certainty is not a requirement for moral proselytizing.

The uncertainty surrounding the question of the epistemological status of religious beliefs raises another problem concerning Newman's objections to proselytizing. Is the ethics of proselytizing even dependent on religious beliefs having a certain epistemological status? J.S. Mill clearly did not think so. It is precisely the difficulties in ascertaining whether opinions are true or false, whether reasons are good or bad, that lead Mill to defend the freedom of thought and discussion, and he makes the point specifically with regard to religious beliefs. To prevent a religious opinion from being heard because one is persuaded that it is uncertain or false is to assume one's own infallibility, which according to Mill is itself a questionable assumption (1978, 17). Therefore, anyone has a right to try to convince another person of anything, according to Mill.

---

[17] On these criteria, see for example Quine and Ullian (1978), and Wolfe (1982, 50–55).

I am not sure that I would want to go quite as far as Mill in disassociating the ethics of proselytizing from providing evidence. There is still something right about the concerns expressed by Newman and others about proselytizing and trying to convince others of beliefs that are somewhat speculative and for which we have good but not compelling reasons, and about which we have some degree of doubt. Surely the levels of certainty and speculation have some implications for how proselytizing is done. It is surely wrong to ascribe a higher degree of certainty to religious beliefs than is warranted by the evidence available. Surely there is some justification for proportioning the confidence with which we proselytize with the degree of evidence and certainty that we have for our religious beliefs. However, we must be careful not to demand more in the area of religious proselytizing than we do in other areas where proselytizing occurs. Therefore, rather than condemning proselytizing outright because religious beliefs are not absolutely certain, and because the reasons we have for them are not universally thought to be compelling, we need instead to define the relation between moral proselytizing and the required levels of confidence and rationality that exist with regard to religious beliefs.

Chapter 4

Proselytizing and the Integrity/Freedom of Individuals and Societies

In the previous chapter I focused specifically on objections to proselytizing that cross the boundaries of epistemology and ethics. This chapter examines the charge that proselytizing is in some way a violation of the freedom and integrity of individuals or societies. For example, some critics maintain that proselytizing is very often, or even by its very nature, coercive, thus violating the freedom and integrity of individual persons. Anthropologists and historians have gone on to apply this charge to entire societies. For example, critics have made much of the link between Western Christian missionary activities and Western colonialism. Thus missionary activity is described by some critics as religious imperialism, or even as an expression of cultural genocide. Here the proselytizing of missionaries is seen as an assault on the integrity and freedom of societies as a whole. Both of these charges are serious and demand a response.

I begin this chapter with a consideration of the coercive charge as applied to the proselytizing of individuals. Some examples of such charges have already surfaced in chapter 1. In a Beliefnet dialogue, one participant complains about "evangelical people going around the world forcing their religion on people". Ibraham Hooper raises a concern about the Baptists and their plans to send in missionary-aid workers into Iraq in March of 2003, immediately upon its so-called liberation by the American and British troops. He suggested that it would be difficult to avoid the perception that such a missionary assault would be seen as a crusade, especially given that these missionaries described themselves as bent on a spiritual warfare campaign to convert the country's Muslims to Christianity.

The issue of coercive proselytizing also often comes to the fore in charges made against proselytizing groups on university campuses.

An article appearing in the student newspaper at Arizona State University, entitled, "Do campus religious groups breach the boundaries of ethics", reported on a talk given by Rick Ross.[1] Ross condemned various religious groups on campus for their recruiting practices. He chastised them for training their professional proselytizers in methods of deception and for proselytizing without completely revealing their affiliations or agendas. In this same essay, a director of a Catholic student center at this same university, recalls a student, who after three days in a cultish group, came to him and said the doctrines of the Catholic Church were wrong. The director's response: "That's when you know you are brainwashed."

Sometimes it is the inducements to convert that are singled out as being coercive in missionary or evangelistic activity. In an important statement of the Central Committee of the World Council of Churches, "Towards Common Witness", the following items are listed as in one way or another coercive:

- Offering humanitarian aid or educational opportunities as an inducement to join another church.
- Using political, economic, cultural, and ethnic pressure or historical arguments to win others to one's own church.
- Taking advantage of lack of education or Christian instruction which makes people vulnerable to changing their church allegiance.
- Using physical violence or moral and psychological pressure to induce people to change their church affiliation. This includes the use of media techniques profiling a particular church in a way that excludes, disparages, or stigmatizes its adherents, harassment through repeated house calls, material and spiritual threats, and insistence on the 'superior' way to salvation offered by a particular church.
- Exploiting people's loneliness, illness, distress, or even disillusionment with their own church in order to 'convert' them. (Central Committee of the World Council of Churches 1997, 468)

While the problems identified above are linked with proselytizing in the narrow sense, of sheep-stealing, these methods need to be evaluated quite apart from the specific ecumenical concerns about intra-church competition. Besides, these same problems are often

---

[1] Jim McCleary, "Salvation and Cultivation", *Arizona Campus Weekly Tempe* 1.4 (Feb 28 – Mar 6, 1985).

associated with proselytizing understood in the broader sense. For example, Alexander Berzin, a research fellow at Columbia University, in an interview in *Newsweek*, complains about Christian missionaries in Mongolia: "All the missionaries come in the guise of English teachers . . . They give money, computers to universities, scholarships to children of influential officials. They buy their way in."[2]

The charge of coercive proselytizing also appears in academic discussions of proselytizing. David Novak, for example, describes proselytizing in terms of "cajoling" the adherents of other faiths to cease being what they have been and to change their identity by becoming what the missionaries are (1999, 43). It is important to note that for Novak this would appear to be an inevitable part of proselytizing efforts. Similarly, Antonio Cal suggests that proselytizing "constitutes an assault upon human freedom" (1997, 222). Others make the weaker claim that many or most forms of proselytizing "accompany, foreshadow, and promote more radical forms of religious harassment" (Newman 1982, 88).

The charge of coercion in proselytizing has been applied particularly to what are often identified as cults or new religious movements or NRMs. Various models have been used to describe the supposedly coercive methods used by the cults – brainwashing, thought reform, mind control, and coercive persuasion (Robbins 1984, 248). Again I caution against the danger of singling out the cults as being uniquely liable to having this charge made against them. In fact it might be difficult to distinguish between what is done in the cults and what is done in other more mainstream religious groups by way of proselytizing.[3] The charge of coercive proselytizing needs to be dealt with wherever it is found and whatever its application.

I will grant at the outset that the charge of coercion against the proselytizing efforts of cults and various religions, past and present, is sometimes quite legitimate. Various examples of coercion have already been identified in chapter 2 – Charlemagne's very effective baptisms by the sword, Mohammed's order to one of his generals sent to a tribe

---

[2] The quote is taken from *Newsweek Magazine*, Asia and Atlantic editions, (13 Jan, 1997), p. 56.

[3] I agree with some writers who have pointed to a strange myopia on the part of some evangelical Christians who fail to recognize that arguments being made against the proselytizing activities of so called cults can be, and sometimes are, directed against all evangelistic outreach, including that of evangelicals. See, for example, Sawatsky (1986) and Robbins (1984).

in Arabia – "invite them to Islam three days before [you] attack them", and, in Jewish history, the forced conversion of the Itreans and the Idumeans by the Maccabean king in the second century B.C.E. Jesuit missionary, Jose de Acosta, says this in his 1588 work on missionary activity in the new world:

> Without doubt, and experience confirms it, the barbarians are of a servile nature, and if you do not make use of fear and compel them by force . . . they refuse to obey. What should be done then? . . . It is necessary to use the whip . . . In this way they are forced to enter salvation even if it is against their will.[4]

These are obvious examples of coercive proselytizing, and they can only be characterized as blatantly immoral. But things become much more complicated when we consider less obvious examples of coercion. And there is a tendency not to distinguish between these less obvious cases and paradigm cases of coercive proselytizing. Often all proselytizing is simply painted with the same coercive brush. Before moving on to consider the difficulties in making distinctions between obvious and less obvious cases of coercive proselytizing, I want to consider some all too frequent problems underlying the labeling of proselytizing as coercive.

Problems of question-begging

I have already alluded to the problem of arbitrarily defining proselytizing as immoral in the previous chapter. This problem arises particularly with regard to the charge of coercion. As we have already seen, Margaret Battin seems to assume that proselytizing is aggressive by its very nature, allowing only for varying degrees of aggressiveness (1990, 136–40).[5] Novak describes proselytizing in terms of "cajoling" others to convert (1999, 43). Others revert to warlike language when they talk about proselytizing, describing it in terms of stalking and pouncing on a potential convert.[6] Michael Langone, in an essay exploring the ethics of social influence in relation to the proselytizing activities of evangelicals

---

[4] Quoted in Rivera (1992, 218, 220).

[5] For a more careful analysis of Battin's position, see chapter 1, p. 18, and n. 34.

[6] For example, Daniel Polish describes missionaries as making an "assault" on potential converts (1982, 164). Keiner argues that "proselytizing by its very nature is a direct assault" upon the identity of the recipient (2007, 107).

and the cults, proposes a "continuum of influence" (1985). At the one end of this continuum are "choice respecting" methods of influence while at the other end there are "compliance gaining" methods. What is significant here is that persuasion is placed in the same category as coercion, though persuasion is seen as a milder form of a compliance-gaining mode of influence. In the popular mind too, persuasion is associated with brainwashing, mind control, hypnotic suggestion, mass conformity, coercion, and propaganda (Perloff 1993, 11).

Now it should be rather obvious that the popular association of persuasion with brainwashing, mind control, and hypnotic suggestion is just plainly mistaken. There is all the difference in the world between brainwashing, and a lover gently and carefully trying to persuade his beloved to marry him. To describe as mind control an attempt to persuade a friend that a certain movie is not worth watching is just inappropriate. Such associations can only be made by arbitrary fiat. I believe the same kind of arbitrariness is found in the other descriptions of proselytizing that I have listed in the previous paragraph. Links between proselytizing and coercion are simply being assumed. Proselytizing is simply being defined as coercive. But this is to beg the question.

There is another way in which suspicions about persuasion and proselytizing and their association with coercion often beg the question. I have already mentioned that the charge of coercion is frequently made against the recruitment activities of the cults. But, as Thomas Robbins has noted, arguments imputing extreme mental coercion, mind control and brainwashing to cultist practices, tend to depend on arbitrary assumptions, definitions, and interpretive frameworks (1984, 242).[7] The same can be said about proselytizing generally. I would suggest that a deterministic framework is often at the root of the charge that proselytizing is coercive.[8] Obviously, if human beings are completely determined, whether physically, psychologically, or sociologically, then of course all proselytizing is coercive. But this begs the question.

It is far beyond the scope of this chapter to try to resolve the debate between freedom and determinism. Philosophers have wrestled with

---

[7] Perhaps some cautionary comments are in order here. I am well aware of the polarization that exists between the sympathizer and anti-cult camps with regard to the cults, and that Robbins' comments reflect the former camp (see Appendix 2, #D4 for a review of this polarization).

[8] For other writers who point to the deterministic assumptions underlying the charge that proselytizing is coercive see, Barker (1984), Bromley and Richardson (1983), and Dawson (1998, 113).

this problem over the centuries and the debate continues. Here I can only articulate my assumption and outline my approach to the problem of free will and determinism. I am assuming that human beings have limited free will. The extent of freedom possessed by an individual varies in light of background and context. Heredity and environment do serve to limit the freedom of individuals. But these constraining forces, while they limit freedom, do not eliminate freedom as determinists maintain (see Figure #1: Circle of Choice).[9] We must therefore allow for varying degrees of freedom of individuals, depending on their background. But all individuals have some degree of freedom.[10] Hence we must be careful not to describe all proselytizing as coercive, based on the assumption of a determinist interpretative framework. At the same time, we must define the parameters of freedom so as to be able to distinguish between coercive and non-coercive approaches to proselytizing.

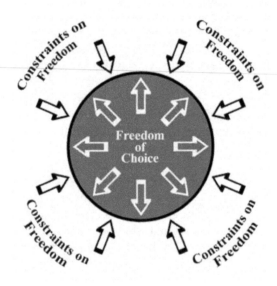

Figure #1: Circle of Choice

Robbins identifies a final question-begging assumption that tends to underlie charges of coercion against proselytizing, and more generally,

---

[9] My approach to freedom draws on essays by Frederick Ferre (1973) and Richard Taylor (1992, 44–53).

[10] My model of the relation between freedom and determinism is similar to Janja Lalich's notion of "bounded choice" in a recent book by that title (2004). However, Lalich overemphasizes the bounded nature of choice in describing the true believer.

charges against proselytizing as a whole. Although Robbins is more narrowly concerned with charges of coercive mind control against the cults, his point can be applied to all religious proselytizing. Robbins maintains that "the overwhelming popular, legal and scholarly focus on the *processes by which individuals become and remain committed to cults* is misleading in the sense that it shifts attention away from what we consider the ultimate sources of social and professional hostility to cults" (1984, 242). I believe the same can be said for opposition to proselytizing generally.

Charges against religious proselytizing, including the emotively loaded charge of coercion, are rooted more deeply in hostility against religion generally (Robbins 1984, 243). Religious conversions just should not happen in a supposedly secular culture. Secularists find it difficult to admit that individuals would turn to religion to find answers to the deep void that they feel. Mystery militates against scientific explanation. The emphasis on community in various religions contravenes the deeply rooted individualism of Western societies (242). There is also a conflict between "the socially adjustive ethos of mental health" and the alternate holistic models of health that include the spiritual and the transcendent (242–43). Pastors, priests, and rabbis compete with certified secular therapists and healers. In short, opposition to religious proselytizing and the charges of coercion against the same may be rooted in plain anti-religious prejudice. At the very most, liberal scholars will tolerate "benign religious groups" (West 1990, 126). How tolerant of them! And of course, any scholar who dares to defend proselytizing religious groups and cults is declared mentally unfit or incompetent.[11] Really?

The main thrust of this section is that we must be careful not to beg the question when we object to persuasion or proselytizing as coercive, and hence immoral. We must be especially careful not to arbitrarily *define* proselytizing as coercive. At the same time, we must not

---

While I agree that it is very difficult for a true believer to leave a cult, it is still possible, and Lalich herself is forced to admit the same. She also admits that commitment is "a recurring, renewable, and renewing process", but this again entails that the boundaries of her notion of bounded choice are somewhat porous (18).

[11] West, for example, characterizes anyone who dares to defend the cults as having been "successfully deceived by charismatic cult leaders or their representatives" (1990, 133). "There are even some armchair philosophers who have either never seen the destructive effects of cults or prefer to deny their reality", and who discuss them in an "uncritical way" (134). And, of course, apologists have been bribed. All this with no supporting evidence!

preclude the possibility of proselytizing becoming coercive. What we need are criteria to distinguish between coercive and non-coercive proselytizing. That task will be taken up in later chapters. What still remains to be done in this chapter, is to explore the validity of arguments that suggest that coercion is very common when proselytizing. We are still left with questions about the probability of coercion in proselytizing. These questions are particularly troublesome given my suggestion that we need to talk about degrees of freedom with regard to the human condition. In the following section I want to argue that there is a problem of vagueness that pervades assignments of probability of coercion to proselytizing.

Physical coercion and the problem of vagueness

The most obvious examples of coercion in proselytizing would seem to be those that involve the use of physical force. The twelfth-century crusader threatening someone with a sword if he/she didn't convert surely is a case of physical coercion. The sixteenth-century Anabaptists who were given one last chance to convert back to Catholicism before being burned at the stake were surely subject to physical coercion. However, even here some caution is in order. There were after all individuals who refused to convert even in the face of such physical threats. So even cases of physical coercion are not as clear as is often assumed. A degree of freedom exists even in such extreme cases. So the problem of vagueness in defining coercion can even arise with regard to physical coercion. But, I'm sure most of us will want to grant that coercion is involved in these cases. It is only heroes who have the courage to resist physical coercion.

The problem of vagueness becomes much more pronounced as soon as we move beyond examples of physical coercion. The following questions cry out for answers. Exactly what does it mean to be invasive, cajoling, or, coercive? In what sense does the missionary make an assault on the potential convert? Is the Jehovah's Witness, quietly standing on a city street-corner, holding out a *Watchtower Magazine* for any passer-by to take, really being coercive? Is it really fair to talk about stalking and pouncing and coercion when a person has responded to an advertisement on a billboard for a Billy Graham Crusade, and freely walks into the arena to hear him speak?

If I as a Christian, at some point in my long-standing friendship with a Jewish colleague, suggest to her that my religious position is "the highest truth and the greatest good" (to use Novak's terms), and if I even go on to argue the same and seek to persuade her to adopt the better religion, and if she then rejects my argument and my appeal, and if despite all this, our friendship continues to flourish, am I cajoling her? And, if, in giving aid to the many who are starving in various parts of the globe, the Mennonite Central Committee puts on each sack of grain shipped overseas the words, "In the name of Christ", with nothing more being said when the grain is being distributed, can this really be described as coercive? The answer to all of these questions is, surely not! But each of the scenarios described are obviously cases of proselytizing, though the latter example is perhaps better classified as a case of covert proselytizing. And yet, these are the sorts of things that are listed as examples of coercion in the literature that is critical of proselytizing.

Given the frequently made charge of coercion against cults or NRMs, one would expect to find that more attention has been paid to trying to define coercive proselytizing in this literature. But even here, as Robbins notes, critics appeal to "a broad and only tenuously bounded concept of 'coercion'" (1984, 243, 247). Let me give just a few illustrations of this. The influence techniques of cults are often described as being taken to an extreme and thus they are deemed to be coercive. Singer and Addis, for example, talk about "intense and frequent attempts" to undermine a person's confidence and to cause them to reevaluate themselves, their values and beliefs (1992, 171). But how intense? How frequent? We must also keep in mind that conversion resulting from proselytizing will necessarily involve some degree of destabilizing of an individual's sense of self – after all, the person is undergoing a serious reevaluation of core beliefs that may have been held for a long time.[12]

Another attempt at defining coercion in the cults is to introduce the notion of a coordinated program of a variety of techniques, the combination of which can be seen as psychologically coercive. For example, Ofshe and Singer talk about "coordinated programs of coercive influence and behavior control" (1986). But, how coordinated does a program of influence have to be in order to be coercive? Another problem here is that there are other contexts in which you find coordinated efforts at influencing beliefs and behavior, but which are generally considered to be quite

---

[12] Edgar Schein correctly identifies three distinct sub-phases in the overall process of coercive persuasion – unfreezing, change, and refreezing (1961, 111–39). But, these phases are simply an accurate description of conversions generally, whether coerced or not.

acceptable. For example, as Singer and Addis point out, sales programs, recruitment programs, and political campaigns, all include "planned influence procedures" (1992, 171). But unless critics can identify a difference between these coordinated programs of influencing beliefs and behavior, and proselytizing programs, they are being inconsistent in calling one kind of program coercive and the other non-coercive.

In fact Singer and Addis try to define this difference in terms of various efforts made by the cults "to establish considerable control over a person's social environment and sources of social support" (1992, 171).[13] The purpose of such environmental manipulation is to undermine a person's confidence and judgment, to cause people to reevaluate themselves, and to isolate them from previous social contacts where disconfirming information and non-supporting opinions might be expressed. Social, psychological, and spiritual threats and punishments are used to bring about compliance.

Here again vagueness abounds. What is meant by establishing "considerable control" over a person's social environment in order to undermine a person's capacity to make genuinely free choices? It is also all too easy to exaggerate human vulnerability in this regard. Surely, as Robbins points out, three weeks of indoctrination, presuming that brutality and torture were not used, are not sufficient for an adult to actually "lose capacity" to make choices (1984, 252). Indeed, as various studies have shown, the high rates of defection from cults and NRMs would suggest that individuals have not at all lost their capacity to make choices.[14] There is also a problem with the idea of contrived and manipulated environments. If ever there is an institution that can be characterized as a contrived environmental setting and where potential converts are isolated from previous social contacts, it is the state-maintained public schools of Western societies.[15] If we accept control over a person's social environment here, should we not also accept it in the

---

[13] Robert Lifton referred to the totalistic quality of institutions to describe the extraordinarily high degree of social control characteristic of some organizations that operate reform programs (1961). But, how high a degree of social control is required before one calls it totalistic?

[14] For example, in her detailed study of the Unification Church, Eileen Barker found that one-third of those who had initially joined the group left of their own accord after four months, and few lasted more than two years (1984, 144–48, 259). Another study of a more diverse array of groups found that two-thirds of the most highly involved members eventually left (Dawson 1998, 119). Dawson suggests these data call into question the entire credibility of the brainwashng explanation of cult conversions (119).

[15] I have argued this point at length elsewhere (Thiessen, 1993, ch. 7).

religious context? We must also be very careful not to rule out the possibility that there will be a natural tendency for recent converts to disassociate themselves to some degree from previous social contacts. A degree of isolation can be a result of uncoerced individual choice.

So much for the charge of coercion against the cults. More generally, I would suggest that critics of proselytizing are playing fast and loose with the notion of coercion. It is this kind of elasticity in meaning and non-specificity in its applicability that make Young and Griffith reject coercive persuasion as a useful way to distinguish between moral and immoral methods of proselytizing (1992).

Further, the language used in making the charge of coercion against proselytizing is invariably strident and exaggerated. For example, a dissertation critical of Christian missionaries proselytizing Jews uses the heading "power strategies" to cover coercive proselytizing (Stiebel 1982, 35). "The simplest form of 'power' technique was to intrude uninvited into the homes of Jews" (53). But does door-to-door evangelism really deserve to be described in terms of a coercive power strategy? The use of the term *intrusion* is perhaps legitimate. But surely not coercion, as anyone is perfectly free to shut the door on a door-to-door evangelist. This dissertation goes on to describe Campus Crusade methods of evangelism on university campuses as "strong arm evangelism" (99). Attempts by university campus ministries to evangelize student leaders under the assumption that others will then follow are criticized: "These groups exert pressure on the lonely, confused student who would like to be in the cavalcade of campus stars corralled by Campus Crusade or Inter-Varsity" (100). But, in what way do these groups corral campus leaders? No evidence is given. Is love coercive? Is it coercive to share good news to students many of whom are struggling with problems of hopelessness, meaninglessness, and despair, as any number of sociological studies will tell you?

My main point here is to draw attention to the strong language being used. Such rhetorical flourishes do not contribute to careful reasoned analysis. A civil rights lawyer criticizes "the name calling which is typical of programs of denigration", particularly as applied to controversial religious groups: "A religion becomes a cult, proselytization becomes brainwashing; persuasion becomes propaganda; missionaries become subversive agents; retreats, monasteries, and convents become prisons; holy ritual becomes bizarre conduct; religious observance becomes aberrant behaviour; devotion and meditation become psychopathic trances."[16]

---

[16] Quoted in Robbins (1984, 244).

There are also some strange inconsistencies that emerge in attacks against proselytizing. Whereas love and care are described as "love bombing" and a sinister coercive technique when applied to the cults, these same features are lauded in deprogramming and rehabilitation centers by deprogrammed ex-devotees who have praised the warmly supportive and "familial" atmosphere of these centers (Robbins 1984, 245). Whereas missionaries are criticized for having adopted tactics used in selling, marketing, and advertising, the latter capitalistic techniques would seem to be exempt from criticism when applied to business (Stiebel 1982, 163).

Again I stress that all this is not meant to be an indiscriminate defence of all proselytizing techniques against the charge of coercion. I am only arguing that we need to be more consistent, more objective, and more cautious in making this charge. Further, the inherent vagueness in the charge of coercion, might suggest that there is not as much coercive proselytizing occurring than is often assumed.

Psychological coercion

I now want to examine some of the more specific expressions of the charge of psychological coercion as made against proselytizing. One of the characteristics of religious proselytizing which is widely excoriated is the alleged tendency of religious groups to exploit the vulnerability of young persons who are lonely, depressed, alienated, or drifting away from social moorings (Robbins 1984, 248). The website of the chaplains of The United Ministry at Harvard University, issues this warning: "You're especially vulnerable to destructive religious groups if you're lonely – or feel overwhelmed by decisions or responsibilities – or find yourself wishing for someone else to organize your life or your priorities."[17]

But I am not sure that exploiting the vulnerability of young persons will serve to define coercive proselytizing. It is not just young people who are vulnerable. We are all vulnerable, that is, if we are honest about the human condition. And it is precisely the realization of human vulnerability and need that causes people to reach out to religion. Of course, this has led to skeptical arguments about religion, but that is another question that need not concern us here. Let us assume for the sake of argument, that human vulnerability and need

---

[17] Retrieved July 27, 2009 from http://www.chaplains.harvard.edu/about_us.php.

characterize the human condition. Then surely it would be wrong for religious groups who feel they have an answer to these needs, to fail to respond to them out of fear of being coercive. And surely it is unfair to interpret this in terms of exploiting vulnerability and need. Responding to vulnerability and need does not in itself make religious proselytizing psychologically coercive and hence immoral.

We also are not entirely consistent in the way in which we apply the charge of exploiting vulnerability. Somehow we seem to exempt our public high schools and universities from this charge even though these institutions are full of vulnerable young people, and they are being influenced very significantly by teachers and professors, many of whom are conveying highly controversial ideas, and are doing so in semi-totalistic environments. What is also rather curious is that in this context young people are generally seen as autonomous individuals, quite capable of making their own choices. Is it not inconsistent to suddenly view them as confused youth, or as helpless college students away from home, and therefore as unable to fend off religious proselytizers?[18]

The same can be said for the frequently made charges of exploiting guilt.[19] What if guilt is a reflection of an ontological reality? Many people do genuinely feel guilty about what they have done. For religious people who believe in a moral universe, this guilt is in fact an appropriate feeling to have after one has done something that is morally wrong. Surely it is unfair to charge a religious group of coercively exploiting this guilt when they offer forgiveness and moral healing as part of proselytizing activity. Surely this should be seen in positive terms, as something healthy and even moral.

At the same time, conversions typically also result in alienation from relatives and former friends, and sometimes even persecution. There may be anxious periods of doubt. Then there are the trials of faith.

---

[18] See, for example, the 1987 statement approved by the Executive Board of the Interfaith Conference of Metropolitan Washington: "Deceptive proselytizing efforts are practiced on the most vulnerable of populations – residents of hospitals and old age homes, confused youth, college students away from home. These proselytizing techniques are tantamount to coerced conversions and should be condemned" (Interfaith Conference 1989, 224). The charge of exploiting vulnerability is also frequently made against the cults. For example, in a preface to a book, *Cults on Campus*, the author describes college students as "youngsters", who therefore need protection from cults (Rudin 1996, 1). How insulting! Young people who join the new religious movements are not generally vulnerable and immature (Barker 1984, 198, 203). Indeed, they are often well educated and come from middle and upper class homes (Dawson 1998, 120, 87–88).

[19] See, for example, Ofshe (1992, 216) and Delgado (1980, 26).

Surely all these accompanying negative consequences should make us more cautious about describing proselytizing as coercive in nature. As Jeff Spinner-Halev has pointed out, resisting the mainstream in today's Western liberal democracies by choosing to adopt what is generally perceived to be a strange religious way of life, is not easy to do (2000, 25). It takes courage, depth of commitment, and character. In other words, autonomy is a requirement for responding to proselytizing appeals and following through with an alternative lifestyle. The charge of coercion is hardly appropriate.

A final expression of the charge of psychological coercion against proselytizing involves concerns about appeals to emotions. Insofar as proselytizing involves persuasion, it makes use of rhetoric and emotion, which are commonly thought to be dishonest devices to manipulate people into accepting what they would not accept by reason alone (Marlin 2000, 164). Religious proselytizers sometimes appeal directly to fear. A famous example of this is the fire-and-brimstone sermon delivered at a church in Enfield, Massachusetts in 1741, by American revivalist, Jonathan Edwards. The title, "Sinners in the Hands of an Angry God", is already indicative of the language and the vivid imagery Edwards used to scare sinners into the Kingdom of God.[20]

But our suspicions about emotions are problematic in that they rest on an overemphasis on rationality. We are whole beings who are moved by both reason and emotion. Indeed, we may just need some pathos and emotion in addition to rational arguments to move us to do the right thing. Randal Marlin, drawing on nineteenth-century writer on ethics and rhetoric, Richard Whately, exposes our tendency to assume that "whenever the feelings are excited they are of course overexcited" (Marlin 2000, 165). In fact, the reverse is the case, as people are often dispassionate and disinterested when they should be moved to action. And this would suggest, according to Marlin, that "appeals to emotions are not necessarily wrong, and may well be justified in a majority of cases" (165). Thus, for example, we generally assume that there is nothing wrong with charities featuring pictures of starving children when soliciting donations (Baber 2000, 339). Even Aristotle, who defined man as a rational animal, recognized the place of emotions in rhetoric, and proposed a golden mean between reason and emotion (Johannesen 1996, 46–47). Indeed, research would seem to show that emotion and cognition are intimately linked (Littlejohn and Jabusch 1987, 62–66). Robbins goes so far as to suggest that the

---

[20] Quoted in Marsden (2003, 223).

suspicions about emotional manipulation in proselytizing "reflects a secularist premise that only a deracinated intellectualist religion which does not control one's practical activities is legitimate" (1985, 360).

Of course, emotional appeals can be taken to an extreme. And such extreme appeals to emotion can undermine a person's ability to reflect on what is being said in a rational matter, thus upsetting what should be a healthy balance between reason and emotion. But exactly when is this balance upset? When are appeals to emotion taken to an extreme? Here we again encounter the problem of vagueness already dealt with in this chapter. So again caution is in order when making the charge that proselytizing is coercive because appeals are being made to emotions.

Inducements to convert

Many of the above considerations also apply to the frequently made charge concerning inducements to convert, examples of which I have already given in the introduction to this chapter.[21] Sometimes the charges are based on blatant misrepresentations of religious activities, and can only be attributed to anti-religious prejudice. Take for example, Astro5, in a dialogue on Beliefnet: "The Salvation Army will only give food to people that recite a Bible verse."[22] Anyone with any knowledge about the Salvation Army knows that this kind of accusation is obviously mistaken, as some respondents to this dialogue were quick to point out. And yet, these kinds of generalizations are made all too often with regard to proselytizing and any kind of inducements to convert.

The fundamental problem with this kind of a charge is that it is very difficult to define when an inducement might be viewed as coercive and hence morally blameworthy. This problem is well illustrated by Catholic scholar, Anand Nayak, in a response to an academic email discussion on this topic. Nayak, teaching at the University of Fribourg,

---

[21] The topic of material inducement to convert is one of the key concerns in a Hindu-Christian email discussion group prompted by a statement from the Dalai Lama in January of 2001 (hcs-l@lists.acusd.edu Jan 26 – Feb 2, 2001). The Dalai Lama's statement, while condemning all proselytizing, at the same time expresses opposition to "conversions by any religious tradition using various methods of enticement". Rajiv Malhotra objects to "preying upon the prospective client's poverty" (Jan 28, 2001). Dave Freedholm says missionary activity often uses the unethical method of providing material incentives for conversion (Jan 29, 2001).

[22] Retrieved July 21, 2009 from http://www.beliefnet.com/boards/message_list.asp?boardID=426&discussionID=208381 (listed Jan 1, 2003).

cites a concrete case from his neighborhood in Mangalore, and invites the members of the discussion group to tell him if the following case involves a forced conversion:

> Madhusudan, a Harijan, was living in a small shed of thatched roof at the foot of a hill with his wife and six small children. They were living on their handicraft trade of making baskets. Their daily income three years ago was Rs.20. – per day (about 45 cents or 27 British pence). When his wife was dying he came to the Catholic priest for help. The priest got his wife admitted in the hospital and gave some help to the family. When she recovered she found a job in the priest's compound. The children, who never saw a school before, were admitted in the Catholic parish school. Madhusudan had by now come to know other Christian homes where he got regular job[s]. One day the whole family decided to become Christian and the priest baptized them and lodged them in a simple home built by a cooperative society.[23]

Now, Nayak asks, is this enticement? Of course it is, he responds. But then he probes with another penetrating question: Or should the priest have left Srimati Madhusudan and the children to die out of fear of enticing people to convert? Surely dire medical and economic needs call for a caring response. And if people convert as a result of such care, is it really fair to criticize the initial response as an exploitation of need, or as providing a material inducement to convert? Besides, are we really in a position to assess what prompted the conversion in the first place? Nayak prefaces this case description by pointing out that conversion is a personal act of faith, and it is only the convert who can really tell what his or her motivations are. Besides, we must be very careful not to assume an impossible level of purity for any motivation behind actions. Here it might be well for the critics of proselytizing to do some introspection on what motivates them to criticize missionaries and evangelists!

Nayak further reminds us that all religions would themselves condemn any seeking of conversions through a blatant use of material incentives.[24] As noted in chapter 1, the three religions being referred to

---

[23] Nayak's contribution was made on Jan 29, 2001, from hcs-l@lists.acusd.edu Jan 26 – Feb 2, 2001.

[24] Vincent Donovan, Catholic missionary to East Africa for many years, makes this point so well: "To bring freedom or knowledge or health or prosperity to a people in order that they become Christians is a perversion of missionary work" (1988, 12).

for illustrative purposes in this book all see it as part of their mission to provide aid for the poor, help for the underprivileged, and justice for the exploited. A religious outlook that prompts this sort of activity will obviously be rather attractive to people who are suffering from exploitation from the rich and the powerful, and it might prompt some of them to convert. It is only a perverse logic that seeks to reinterpret all such actions in terms of "preying upon the prospective client's poverty".

On the other hand, proselytizers need to be sensitive to the possibility of inauthentic conversions based on advantages that are incidental to the conversion process. Here Western Christians in particular need to recognize that simply being rich or Western can be viewed as an inducement in certain contexts. These factors can have a powerful psychological influence and become an inappropriate motivator toward conversion or transfer of religious affiliation (Nicastro 1994, 226–27). But it is difficult to specify exactly when such an influence becomes coercive. Strangely, those making the charges of using inducements to bring about religious conversions seem to hesitate making such charges when they are talking about exporting other Western influences such as the ideas of liberalism or capitalism, or when selling Coke or Pepsi to Majority World countries.

What these examples highlight is the inescapability of some level of social or political inducement. Individuals always make decisions in a particular social, economic, and political context. Thus while there needs to be sensitivity to this broader issue of social and political inducement, we must not be too quick to label this inducement as coercive. As I have illustrated earlier in this chapter, our freedom is always expressed within the context of some constraining forces. It is only if the social, economic, and political constraints become extreme that we can begin to make the charge of coercion in relation to inducement to convert.[25] Here again we encounter the problem of vagueness that I have already dealt with under psychological coercion.

Unfortunately, Donovan makes this statement as part of a critique of the past 100 years of missionary work in East Africa, and he seems to be oblivious to the problems I have already articulated. Strangely, he seems to be equally critical of aid for its own sake. While he might be justified in highlighting the need to focus on "direct evangelism", Christians surely ought to be engaged in all dimensions of kingdom building and mission work.

[25] Here I take issue with Herbert Butterfield's careful analysis of the coercive power of Christian culture after Constantine's initial protection, and then establishment of Christianity, as the official religion of the Roman empire (see my reference to Butterfield in ch. 2, p. 38). He fails to see that a secularist culture would be just as

We must also not forget that there are most often powerful social and even economic inducements *not* to convert. Those who make the inducement charge are all too often strangely inconsistent when it comes to recognizing the power of material disincentives to change a religion. Durham draws attention to this problem in relation to the narrow sense of proselytizing: "My sense is that whatever material inducements proselytizing groups may use to encourage conversion pale in comparison with the economic and social disincentives larger groups can mobilize to deter an individual from leaving a religion: disinheritance, reduced job and educational opportunities, social isolation, and the list goes on" (Durham 2001, 30). The charge of material inducement is a two-edged sword, and not a very sharp one in any case, and so I would suggest more caution in making the charge.

Coercion and informed consent

As a final specific expression of the charge of coercion against proselytizing, I would like to deal with the notion of informed consent that is at the heart of the modern ideal of free choice. Newman complains about proselytizers failing to tell the whole truth, or methodically concealing truths, and it is safe to assume that part of his concerns have to do with the fact that these failures make it impossible for a potential convert to give informed consent (1982, 100). Stiebel highlights deception as a separate category of persuasion strategies that he finds objectionable in Christian efforts to proselytize the American Jew (1982). The charge of deception has been applied particularly to the cults as is highlighted in the writings of Richard Delgado: "The process by which an individual becomes a member of certain cults appears arranged in such a way that knowledge and capacity, the classic ingredients of an informed consent, are maintained in an inverse relationship: when capacity is high, the recruit's knowledge of the cults and its practices is low; when knowledge is high, capacity is reduced (Delgado 1980, 28–29).

I want to state at the outset that I concur entirely with the condemnation of some methods of proselytizing as coercive because they are deceptive. I agree with Stiebel that it is wrong for missionaries to inflate the number of their converts so as to encourage others to

---

coercive. We need to face the inevitability of there being some kind of cultural constraints in any society. Only when these cultural constraints are excessive should we speak of individual coercion. On this, see also Alan Kreider (1999, 38–39), and my additional comments in chapter 2, p. 38, n. 22.

convert (1982, 49). It is coercive to invite youth to programs, meetings, movies, and camps while hiding the identity of the sponsoring body, or the missionary aim of these activities. To conduct a religious survey as a pretext for doing evangelism is underhanded. But I would add that I also condemn the all too frequent occurrence of using telephone surveys for the purpose of marketing various products, from toothpaste to television sets. Oddly enough, many critics of proselytizing have no problem with the ethics of conducting surveys in the field of advertising. We need to be more consistent.

The charge of deceptive coercion is not as strong as is generally assumed, even with regard to the cults. Robbins (1984) has challenged Delgado's account on several fronts. We must first of all be very careful about hasty generalizations. Robbins suggests that allegations of widespread cultist mind control are all too often constructed on the basis of overgeneralization of extreme deceptive proselytizing on the part of a few notorious sects. Clearly debilitating deception is used by some cults and proselytizing religions. But, how typical is Delgado's account really? With some of the cults it would be very difficult for a potential convert to become involved without knowing at the very outset that he/she had encountered an eccentric and somewhat regimented communal sect (e.g. Hare Krishna). Similarly, if an Inter-Varsity, IFES, or Campus Crusade group invite college students to a program of some kind, most respondents surely come prepared to expect some proselytizing. Any parent sending a child to a Catholic camp should be aware of the fact that the child might experience some implicit and even explicit proselytizing.[26]

More generally, it needs to be noted that the modern notion of informed consent is not without its own problems. It is a legal term and we should therefore be cautious in using the term in other contexts. The term is further highly individualistic, and fails to take into account the inter-dependence that is a natural part of normal human relations. There is also vagueness inherent in the ideal of being informed. Complete information is impossible for finite human beings. Caution is therefore in order when claiming that proselytizers are rarely committed to making known the whole truth. And again, where are the data to back up this empirical claim? The notion of consent is further all too frequently based on an ideal of absolute freedom. What is needed is a more realistic ideal of normal autonomy and freedom.

---

[26] Here I am commenting on Stiebel's concern about targeting Jewish youth (1982, 96).

There are additional problems with applying the notion of choice to the area of religion. Questions can be raised about the extent to which religious commitment is really an act of the will. William James has underscored the fact that believing in any area is not obviously a matter of choice (1968, 90–93). We do not choose to believe that the sun is shining, when in fact it is shining. Rather, we find ourselves believing. Similarly, with regard to religious commitment. A more defensible approach to choice in regard to religious belief would make reference to dispositions to believe, and this will lead to a more moderate assessment of the place of the will in religious commitment (Astley 1994, ch. 8). All this is not to negate entirely the element of choice in conversion and the need to respect choice when proselytizing. However, we must be careful not to exaggerate the degree of choice that exists in conversion and hence also the dangers of coercion when proselytizing.

I therefore conclude that critics of proselytizing must be careful to avoid hasty generalizations when making the charge of coercion. While admitting that coercion is possible, and does indeed occur, it is not necessarily an accompaniment of proselytizing. So, instead of making wholesale condemnations of proselytizing as coercive, more care needs to be taken in defining the distinction between coercive and non-coercive proselytizing.

Missionary colonialism

It is important, when discussing the ethics of proselytizing, to take into account the broader context within which proselytizing occurs. However, as has already been pointed out in the previous section, the charge of coercion against proselytizing becomes more complex when contextual issues are introduced. In this section, I want to address a dimension of Western Christian missions that is much criticized in our day, namely its links with Western imperialism. It is beyond the scope of this book to provide a detailed response to this larger contextual issue, but at least a brief response is called for.

Here the charge of coercion takes on the vocabulary of religious colonialism and cultural genocide. Here we are being asked to listen to the cries of pain and loss by aboriginal peoples in North and South America, and by artists and intellectuals from Majority World countries in Africa, Southeast Asia, the Pacific islands, and elsewhere.[27] Surely there is something very suspicious about prose-lytizing that is hitched to the wagon of British imperialism. Or, to the Spanish conquests of past centuries (Rivera 1992). Or, to the ruthless exploitation of the Congo by Belgian King Leopold II (Hochschild 1998).

Norman Lewis, in his book entitled simply, *The Missionaries*, tells a story of corruption, exploitation, and forced conversions, and impli-cates missionaries in all the evils of Western colonialism. In one account he describes the appalling atrocities in modern Brazil, includ-ing mass murder, citing an authoritative newspaper report to show that: "In reality, those in control [of the areas where the majority of the atrocities had occurred] are North American Missionaries . . . they dis-figure the original Indian culture and enforce the acceptance of Protestantism . . . It was missionary policy to ignore what was going on" (Lewis 1988, 99, 103). Jomo Kenyatta famously said, "When the white man came we had the land and they had the Bible. They taught us to pray with our eyes closed and when we opened them, they had the land and we had the Bible."[28]

Inga Clendinnen (1987) provides a careful and graphic description of the sixteenth century Spanish exploration and conquest of Yucatan, a peninsula in the Caribbean, inhabited by the Maya Indians. Hernan Cortes, an early explorer of the New World, shortly after the conquest of Yucatan, "petitioned Pope and Crown that the establishment of the new Church in the Indies be entrusted to the Franciscans" (16, 46). Cortes had a special tenderness for St. Francis and his followers, and thought that the Franciscan's simplicity, self-forgetfulness, and devo-tion to poverty fitted them to this new task. Pope and Crown con-curred, the Crown "probably also responsive to Cortes' reminder that the friars would ask for minimal material support, for the Crown would bear the cost of the mission" (47).

Though initially small in number, the Franciscans did not despair, as they were working in "a context of coercion".

> Among Indian commoners, adults were obliged to attend weekly, and children daily instruction in the catechism. More important, those natives in authority were compelled to accept baptism, while the sons of native lords were gathered up and sequestered in the schools attached to

---

[27] See, for example, stories of European mission activity to the North American Indians, stories that are now being told in all their painful detail – listed in Appendix 2, #D1.

[28] Cited in Sampson (2001, 94).

every monastery, to be drilled in the catechism, in Christian-Hispanic patterns of living, and in contempt for their fathers' ways (Clendinnen 1987, 47).

While the Spanish settlers themselves had no interest in tampering with the institutions of native life at the village level, the missionary friars "were determined to reshape those institutions root and branch" (49). They worked cooperatively with the Crown in enforcing law and order and civilized behavior, however artificial it might seem. The Franciscans even went so far as to enforce Spanish notions of propriety at meals – "the sitting around the table, the cleanliness of the table cloth, the folding of the hands, the saying of Grace, all being laid out in obsessive and wistful detail. (The Maya lacked tables, chairs, and table-cloths.)" (58).

The year 1562 was to become "something of a watershed year for the Yucatan Franciscans" (Clendinnen 1987, 72). "In essentials the web of control had been established and the people tamed to the Christian order", though the missionaries were aware of some vestigial idolatry in scattered rural regions (73). Tensions were growing and reached crisis proportions with the discovery of a cave in which were found a number of idols together with human skulls. This led to an initial attempt by the friars to gain confessions by means of torture. The initial offenders were publicly humiliated, exposed to the lash, and fined. A more formal episcopal inquisition was then conducted. "More than 4,500 Indians were put to the torture during the three months of the inquisition, and an official enquiry later established that 158 had died during or as a direct result of the interrogations (76). Others were known to have committed suicide to escape the torture. Many more were left crippled because of the treatment they received. A massive festival was organized in order to highlight "the terrible majesty of the combined power of Church and Crown" (77). However, Clendinnen concludes that the Franciscans never succeeded in entirely eliminating Maya human sacrifices, all this underscoring their determination to sustain the old ways and their ability to reinterpret Christianity into their own traditions.

I have told this story in some detail (and there are many more that could be told), because it provides such a graphic illustration of obviously immoral proselytizing and missionary imperialism. Inquisitions, cruelty, and torture are a complete betrayal of any moral framework that deserves the name, let alone a Christian moral framework. The blatant harnessing of the church to the Crown is wrong, terribly wrong. The imposition of the Western way of life as though it were the Christian way of life, and the resulting lack of sensitivity to Mayan customs and culture involves not only a lack of respect for persons, but is also a complete betrayal of biblical Christianity and the doctrine of the Incarnation – the universal Word becoming particular flesh. The failure of most of the Franciscan friars to even bother learning the Mayan language, at least not well enough to preach fluently or to hear Indian confessions, displays an arrogance and lack of plain love that deserves to be condemned in the strongest language possible (Clendinnen 1987, 72–73).

The acceptance of coercion as a way to propagate the faith, from obligations of Indian commoners to attend catechism, compulsion of native chiefs to be baptized, and the sequestering of the sons of native lords to be taught in schools attached to every monastery, all of this can only be condemned as morally wrong. Despite the official requirements of the missionary program to ensure that Indians were taught the basics of the Christian faith before they were baptized, in actual practice the friars settled for much less, baptizing them if they knew how to cross themselves, say the Pater Noster (Our Father), the Ave Maria, and the Articles of Faith. Indeed, even this modest aim was rarely achieved at least among the commoners (Clendinnen 1987, 183–84). Such standards of minimal instruction made room for "successful" mass baptisms, one Franciscan recording the feat of a brother baptizing "four or five or six thousand in a day" (48). In the end, of course, serious questions can be raised as to whether the Franciscans did indeed succeed to convert the Maya of the Yucatan. But regardless, the means they chose to do so were terribly wrong.

Having conceded all this, it might seem to the reader that there is not much more that can and should be said in response to missionary colonialism. Surely it is immoral, period! But even here we need to be careful and look out for possible overstatements and hasty generalizations. Kenelm Burridge, in an anthropological study of Christian missionary endeavors suggests that all too often the negative stereotypes of the Christian missionary are based on a failure to understand the theory or logic, and the various components of Christian mission (1991, xiii). Too much is taken for granted and subsumed under the rubric of colonialism, says Burridge. What is forgotten is that Christian missionaries were also invariably "in the way", a phrase that he uses in the title of his book. As part of their overall missionary work, they were also defending the "natives" from exploitation and serving as mediators (244). Luis Rivera, in his careful documentation of the political and

religious conquest of the Americas in the fifteen and sixteenth centuries devotes two chapters to highlighting the denunciations and ethical evocations coming from brave prophetic voices of the same time
per-iod (1992, chs. 13 and 14).[29]

We see this even in the work of the Franciscan friars in Yucatan.
During the military phase of the Spanish conquest when sexual abuse of
native women was taken for granted, and when colonists continued to
regard all native women as sexually available, it was the missionary
friars who discouraged this by "vigorous intervention" (Clendinnen
1987, 43). They mounted "a magnificent campaign" to reduce to law all
exactions that the conquerors made on the Indians (48). One friar, upon
witnessing the cruelty of a punitive expedition of Spanish soldiers after
a Mayan uprising, wrote a long and furious letter to the Crown, making
clear "how complete was his identification with his new flock, how total
his repudiation of his compatriots, and how powerfully in this new
milieu the friars' sense of themselves as the Indians' protectors against
rapacious and brutal encomenderos had been reinforced" (52–53).

Many other stories of missionaries standing in the way could be
told. Indeed, when governments found that they could not control the
independence of missionaries, they were often expelled to prevent
their publicizing atrocities or intervening to help the native people.[30]
Missionaries to this day continue to be supporters of native rights and
culture.[31] The late Lesslie Newbigin, one of the last century's most dis-
tinguished missionary statesmen says this about missionary contributions to native cultures:

> On page after page of the history of Asia, Africa, and the Pacific Islands,
> you will find missionaries laying the foundations for the cultural
> revivals of the twentieth century, reducing languages to writing, revital-
> izing stagnant languages, rediscovering the forgotten past of ancient

[29] For example, Bartolomé de Las Casas devoted his entire life to fighting against a
system that continued to deny human dignity and freedom to the natives of the
Indies. Kusumalayam (2004) provides an inspiring summary of his attempts to
fight for freedom of conscience, and his well-earned reputation as "Protector of the
Indians".

[30] For example, Portuguese authorities imprisoned the Jesuit missionary Padre
Samuel Fritz and destroyed the mission he had established in Peru in the early
eighteenth century in order to extend their territorial control and enslave the native
people (Sampson 2001, 101).

[31] David Stoll, no friend of missions, is forced to concede that much of "the leader-
ship of current native rights organizations in the Peruvian Amazon comes out of
[the missionaries'] bilingual schools" (Cited in Sampson 2001, 101).

cultures and creating a new pride in them, and protecting the living cultures from destruction. You will find them also in countless cases standing up, often alone, on behalf of the peoples unable to stand up for themselves against the slave-trader and the blackbirder, the exploiting of cheap labor by industry, and the over-riding of native interests by colonial governments. These things must be taken into account if a balance sheet is to be drawn (Newbigin 1961, 107–8).

We also need to recognize the diversity and complexity of native cultures. While clearly there were and are many native practices which western cultures might emulate (e.g. respect of the elderly, land being understood as held in trust), there were and are nevertheless some practices that must simply be condemned as immoral. The human sacrifices of the Maya Indian and the crucifying of children and cutting out their hearts while still alive is simply immoral. And no amount of re-interpretation, as attempted by Clenninden, will eliminate the wrongness of these activities.[32] In this context, surely a Christian missionary telling the Maya that the true God does not require human sacrifice is "good news". There is nothing wrong with this dimension of missionary imperialism, if indeed it is even appropriate to use the label "imperialism" here.

The possession and ritual killing of slaves has been widespread throughout the world. Yet it was Christian missionaries who were often at the forefront of opposing slavery in practice, often at great personal cost.[33] It was the Christian doctrine of all persons being created in the image and likeness of God that lay behind the reform and eventual abolition of slavery. Thus William Wilberforce, of the evangelical Clapham sect, formed the Society of the Abolition of the Slave Trade in 1787 and cultivated links with missionaries. More generally it is the

---

[32] Although there is something to be said for Clenninden's suggestion that we need to try to understand what human sacrifice meant for the Maya Indian, this can be taken too far (1987, 177). For Clenninden, the real object of human sacrifice for the Maya Indian was not to kill, but to let blood spring forth as "a substance of great fertilizing power". But in the end, human sacrifice involves unnecessary killing of persons, and it is wrong. Of course, it is possible, in today's postmodern climate, to deconstruct or reinterpret most anything and thereby also to make ethical evaluation impossible. But even postmodernists will become strangely absolutist if these actions are personalized and applied to their own children, for example.

[33] For example, in Brazil, Jesuits took courageous stands against the abuses of slave raids and evoked great wonderment from the natives as word sped through the jungles that among the Portuguese there were some who defended them (Sampson 2001, 100).

Christian gospel's concern for the poor, the powerless, and the vulnerable, that has been at the root of much of the active opposition to the
exploitation of those most vulnerable to abuse, whether widows,
slaves, children or the elderly.

So, while admitting that there is some truth to the story of missionary colonialism, I want to suggest that it is in part a misleading
stereotype. I don't think the generalized charges of missionary imperialism are quite as strong as generally thought. More importantly,
Christian proselytizing *need not* take the form of cultural imperialism,
and it *need not* be a handmaiden of Western capitalistic imperialism.
Sadly, sometimes it has failed in this regard. But even here we must
be careful not to exaggerate past failures. We must at least be fair.
There were also always courageous prophetic voices that spoke out
loudly against the abuses of the conquerors, the use of force to convert, and the disturbing subversion of values where the idolatry of
mammon was hidden behind rhetorical allegiance to the crucified
Christ. We must also not forget the good often associated with the
cultural transformation brought about by the proselytizing of
Christian missionaries.

In the end, we will need a more nuanced analysis of the interaction
of Christianity and local cultures. Thankfully, there has been significant
evolution in the understanding of Christian interaction with culture,
though here we must be careful not to assume that these ideas are
entirely new.[34] By and large missionaries no longer aim to reshape the
institutions of native cultures "root and branch".[35] Given a more
nuanced analysis of the interaction of Christianity (or any other reli-

---

[34] For example, Dominican theologian Francis Vitoria (1480–1546) provided a careful
analysis of various positions on the legitimacy of the Spanish conquest and occu-
pation of the Americas (Muldoon 1999, 169). He very clearly rejected the argument
that the Indians' refusal to accept Christianity justified their conquest. His reason
was that nonbelievers cannot be forced to accept baptism. On the other hand, if a
non-Christian society refused to admit missionaries or harassed them, then this
would constitute a legitimate basis for occupying their lands, according to Vitoria.
[35] For example, Catholic missionary, Vincent Donovan, documents his own radical
shift in understanding his work in East Africa (1988). He stresses that the Christian
gospel cannot be identified with any social, political or economic system. The main
theme of his book is that the preaching of the gospel is the affair of the missionary
and the interpretation of the gospel is the affair of the people who hear the gospel
(164). Lesslie Newbigin, Presbyterian missionary and eventual Bishop of the
Church of South India, an influential leader in the ecumenical movement, and pro-
lific author, in his book, *The Gospel in a Pluralistic Society*, warns about the danger
of linking the gospel too closely to a particular culture (1989, ch. 12).

gion) and culture, we can then move on to provide a more carefully defined distinction between moral and immoral forms of such interaction.

Chapter 5

Liberal Objections to Proselytizing

In this final chapter of responding to a variety of objections to proselytizing, I want to focus on those that can be loosely collected under the rubric of liberalism. Modern liberalism can be understood both as a political movement and as an identifiable strand in thought and practice, having its origins in the seventeenth century, whose central values are freedom, autonomy, tolerance, equality, a stress on common human nature, an emphasis on neutrality as a way of achieving unity within a society, and a belief that human life can be improved by the use of critical reason. A more accurate heading of this chapter would perhaps be "Liberal/Kantian/Utilitarian Objections to Proselytizing". Hopefully this grouping doesn't sound too arbitrary, but some arbitrariness seems inescapable with any classification.

Let me first of all review some more popular expressions of the objections to be considered in this chapter. In the summer of 2000 the Southern Baptist Convention (SBC) planned to send 100,000 volunteers to the city of Chicago to evangelize the unsaved population. This led to tensions with the local, inter-faith council. The Council of Religious Leaders of Metropolitan Chicago wrote a letter to the President of SBC, asking that they not send thousands of missionaries to Chicago for fear they would create a climate conducive to hate crimes. The Southern Baptists pointed out, "Neither spokesmen for the Catholic Archdiocese of Chicago and Council of Religious Leaders, nor organizations and agencies that track hate crimes cite any studies linking them with evangelism." A leader of the Southern Baptists went on to suggest that these charges are themselves an expression of intolerance. These charges and counter-charges led some of the country's top evangelical leaders to formulate "The Chicago Declaration on Religious Freedom", which reasserted the constitutional right to evangelize. This declaration also denied that evangelism undermines "a peaceful, pluralistic society and may lead to intolerance, bigotry, and even violence".[1]

The website of the chaplains at Harvard University who are associated with The United Ministry at Harvard, warns about "destructive religious groups". By contrast, they describe themselves as "subject to the collaborative code of non-proselytization and mutual respect".[2] It would seem here that proselytizing and mutual respect or tolerance, are viewed as mutually exclusive.

In a U.S.News/PBS poll, 71 percent of those polled, including 70 percent of Christians, said that Christians should be tolerant of people of other faiths and leave them alone.[3] It is this attitude that perhaps best sums up liberal objections to proselytizing.

Intolerance

Tolerance has clearly been a dominant virtue in the history of liberalism. The association of proselytizing with intolerance serves as the primary concern of Jay Newman in a chapter devoted to this subject in his work, *Foundations of Religious Tolerance* (1982, ch. 5). He makes two different claims in this regard. "There is something essentially intolerant about the missionary, the proselytizer", Newman maintains, early in the chapter (88). In support of this claim, Newman points out that the proselytizer "has much more trouble than the average religious believer in accepting the fact that men of other faiths and philosophical persuasions do not share his religious convictions" (88). The proselytizer is further "impatient and feels that it is urgent that religious outsiders immediately embrace his religious outlook" (88). Newman also worries about the tendency to "confuse genuine religious dialogue with the missionary's monologue" (104). The latter, he says, "does not promote tolerance" (104). At other times Newman makes a more modest claim, namely that "most proselytizing tends to promote resentment", which in turn promotes intolerance (110). I want to concentrate

---

[1] B.A. Robinson, "Is Christian Proselytizing Linked to Religious Hate Crimes?" Retrieved on Aug 3, 2009, from http://www.religioustolerance.org/chi_decl.htm. The article describing this controversy was written on June 12, 2000, and updated on June 28, 2004.

[2] Retrieved on July 27, 2009, from http://www.ministry.chaplains.edu/about_us.php.

[3] Jeffery L. Sheler, et. al. "Faith in America", *U.S. News & World Report* (6 May 2002), p. 40.

on Newman's more extreme position, though in refuting this, I will at the same time be weakening the more modest claim about the probability of proselytizing fostering intolerance.

The objection that proselytizing is intolerant is really implicit in the objections we have already considered in chapter 3. Making exclusive truth claims is viewed as intolerant by many people. Arrogance and the denigrating of other faiths are also often interpreted as expressions of intolerance. However, I believe the intolerance objection deserves separate treatment, because it comes up so often, and because it rests on some additional errors.

The key problem with this objection to proselytizing is that it rests on some misconceptions about the nature of tolerance. A look at the history of the notion of tolerance illustrates the problem. The promotion of tolerance as a virtue is of relatively recent origin. Tolerance is not identified as a virtue by Aristotle, or by the Stoics, or by St. Thomas Aquinas. Indeed, prior to the Enlightenment, tolerance was seen as a weakness, or as an expression of cowardice, that is, a lack of commitment to one's professed beliefs (Kimball 1986, 121). Today it is seen as a virtue. This shift in evaluations should cause us at least to question our contemporary attitudes to tolerance. Maybe the contemporary preoccupation with tolerance, and our seeing it as the central, if not the only virtue, is mistaken. Lest I be misunderstood, let me hasten to add that I do place a high value on tolerance. My own Mennonite ancestors were burned at the stake in the sixteenth century, routed in the seventeenth, and forced to emigrate twice in subsequent centuries. There were some very good reasons behind the emphasis on tolerance that arose during the Enlightenment. The religious wars of the time were not pretty, and there was a desperate need for religious adherents to learn to tolerate each other.

But what exactly needed to be tolerated during that stormy period of history with its religious wars? Religious adherents needed to learn to tolerate each other. The traditional modern notion of tolerance had to do fundamentally with *persons, not with ideas*. Heyd captures this emphasis well when he describes tolerance as requiring "a perceptual shift: from beliefs to the subject holding them, or from actions to their agent" (1996, 11). Tolerance requires that we distinguish between beliefs and the believer, and it allows us to evaluate the opinions and beliefs of another in abstraction from the subject holding them. Toleration is therefore a sub-category of respect, which in the end will lead to restraint in how one responds to that with which one disagrees. Today, unfortunately, tolerance has come to be associated primarily with ideas, not persons.

Another fundamental shift in meaning has occurred with regard to the notion of tolerance. The traditional concept of tolerance meant only to endure, to put up with (from the Latin *tolerare*); nothing more than that. It did not mean one had to *like* something. It meant *putting up with something you dislike*. Indeed, the need for tolerance arises precisely because one doesn't like the other person's ideas. We tolerate an item always in relation to some other priority that we consider higher. We believe respect for persons is more important than fighting over a disagreement about ideas. This does not mean that truth is not important. It has been well said that error has no rights, but people do. That is why we endure or put up with ideas and practices and institutions that we do not like.

Today, however, this is condescendingly spoken of as *mere* tolerance, and it is not seen as good enough. Today a further demand is made of the tolerant person, namely the requirement of fully accepting and even agreeing with what is different. Indeed, to disagree with someone is to be intolerant. The preferred substitute for tolerance today is mutual acceptance of each other's ideas as equally valid.

Bernard Lewis, who has written much about the history and the perplexities of Islam, gives expression to this change in the notion of tolerance in an essay suggestively entitled, "I'm Right, You're Wrong, Go to Hell" (2003). Christianity and Islam, he argues, have a problem with tolerance towards other religions because they have the final truth revealed by God, and they believe everybody else is going to hell. Lewis highlights the seeming arrogance of the traditional notion of tolerance. "Tolerance is, of course, an extremely intolerant idea, because it means 'I am the boss: I will allow you some, though not all, of the rights I enjoy as long as you behave yourself according to standards that I shall determine.'"[4] What is needed instead of the triumphalism inherent in Christian and Muslim religions, according to Lewis, is relativism, which is the only way in which to achieve genuine mutual respect.

For a detailed response to the problem of relativism, I refer the reader to my discussion of the notion of absolute truth in chapter 3. The basic problem with epistemological relativism is that it is inconsistent, and those adhering to this doctrine invariably contradict themselves. Here it should be noted, that Newman devotes an entire chapter to refuting "the pernicious doctrine of relativism" (1982, 8; see

---

[4] Bernard Lewis, "I'm Right, You're Wrong, Go to Hell." *Atlantic Monthly* 291.4 (May, 2003), p. 39.

ch. 3). In places he clearly states that relativism is not compatible with genuine tolerance (47). A relativistic approach to truth "not only conflicts with the actual nature of religious commitment but also conflicts with the true nature of tolerance", i.e. it undercuts the possibility of accepting something one has a negative attitude towards (9). Newman clearly accepts the traditional understanding of tolerance as being half-hearted in some sense – it involves "accepting, enduring, bearing, putting up with" something "that is not liked, loved, respected or approved of" (6).

How then does one explain Newman's opposition to proselytizing and his associating of the same with intolerance? Unfortunately, Newman is not entirely consistent in his opposition to relativism. He devotes two chapters (5 and 6) to what he calls the theological dimension of religious intolerance (1982, 147). Religious fanaticism and intolerance are due to doctrines of universalism and exclusivism inherent in religions, Newman argues. The Roman church, for example, conceives of itself as a catholic institution, insofar as it strives to be universal, seeking to incorporate all human beings into the one church, the Body of Christ (111). All the well-known Western religions are also exclusivistic in holding themselves up as the true and/or best religion (118–19). Both of these doctrines underlie programs of evangelism and proselytizing, characteristic of well-known religious bodies. Newman therefore suggests that in order to combat religious intolerance we must induce religious leaders "to play down" those doctrines that tend to foster intolerance (148).

Here Newman seems to be advocating the very relativism that he has previously condemned. He seems to have forgotten his earlier argument that a thorough-going relativism undermines the very need for tolerance (1982, 9, 22). Indeed, at one point he suggests that "the relativist's 'cure' for intolerance is not only ineffective but worse than the disease" – it breeds a "kind of paralyzing skepticism and lack of commitment" (61).

Newman also fails to take religion and religious commitment seriously and at face value, a problem he himself criticizes others for, elsewhere (1982, 173, 9). Indeed, at one point he says that the relativist is not doing justice to the notion of religious belief – he is "trying to pass off as *believing* a kind of propositional attitude, some kind of 'holding' a belief, that falls short of being genuine believing" (61). Why then the call to play down doctrines of exclusivism and universalism? As Harold Coward has emphasized, "Religious belief is not filled with provisional faith or possible propositions, but with knowledge of the truth. Any theory of tolerance that does not make room for such genuine believing is simply inadequate in its formulation and untrue to the data of experience" (1989, 15).[5] At times, Newman recognizes the need to take into account "the actual nature of religious commitment" (9). Unfortunately, he fails in this when he attacks the doctrines of exclusivism and universalism.

Further, a relativistic dismissal of those who disagree with us, is, in the end, not tolerance but indifference, what Jonathan Rauch has labeled apatheism – "a disinclination to care all that much about one's own religion, and an even stronger disinclination to care about other people's [religion]".[6] One problem with apatheism and indifference is that it is the ultimate insult to the other as a person. This is one of the errors of the live and let live ideal that is often suggested as an alternative to proselytizing. Take, for example, a favorite question of those who adopt a liberal mindset: "Why doesn't everybody just leave me alone?" Good question! But another question needs to be asked as a response to this seemingly rhetorical question. What if everyone did always leave you alone? In doing so, you realize you can't really solve the problem of the ethics of proselytizing by asking this question. It is just too simplistic. It requires indifference, and is finally a betrayal, not only of genuine caring, but of genuine tolerance. At least a proselytizer is not being indifferent to the other.

Finally, Newman's attack of adherents to the doctrines of exclusivism and universalism is ultimately an expression of intolerance. Coward has correctly argued that relativism is the breeding ground of intolerance rather than tolerance (1989, 15). "The thesis of the religious relativist with regard to tolerance may be fairly characterized as: 'Tolerance requires that you believe in nothing!' or 'The only way to have religious tolerance is for everyone to have no religious belief'!" (15). Newman himself sees this problem in places. He concludes his book with a stern and I believe appropriate condemnation of liberal intellectuals. "Many liberal intellectuals are themselves intolerant

---

[5] Unfortunately, Harold Coward's otherwise excellent treatment of tolerance and religious pluralism suffers from the same kind of ambiguity as found in Newman. In describing the causes of intolerance, Coward cites as one cause, the tendency of religions to see the revealed scripture of each religion as the truth (1989, 6–8). He then goes on to talk about the theological basis of religious intolerance. The chief culprit is theological imperialism where one's own position is seen as superior, and others – good though they may be – are seen as inferior. Here Coward is succumbing to the very relativism that he later condemns.

[6] Jonathan Rauch, "Let it Be", *The Atlantic Monthly*, 291.4 (May, 2003), p. 34.

men", he argues, and his reason for making this statement is that they "are irrationally hostile towards religious people in general" (Newman 1982, 173). I quite agree, but unfortunately, Newman himself is not entirely immune to this same charge in his hostility towards proselytizing in the name of exclusive truth.

So, how do we encourage Christians and Muslims to be tolerant? Not by demanding that they relativize their claims to truth. This would in fact be an expression of intolerance. Instead, tolerance and respect for other religions must take seriously the truth claims made by proselytizing religions. Tolerance must also be encouraged as developing from within the truth of these religions. As Richard John Neuhaus was fond of saying, "The reason we do not kill one another over our disagreements about the will of God is that we believe it is against the will of God to kill one another over our disagreements about the will of God."[7] So, while tolerance might seem a little half-hearted, as Newman points out, this is in fact its strength. It alone does justice to the deep sense in which religious people are committed to their understanding of religious truth. Such commitment requires at the same time, a very practical accommodation to those who differ – tolerance. Nothing more (*and nothing less*) should be demanded than tolerance.

Is it possible for someone who proselytizes in the name of exclusive truth to be tolerant? Yes! It is quite conceivable for a proselytizer to respect *people* who have differing religious beliefs. Remember, respecting *persons* is at the heart of tolerance. To disagree with someone is not to be intolerant. Clearly the proselytizer will disagree with the beliefs of others. But even here, it is quite conceivable he or she is willing to allow others to have differing beliefs, and is even willing to protect their right to have differing beliefs. Being tolerant is quite compatible with trying to convince other persons of the error of their ways, but at the same time it respects their freedom and their right to believe whatever they want to believe, as well as their right not to listen to those who claim to have the truth.

Equally clearly, there is a danger the proselytizer becomes impatient with those who disagree with him, and that he feels that it is so "urgent that religious outsiders immediately embrace his religious outlook" that he gives up on "the safe but slow method of rational persuasion" to win converts (Newman 1982, 88). But this danger can be avoided. Proselytizing does not necessarily have to become impatient and resort to "unwholesome methods of winning converts." Newman's claim

---

[7] Richard John Neuhaus, (2003). "Why Aren't Muslims Like us?" *First Things*, 134 (June/July 2003), p. 61.

that there is something essentially intolerant about the missionary or proselytizer is therefore fundamentally mistaken.

Indeed, many examples can be found where proselytizers have been tolerant and where religious leaders have exhorted adherents to be tolerant of other faiths. The Buddhist attitude towards other religions, for example, has been described as exemplary in combining tolerance and missionary zeal (Coward 2000, 126, 153). Evangelicals, who are very committed to evangelism, have been found to be strongly committed to toleration of diversity (Smith 2000, ch. 2).

Another interesting historical example is the subject of two recent books, both focusing on Constantine, who might be seen as a counterexample to my thesis. H.A. Drake's book, entitled, *Constantine and the Bishops: The Politics of Intolerance* (2000), challenges the widespread assumption that intolerance is endemic to Christianity. The subject of Elizabeth Digeser's book is Lactantius, a Latin Christian apologist and contemporary of Constantine (1999).[8] In the years before Constantine took the throne, Christianity was rapidly winning the hearts and minds of millions of Roman citizens. Attempts at halting the growth of Christianity through persecution by Constantine's predecessors, most notably by Diocletian, had simply failed. Early in the fourth century, the Christian church was simply too large and too influential for Christianity to be halted by the sword. Interestingly, at the time of Diocletian's persecution, it was the polytheism of Rome that was in fact very intolerant. By contrast, though making exclusive claims, early Christianity was very tolerant. Indeed, Constantine, influenced by the writings of Lactantius, developed a religious policy that advocated tolerance.[9]

---

[8] Both books are reviewed by Robert Louis Wilken, "In Defense of Constantine", *First Things*, 112 (April 2001), pp. 36–40.

[9] Drawing on Cicero, Lactantius gives a theological justification of tolerance (Digeser 2000, 109). Religion, he says, has to do with love of God and purity of mind, neither of which can be compelled. Religion cannot be imposed on someone, it can only be promoted by words, i.e., by persuasion, for it has to do with an interior disposition, and must be voluntary. Drake and Digeser both see the hand of Lactantius in the famous Edict of Milan of 313 A.D., that granted Christians the right to practice their religion without interference from Roman authorities. But this Edict was not limited to Christians. It gave to "all persons the freedom to follow whatever religion each one wished" (Digeser 2000, 122). Thus it is significant that there is no evidence that traditional pagans in the early fourth century found Constantine's religious policy favoring Christians to be a threat to their religious beliefs and practices. Drake therefore argues that the claim that Christianity is in itself intolerant is a mistaken notion, indeed, a modern prejudice. Nederman (2000) extends this argument further, arguing that medieval theologians and philosophers also developed and defended a Christian notion of *tolerantia*.

A modern example of a Christian advocating tolerance is Roger Williams, founder of Rhode Island. Williams was a staunch and zealous Calvinist, and yet he was a champion of tolerance and religious liberty, and thus an exemplar in colonial American history.[10] Pope John Paul II, in an address to the United Nations in 1995, gave us a contemporary theological justification of tolerance.[11] Newman himself acknowledges that history provides us with examples of tolerant proselytizing (1982, 12, 36, 81), but he fails to see that such an admission is inconsistent with his claim that proselytizing is essentially intolerant.

This is not at all to deny that Christian thinking and proselytizing sometimes does express itself in an intolerant manner. Indeed, the later Constantinian period provides ample illustration of this very disease. All too often in Christian missionary endeavors, the heathen are viewed as barbarians. For example, José de Acosta, Jesuit missionary to the Americas during the Spanish conquest had a rather sophisticated taxonomy of barbarian nations, distinguishing between three types of barbarians. In the New World, "a great many" of those who fall under the third category of barbarians, are described as, "savage-like wild animals who hardly have any human sentiments; without laws, nor pacts, nor judges, nor republics."[12] The arrogance and intolerance of such a categorization needs to be condemned in the strongest language possible.

Contemporary equivalents of intolerant attitudes and intolerant Christian proselytizing can also be given. For example, some of the name-calling that has been characteristic of televangelists with regard to Muslims after 9/11 is a case in point. Jimmy Swaggart in a Nov 10,

---

[10] For a biography of Roger Williams, see Guastad (1999). While in England in 1644, getting a charter for his colony, Williams wrote, "It is the will and command of God that (since the coming of his Son the Lord Jesus) a permission of the most paganish, Jewish, Turkish, or antichristian consciences and worships, be granted to all men in all nations and countries; and they are only to be fought against with that sword which is only (in soul matters) able to conquer, to wit, the sword of God's spirit, the Word of God" (retrieved Aug 3, 2009, from http://www.constitution.org/bcp/religlib.txt; quotation also found in Feldman 1997, 129).

[11] "As a Christian, my hope and trust are centered on Jesus Christ . . . [who] is for us God made man, and made a part of the history of Christianity. Precisely for this reason, Christian hope for the world and its future extends to every human person. Because of the radiant humanity of Christ, nothing genuinely human fails to touch the hearts of Christians. Faith in Christ does not impel us to intolerance. On the contrary it obliges us to engage others in a respectful dialogue" (quoted in Weigel 1999, 9).

[12] Cited in Rivera (1992, 221).

2003 broadcast, called Muhammad a sex deviant and pervert, called for the expulsion of foreign Muslim university students from the U.S., called for profiling airline passengers "with a diaper on their head and a fan-belt around their waist", and said, "We ought to tell every other Moslem living in this nation that if you say one word, you're gone."[13] This is not only a sad example of intolerance but also a colossal betrayal of the Christian gospel. One can only imagine the perversion of proselytizing that must characterize Jimmy Swaggart's supposed Christian ministry.

A final response to the charge that proselytizing based on strong religious convictions is inherently intolerant. A good case can be made that in fact exactly the opposite is true. As S.D. Gaede observes, "Intolerance of differences comes from those whose confidence in truth is shaky, who think truth depends on them. Thus it is not the genuine truth lover we ought to fear, but those whose love of truth is not genuine. And that includes the hypocrite and the cynic as well as the relativist," according to Gaede (1993, 59). Those who genuinely believe in truth will be the least likely to come to blows over it, since they know truth will stand regardless of their ability to defend it. Intolerance arises when truth is *used* rather than genuinely believed, according to Gaede. The genuine believer is able to conduct his or her life "in the gentle confidence that [what he or she believes] is true" (118, n. 5). Indeed there is empirical evidence to back this up. George Gallup and Timothy Jones, in a study of Americans who are strongly committed religiously, found that "The Saints Among Us", are more tolerant of other creeds and cultures than the uncommitted (1992). In fact, the further down the scale of religious commitment, the less tolerant people are.[14]

My criticisms of Newman's extreme position also provide a partial answer to his more modest claim suggesting that most proselytizing causes intolerance. This empirical claim rests on the same conceptual misunderstandings about the nature of tolerance that I have already dealt with. Once these misunderstandings are corrected, the evidence

---

[13] Reported in the *Mennonite Brethren Herald* (March 21 2003), p. 24, and based on a report of the Council on American-Islamic Relations. See http://www.caircan.ca/itn_more.php?id=P97_0_2_0_C (accessed Dec 12, 2009).

[14] Gallop and Jones found that 84 per cent of the spiritually committed would not object to a person of another race moving in next door, a score that was twenty points better than that of the spiritually uncommitted (1992, 40). I cite further evidence of this claim, with respect to religiously committed schools, in Thiessen (2001, ch. 3).

for intolerant proselytizing will be seen to be much weaker than is commonly assumed. However, I concede that sometimes proselytizers do become too obsessed with the urgency of their task and this then leads them to become impatient and to adopt unwholesome methods of proselytizing which do indeed foster resentment and intolerance. But again, rather than making unsubstantiated claims about proselytizing fostering intolerance, we need to pay more attention to distinguishing carefully between tolerant and intolerant forms of proselytizing. And when we do so, we need to make sure such distinctions rest on a philosophically defensible ideal of tolerance.

Consequences of proselytizing

Jay Newman devotes a lengthy section of his treatment of the ethics of proselytizing to utilitarian considerations (1982, 89–96). Newman recognizes the difficulties of taking into account all the consequences of proselytizing and on that basis coming to a final assessment as to whether or not proselytizing as an institution is "basically morally sound" (92). Despite this, he repeatedly makes generalizations about the consequences of proselytizing. It is because many missionaries have difficulty discussing religious subjects in a rational manner that "religious teaching (or proselytizing) has often given way to religious propaganda and why religious propaganda has often given way in turn to religious persecution" (94–95). Newman goes on to highlight the risks inherent in proselytizing activities, especially "the risk of promoting social disunity, hatred, bitterness, and conditions of barbarism" (101). Again at the end of this same chapter: "Most religious proselytizing tends to promote resentment. Resentment promotes intolerance, which in turn promotes barbarism" (110).

Kenelm Burridge, in his anthropological study of Christian missionary endeavors, draws attention to the usual stereotype of such endeavors: Missionaries, he says, have today popularly "emerged more as robots programmed to convert the heathen and making an unholy mess of things" (1991, xiii). Others have pointed to the damaging consequences for individuals who are the subject of conversionary efforts. There is the mental turmoil involved in the process of conversion itself. Conversion can lead to alienation from family and friends.[15] Some

---

[15] Greenway highlights this problem, and gives a concrete example of the alienation experienced by a Hindu convert to Christianity (1993, 150).

critics argue that religious conversion has the result of making individuals more prone to feelings of guilt and less capable of bearing the misfortunes of life (Newman 1982, 91).

Consequential arguments involve empirical claims. As such it is of utmost importance that they are backed up with sufficient evidence. All too often, however, when utilitarian arguments are used against proselytizing, sweeping generalizations are made without adequate evidence. Sometimes they are based on nothing more than a hunch. Is it true that *most* proselytizing fosters resentment, intolerance, and even barbarism, as Newman claims? Where are the statistical studies? And is the popular stereotype of missionaries making an unholy mess of things accurate? Again, where is the evidence to prove that this is most often or even always the case?

Here it should be noted that Newman's consequential argument is also a slippery slope argument – proselytizing fosters resentment, which in turn fosters intolerance, which again leads to barbarism (1982, 110). The central problem with slippery slope arguments is that they tend to get very slippery. For the argument to be valid, each causal link in this chain has to be strong. Clearly, sometimes proselytizing has the consequences that Newman postulates. But how often? Always? Sometimes? Seldom? Newman also tends to load the dice by talking about fanatic, irrational, or aggressive proselytizers (1982, 96–97). "When two groups of aggressive proselytizers meet, the result is inevitably 'holy war'" (97). True, but do proselytizers necessarily have to be aggressive? I do not believe so, and therefore holy wars are not the inevitable (or even the most probable) result of proselytizing.

And what about the counter-evidence – the positive consequences of proselytizing? For example, proselytizing has for many individuals led to a relief from guilt, peace of mind, awareness of being loved, and the ability to love. Empirical studies show that the religiously committed are happier as a result of their conversion. William James, experimental psychologist and philosopher of the nineteenth and early twentieth centuries observed as "a certain composite photograph of universal saintliness, the same in all religions", happiness, a feeling of being in "friendly continuity" with an "Ideal Power", "an immense elation and freedom, as the outlines of the confining selfhood melt down", and "a shifting of one's emotional centre towards loving and harmonious affections", which ultimately leads to an increase in charity and tenderness for fellow-creatures (1902, 47–49, 266–69). George Gallup and Timothy Jones find that the religiously committed lead lives that are fuller, happier, and more satisfying, and this because of their faith

(1992). Newman himself, in a later work, acknowledges that there is a "crisis of commitment" in our society, "as has been increasingly argued by both serious social critics and casual observers of the contemporary scene" (1986, 9). He then recounts the benefits of healthy commitment to a reasonably plausible worldview – "happiness, self-realization, and peace of mind" (9). A society which is not dominated by people who have such a commitment "drifts towards a condition of barbarity", Newman maintains (9).[16]

But the benefits of religious commitment go beyond the personal level. The Gallup/Jones study also shows that devout Christians, regardless of denomination, are more tolerant than the spiritually uncommitted. Proselytizing would here seem to be of benefit even in the area of promoting tolerance, contrary to Newman. Other studies show that caring people tend to give religious reasons for doing so (Wuthnow 1991). A growing body of research on the positive social benefits that correlate with church attendance suggests that evangelism can reduce crime if it brings disadvantaged youth into a supportive church family.[17] Then we must not forget the civilizing effects of missionary efforts in ex-colonial or Majority World countries, as reviewed in the previous chapter. Though the central thrust of Burridge's analysis is not to provide a balance sheet of positive and negative achievements of Christian missionaries, he nevertheless concludes that on the whole the effects have been more positive than negative (1991). All of these studies would suggest that proselytizing which leads to religious commitment should be seen as contributing to the credit side of utilitarian considerations.[18]

Of course, there is also the debit side of proselytizing efforts to consider. I have already drawn attention to various negative consequences of proselytizing in the preceding sections of this chapter, and also in earlier chapters. While in no way wanting to minimize or defend this unfortunate

---

[16] See also David Larson, formerly researcher with the National Institute of Mental Health in the United States, who argues that psychiatric studies actually show great benefits to religious commitment. "What the data showed was that religion was highly beneficial – beneficial in more than 80% of the cases found in the psychiatric research" (from David A. Hall's interview with David Larson, "Holy Health", *Christianity Today* [November 23, 1992], p. 19).

[17] Sider and Unruh (2001) review some of these studies in their defense of faith-based social service organizations.

[18] For another account of the social benefits of proselytizing, see Miss Gordon Cumming's description of the positive transformation of the islands of Fiji as a result of Christian missions in the nineteenth century (Quoted in Battin 1990, 154–55).

darker side of the missionizing and proselytizing ledger, there is one caution that is in order. Are the negative consequences of proselytizing due to immoral forms of proselytizing? It is not at all my intent to defend all forms of proselytizing. I admit that some approaches to proselytizing are wrong, indeed horrendous. I am arguing in this book that proselytizing need not be conducted in an immoral fashion, that it need not be coercive with all the attendant pain connected with coercion, and that it need not be intolerant with the resulting psychological pain associated with intolerance. I am arguing that moral forms of proselytizing are indeed possible. Therefore, to do a fair cost-benefit analysis of proselytizing, we should isolate those consequences that are due to immoral forms of proselytizing. It might just be that if all proselytizing were done in a moral manner, it would be even more obvious that the overall consequences of proselytizing are positive. This argument, of course, begs the question as to what counts as a moral form of proselytizing. Clearly I am also moving here beyond a mere utilitarian foundation of morality.

Indeed, I have problems with utilitarianism as an ethical theory. A utilitarian ethical theory can be used to justify immoral behavior. For example, if it could be shown that the overall consequences of coercive proselytizing are good, then according to utilitarianism, coercive proselytizing would be justified.[19] Augustine, as was noted in chapter 2, in fact used this sort of argument to justify the use of coercion in dealing with the Donatists. After all, we get these people to heaven! But I have already suggested that coercive proselytizing is wrong, a violation of the dignity of persons. Utilitarianism alone cannot provide an adequate basis for morality. There is the further difficulty of doing the extensive cost-benefit calculations required by utilitarianism, a problem which Newman himself admits. To determine the rightness of a particular act (and this applies as well to any sort of rule) would require "a fantastic number of calculations involving a very large number of factors or variables" (Newman 1982, 92). In the end, the ethics of proselytizing simply cannot and should not be decided by utilitarian calculations. Thus I am rather surprised that Newman even draws any sort of conclusion about the past consequences of proselytizing, for example, that "most of the religious proselytizing that has gone on is probably morally unacceptable" (103). His argument becomes even more questionable when he extends this conclusion to include all proselytizing.

---

[19] This problem is carefully explored by Battin (1990). For a critique of her position, see Baber (2000).

The above criticisms highlight a major problem in Newman's treatment of the consequences of religious proselytizing. Generally his approach is to evaluate the institution of proselytizing as a whole, and to prove that this institution is essentially or in the main an immoral one. I have argued, in this section, that he is unsuccessful in this. I want to stress, however, that I am in agreement with Newman that sometimes proselytizing is morally unacceptable, and I believe philosophers have an important contribution to make in clarifying the distinction between moral and immoral methods of proselytizing. That will be the central task of chapters 7 and 8.

Questionable motivations

I move now from consequentialist to deontological ethical considerations. I have already expressed some reservations about utilitarianism as a foundation of ethical decision-making. Various ethical theorists would agree and maintain that right and wrong do not depend on a consideration of consequences at all. Instead, what is right and wrong must be located in something inherent in the action itself or the motivation governing the action. Eighteenth century German philosopher, Immanuel Kant, is the most famous representative of such a deontological ethical theory. Kant's emphasis on the dignity, freedom, and rationality of the individual are of course very much at the heart of modern liberalism. For Kant a good person must not only perform his or her duty, but must also do this duty out of pure respect for the law of reason, or out of a pure motivation. In this section I want to examine some objections to proselytizing that focus on *motivation*. In the next, I want to evaluate proselytizing based on Kant's universalization principle.

Objectors to proselytizing and evangelism often call into question the motivations that underlie these activities. These motivations are for the most part unconscious or latent. Religious adherents will of course appeal to more exalted motivations to explain their proselytizing efforts – concern for the proselytes' salvation or obedience to a divine command. There is therefore a tension between conscious and unconscious motivations, which makes for a good deal of hypocrisy in proselytizing, according to the critics. I want to highlight three of the most common and the most damning motivations attributed to proselytizing, drawing on James Megivern's excellent, though dated, analysis of the phenomenology of proselytism (1976).

The first is the insecurity motive. Religious adherents engage in proselytizing as a way of dealing with their own doubts and insecurities. Seeking to persuade others is a way of bolstering their own faith. This analysis is supported by Leon Festinger's classic theory of cognitive dissonance (1957) as well as by more recent refinements of this theory.[20] The presence of dissonance, a sense of discomfort arising from the disconfirmation of important beliefs, gives rise, according to Festinger, to pressures to reduce or eliminate the dissonance. Proselytizing is one common and effective way for reducing dissonance.

Robert Cialdini (1988) provides a classic illustration of this motivation to proselytize.[21] One of the leaders of a small Chicago cult claimed to be getting messages from spiritual beings whom she called Guardians, located on other planets. The Guardians began to foretell a great impending disaster, a flood that would eventually engulf the world. Later messages reassured the followers of this cult that they would be rescued before the flood by spacemen who would carry them off in flying saucers to a place of safety, presumably on another planet.

Two significant aspects of the members of this cult were noted by three social scientists (including Festinger) who managed to infiltrate the group incognito – the high level of commitment to the cult's belief system despite enormous social, economic, and legal pressures; and their curious failure to spread the word, seek converts, or to proselytize. Indeed, secrecy seemed to be the norm. This all changed after the prophecy was not fulfilled. At first an atmosphere of despair and confusion settled over the group. At one point, several hours after the failed prophecy, the leader broke down and cried bitterly. "She knew,

---

[20] See Harmon-Jones and Mills (1999) for essays exploring more recent developments in cognitive dissonance theory. Elliot Aronson (1992) also reviews a number of theories that social psychologists have proposed more recently which, like the original cognitive dissonance theory, blend cognition and motivation. He argues that these newer theories are better seen as refinements of Festinger's cognitive dissonance theory. Dein (2001) reviews the literature that is critical of Festinger's cognitive dissonance theory.

[21] The original account is found in Festinger/Riecken/Schacter (1956). Peter Kenez provides another example of this phenomenon in his analysis of Soviet propaganda. Youth were recruited to head a branch of the youth group Komsomol, despite their not fully agreeing with Party doctrine. "But as the person was carrying out propaganda on behalf of the new regime, he or she was won over. The propagandists usually were the first to become victims of their own propaganda. There is no better method of convincing someone than by asking him or her to convince others" (quoted in Marlin 2002, 78–79).

she sobbed, that there were some who were beginning to doubt but that the group must beam light to those who needed it most and that the group must hold together" (Cialdini 1988, 119). She then got another message from the Guardians providing an elegant explanation of the events of the night. "The little group, sitting alone all night long, had spread so much light that God had saved the world from destruction" (120). The atmosphere of the group changed abruptly, and after the leader received another message from the Guardians instructing her to publicize the explanation, the once secretive group became fanatical in spreading the good news.

Why this abrupt change in behavior? "Oddly it was not their prior certainty that drove the members to propagate the faith", suggests Cialdini, "it was an encroaching sense of uncertainty" (1988, 121). Group members testified that they had given up too much for the sake of their beliefs to see them destroyed – they had to continue to believe. And since their beliefs had been mercilessly disconfirmed by physical reality, they had to establish another type of proof for the validity of their beliefs – social proof. If they could get others to accept their beliefs this would provide the reassurance they needed in the face of the direct disconfirmation they had just experienced and the conse-quent doubts they were experiencing. They therefore became zealous missionaries – if they could persuade nonbelievers and skeptics, "their threatened but treasured beliefs would become *truer*" (122). This search for social proof therefore explains the impulse behind proselytizing generally – "convince and ye shall be convinced" (122).[22]

The second questionable motivation behind proselytizing might be labeled the domination motive – the desire to gain power or control of some kind over others. Hence the military imagery often associated with missionary and evangelistic endeavors – conquering mission territory, winning converts, spiritual weapons, evangelistic crusades or campaigns, soldiers of Christ, and the Salvation Army. This domination motive becomes especially apparent in the link between missionary activity and political power. Thus Charlemagne wanted new tribes brought under his political domain also to submit to the Catholic faith. Thus also the frequent coupling of Western colonialism and missionary endeavors, as described in the previous chapter. This domination motive can also be seen as underlying the evangelism efforts of twenty-first century North American Christian churches. Successful churches

---

[22] John Gager (1988) uses the Festinger's theory of cognitive dissonance to explain what prompted proselytism in the early centuries of the Christian movement.

have power in the community. Of course, this power motive will be hidden – the overt motives appealed to will be obedience to God's command or the interest of the sinner. But underneath, it is the domination motive that really holds sway over the proselytizers.[23]

Both of the motivations alluded to so far can be subsumed under the more general ego-centric-motive. The search for social confirmation of one's faith, and the desire for power over others are both essentially self-centered in orientation. Bringing others to one's faith can also be a source of self-fulfillment.[24] This self-centeredness again calls into question the motivation behind proselytizing and evangelism. Surely the presence of all of these questionable motivations casts suspicion on the very enterprise of seeking to convert others to one's faith.

Clearly there is a good deal of truth behind this phenomenological analysis. A degree of self-interest would seem to color all efforts at proselytizing. Persuasion involves some exercise of power. Converting others provides some reassurance in the face of one's own residual doubts. I further agree that a full evaluation of the morality of an action must include an analysis of the motivation behind an action. Kant was surely right in suggesting that one can only be said to have really done something good if one has done the right action for the right reason.

But, what exactly is a morally acceptable motivation? Here we must be careful not to be too demanding. As most students taking an introductory ethics course are able to point out, there is something very wrong with Kant's demands of doing one's duty purely for duty's sake. Pure motivation is simply impossible, as Kant himself is forced to admit. Kant's ethical theory might be appropriate for angels, but not for human beings. Thus the suggestion that the motivation to proselytize be cleared of all self-interest or self-advantage is simply too demanding.

There is further a contradiction in Kant's own demands for pure motivation. Kant places much importance on the worth of the individual. The second formulation of Kant's categorical imperative exhorts us to treat people, whether ourselves or others, always as ends in themselves, never as a means only. But to treat myself as an end entails that

---

[23] Juergensmeyer (2000) generalizes on this power-motive to explain religious violence. To see oneself as an actor in a cosmic struggle, gives one a feeling of power.

[24] Battin groups the following under ego-centric motivations: gun-notching, church aggrandizing, and social control (1990, 152–53). This analysis of the ego-centric motive can be extended even further by appealing to the insights of sociobiology. Robert Glassman (1980) has attempted this, interpreting the motivation to proselytize in terms of a more general form of "kin selective altruism".

I must look after my own interests to some degree. Clearly I can take this to an extreme – I will then be said to be selfish, and this is morally problematic. But there is nothing wrong with a minimal degree of self-interest, which is in fact necessary for one's own survival and self-worth.[25] Applying this to proselytizing, we should expect that part of the motivation to proselytize will involve some self-interest. This is an inescapable part of all actions and does not give us grounds to question their moral worth. If however self-interest begins to play a dominant part in the motivation to proselytize, then, of course, we are dealing with something entirely different – the vice of selfishness, which deserves to be condemned.

The same can be said for the other motivations surrounding proselytizing that we have considered. All human relationships are characterized by a degree of power and control. Kant himself acknowledges this when he is forced to qualify his demands regarding treating people as ends in themselves. It is only if we are treating another person as a means to an end *only* that we stand condemned. In fact all relationships involve using the other person to some degree. As long as such using is mutual, understood, and freely engaged in, then it is morally acceptable. So we need to admit that the attempt to convert someone is motivated in part by a desire to have some power and control over the other. In most cases, the other person is well aware of this hidden motivation, and if he or she nevertheless freely listens to a proselytizer's appeals there can be no grounds to condemn such proselytizing efforts.

Another way of putting this is to see efforts at proselytizing as a form of social contract. You agree to allow me to persuade you about my religious beliefs, assuming that I am open about my intentions, truthful in what I say, and there are not any power-imbalances in our relationship. There is surely nothing wrong here. However, if I were your boss, or were knowingly not entirely truthful in what I said, or if

---

[25] Baber provides a bold defence of ego-centric motivations in proselytizing, in response to Battin's objections to "church-aggrandizing" (Baber 2000, 341–43; Battin 1990, 152–53, 175). Baber argues that concerns about church-aggrandizing are rooted in a pietistic form of Christianity which is too preoccupied with psychological benefits of conversion, and is therefore not bold enough in looking at public benefits. Baber defends proselytizing as a win-win situation for the evangelist and the convert alike. He admits that the flourishing of the institutional church is in the interest of the church, but this should not be seen as morally suspect because such flourishing of the church is also in the public interest. Baber draws an analogy between the church and the Public Broadcasting System in the United States – both solicit members in order to continue providing benefits to all people.

I were pretending to engage in a certain philosophical conversation, when in fact I was using this conversation in order, eventually, to subtly turn it into a technique to convert you, then of course the implicit social contract has been broken, and my efforts could be condemned from a moral point of view. Of course, we have to be careful with the last example. In a close friendship conversations often take unexpected turns, and each expects and allows the other to do so, without any incriminations following. In a close friendship, hidden motivations are accepted, though of course they can always be challenged by the other, in which case motivations will be brought out into the open.

Similarly with regard to the insecurity motive. As a philosopher I must confess that I have some lingering doubts concerning some of the claims that I have defended in the philosophical papers and books that I have written. I am always very gratified and reassured when a reviewer agrees with the position that I have defended, or even suggests that he or she was persuaded by what I have written. I want others to agree with me. I am motivated in part, when I engage in philosophical persuasion, to seek social proof of my beliefs. Surely this does not provide legitimate grounds for calling into question the morality of philosophical argument and writing. All of us as human beings, if we are honest, are plagued with a degree of insecurity about the beliefs that we hold. We seek reassurance by finding others who share our beliefs, and by persuading others to share our beliefs. We need plausibility structures as Peter Berger and Thomas Luckmann have argued in their classic study of the sociology of knowledge (1967). But this need for plausibility structures is not in itself morally suspect.[26]

We must further be very cautious when we do motivational analysis. Motivations are, after all, subjective and thus hard to read. While there may be some legitimacy to making a distinction between manifest and hidden motivations, we must at the same time admit that this distinction is often blurred. What is hidden is often revealed, and what seems to be revealed is often hidden. Motivations are incredibly complex. Thus it behooves us to take at face value the legitimate motivations behind proselytizing – concern for the proselytizee, the constraint

---

[26] Here it should be further noted that the experimental evidence for the basic claim underlying the insecurity motive of proselytizing, namely that in order to overcome cognitive dissonance, people seek out supportive information and avoid discrepant information is in fact generally weak. See Freedman and Sears (1965). Berger (1979) also provides a more positive interpretation of the insecurity motive of proselytizing. He argues that proselytizing is a key to self-definition within a pluralistic environment, and as such is a positive response to pluralism.

of love for the lost, and the desire to obey God. Granted that there are always additional motivations lurking beneath the surface, we must be careful not to cultivate a hermeneutic of suspicion.[27] At the same time, we must allow for the possibility of corruption of motivation. Rather than condemning proselytizing outright because of hidden motivations, what is needed is a more careful distinction between a morally appropriate and a morally inappropriate mix of motivations.

Proselytizing and universalization

Another objection to proselytizing that I want to consider introduces the universalization principle made famous by Immanuel Kant. Instead of assessing the consequences of an action, the key to assessing the morality of any action is to ask if you can think of your action as a universal law. For example, it is wrong to make a false promise, Kant argues, because the universalization of false promise-making leads to a contradiction – no-one would believe a promise if all promises were broken. The very institution of making promises would collapse if everyone broke their promises.

Jay Newman uses this universalization principle to highlight a problem with proselytizing. Indeed, it is precisely his treatment of deontological considerations that leads him to his more radical claims – "none of them [i.e. deontological and epistemologico-ethical considerations] suggest that proselytizing in general is morally right, and some of them suggest that it is actually morally wrong" (1982, 103).

Newman introduces three versions of the universalization objection against proselytizing. He asks us to imagine a society in which everyone was trying to proselytize everyone else. In such a society, every time that X came to convert Y, he would find that Y was also trying to convert him. Newman suspects that such a scenario would lead to "a civil war, a holy war" which in the end "would cause our imaginary society to collapse" (Newman 1982, 98). Clearly this argument appeals to consequences, and hence involves a betrayal of a deontological ethical approach – a problem that even Kant was not entirely immune from. Accepting for the time being, the legitimacy of consequential considerations, is it true that holy war is an inevitable consequence of

---

[27] For example, Pelkmans' analysis of a lack of transparency in recent proselytizing efforts in Kyrgyzstan, suffers from a failure to be transparent about the presuppositions underlying his own very critical analysis of these efforts (2009).

universalized proselytizing? No. Newman is here resorting to hypothetical speculation. Consequential arguments require empirical evidence. It should not surprise us that none is provided because this argument begins with an imaginary society. So perhaps we can leave speculative societies and speculative consequences where they belong – in the imagination.

At the heart of Kant's universalization principle is the notion of reciprocity. If one religious group thinks proselytizing is right, then it must accept the rightness of other groups doing the same. Newman therefore expresses his amusement at how the very same Roman Catholic friends of his who look favorably on their church's attempts to convert others express an implacable hostility to others seeking to turn Catholics from their faith (1982, 97). He gives an historical example of this inconsistency. In the Middle Ages, the same Catholic Church that zealously sought converts from Judaism or paganism, condemned and even did not permit non-Christians to attempt to convert Christians. Now I quite agree that there is an inconsistency in these examples. The question is, though, whether proselytizers are *necessarily* inconsistent. Surely Newman's Catholic friends could with perfect consistency accept the idea of reciprocity. Just because it is the case that *some* religious groups who themselves proselytize tend to be hostile to others' attempts at proselytizing does not mean that this needs to be the case, or even that it ought to be the case.

As an aside, I might mention that I also never cease to be amused at how the very same liberal intellectual friends of mine who object to religious proselytizing express unreserved support for the spread of secular and anti-religious propaganda by whatever means available. Examples: the eulogizing of science and technology in our schools and the media, advertising, telemarketing, political propaganda, and Hollywood. Here we have examples of proselytizing which are equally in need of critical evaluation, but which in my opinion are seldom given the attention they deserve by my friends. Reciprocity is a two-edged sword, and I would suggest that my liberal intellectual friends should be just as concerned about secular and anti-religious proselytizing as they are about religious proselytizing.

Newman himself acknowledges that the religious adherent can with consistency accept the idea of reciprocity with regard to proselytizing. He can imagine someone saying, "Everyone has a right to attempt to proselytize, and may the best man win" (Newman 1982, 97). So Newman really accepts my critique of his second version of the universalizing objection to proselytizing. He therefore carries his argument one step further. One condition of proselytizing is that "there are some people who are humble enough to be willing to allow others to attempt to convert them" (98). Now if everyone were engaged in proselytizing, and no one were willing to listen, proselytizing would come to be regarded as silly and futile and the very institution of proselytizing would collapse, according to Newman.

Newman's attempted universalization argument against proselytizing also fails at this third level, and it acquires the appearance of validity only by again taking consequences into account. Proselytizing does not *logically* require people who are humble enough to allow others to attempt to convert them. Just ask anyone who has attempted to proselytize! It is true that "one of the conditions of *successful* proselytizing is the receptivity of the potential convert" (Newman 1982, 98 – my emphasis), but this is again to introduce consequentialist considerations and every religious proselytizer knows that most attempts at proselytizing are in fact unsuccessful. Newman also makes the mistake of thinking that persuading and learning are mutually exclusive activities. In fact, most proselytizing, and especially effective proselytizing, requires that the proselytizer listen to and even learn from the potential convert. That is why dialogue is often proposed as an alternative to proselytizing. I do not want to pursue this alternative here. My central point remains, Newman's deontological objections to proselytizing fail.

Proselytizing and pluralism

The final objection to proselytizing that I want to consider, grows out of a point just made. I have alluded to the fact that most proselytizing is unsuccessful. But what if proselytizing were successful? Would this not then have the very unwelcome consequence of everyone being the same? Would this not violate the principle of pluralism that is at the heart of modern day liberal democracies?

Martin Marty, in seeking to explain how proselytizing has come to carry pejorative overtones and undertones in what might be called the late modern period, draws attention to the fact that this is "an age of pluralism, when free polities assure that differing peoples with differing opinions, beliefs, creeds, or parties can coexist creatively, or at least neutrally. Efforts to convert others across the boundaries of sub-communities violate at least the implicit rules of the pluralist game. The proselytizer seeks homogeneity and resents the persisting presence of the other. He must make all the same" (Marty 1999, 2). This is also an age in which identities are insecure, Marty argues. "People have great difficulty knowing who they are, to whom they belong, whom they can trust, and to what they should show loyalty and commit themselves" (2). Again, the proselytizer is suspect because he "violates boundaries and disrupts traditions. He is more concerned with enlarging his own community than caring for the integrity of others" (2). "The message: proselytizer, stay home" (2). And the implicit message: proselytizing is immoral.[28]

The fundamental problem with the fear of homogeneity as a result of successful proselytizing is that it rests on an imaginary scenario that will in fact never be realized. Proselytizing will never be so successful that there will be only one religion. Imagined dangers are just that – imagined, and there is hardly a need to respond. The much more probable causes of dangerous homogeneity are in fact political, or the mass media, as Sue Jansen (1988) and Noam Chomsky (1988) have amply demonstrated.

There is the further question as to whether all expressions of homogeneity, if in fact they could be achieved, are a bad thing. What would be so terrible about uniformly moral behavior in a society? What would be so wrong about everyone having the same religion, assuming of course, that this uniformity of conviction was achieved by moral means? Surely if everyone arrives at the truth this would be a good thing. It is further quite clear that proselytizing violates existing boundaries and traditions. But perhaps the breaking up of some boundaries and traditions is a good thing. It is not at all hard to imagine identities that are not positive, where some disruption would be a good thing. But again, excessive uniformity is highly unlikely. Plurality is part of the human condition. This surely is part of the meaning of the biblical story of Babel – the confusion of languages entails permanent plurality. Indeed, the story can be read as an affirmation of plurality (Smith 1996).

At the same time we need to acknowledge the reality of a fluidity of boundaries and traditions. As I will argue in the next chapter, proselytizing helps to keep traditions alive. There is therefore a symbiotic

---

[28] Harold Coward, in a discussion of religious pluralism, similarly draws attention to the problems of a universal religion. It leads to a violation of the principle of freedom, Coward argues. "A universal religion would amount to religious coercion. Unity without diversity leads to a denial of freedom" (2000, 141). Although Coward does not apply this argument to proselytizing specifically, the implications would seem to be rather obvious – proselytizing is wrong.

relationship between healthy identities and healthy proselytizing. Both are in danger of becoming corrupted. Both are needed to keep the other healthy. There is nothing contradictory between upholding both the importance of identities and the activity of proselytizing. The contradiction between the two is only apparent. Of course, all this assumes that proselytizing is done in accordance with moral guidelines. But proselytizing cannot be condemned simply on the basis that it would seem to be parasitic on the fact of a continuing plurality.

I would further suggest that those who are objecting to proselytizing out of a concern for protecting pluralism are somewhat dishonest. Surely, within a marketplace of ideas, a favorite term of liberals, we should welcome a competition of ideas. Surely, there is something healthy about individuals and groups trying to persuade each other about the convictions that they hold dear. Let me dare to suggest that those opposed to proselytizing on the basis of protecting pluralism are really not liberals at all but closet totalitarians. Liberal fundamentalists, I like to call them, and they are as dangerous as their religious counterparts.

Conclusion

This completes my review of the important objections to proselytizing that are found in the discussions and literature on this subject. I conclude that it is a mistake to think that proselytizing generally is immoral, that the activity of proselytizing is inherently bad. I quite agree that some forms of proselytizing are immoral, but even here, not as many as is commonly assumed. I would suggest that in responding to the more radical claim that proselytizing, *by its very nature*, is immoral, I have at the same time weakened claims to the effect that *most* or *much* proselytizing is immoral.

One of the central problems with discussions of proselytizing is the tendency to tar all cases of proselytizing with the same brush. But proselytizing is not all of one piece. There is all the difference in the world between an individual witnessing and the holy wars. We need to distinguish between aggressive and non-aggressive proselytizing, between proselytizing that includes psychological manipulation and that which does not. Jay Newman, one of the critics of proselytizing who has been referred to several times, at one point, distinguishes between "the safe but slow method of rational persuasion", and "unwholesome methods of winning converts" (1982, 88). But, generally Newman's approach, and that of other critics, is to evaluate the activity of proselytizing as a whole, and to prove that this activity is essentially, or in the main, an immoral practice. The object of the last three chapters has been to show that Newman and his critics are unsuccessful in this enterprise.

I want to stress, however, that I am in agreement with Newman and his critics that some proselytizing is morally unacceptable, and I believe philosophers have an important contribution to make in clarifying the distinction between moral and immoral methods of proselytizing. That will be the focus of chapters 7 and 8. But first there is a need to consider some positive arguments in favor of proselytizing. So far, my approach has been defensive in nature – answering some standard objections to proselytizing. I now want to switch to an offensive strategy. I want to provide several arguments suggesting that proselytizing as an institution is indeed a legitimate and even moral activity.

Part III:

A Positive Approach to Proselytizing

Chapter 6

A Defence of Proselytizing

In the last three chapters, I have tried to answer a number of standard objections often raised against proselytizing. My primary aim was to refute the more extreme position, namely that proselytizing as a whole, and by its very nature, is immoral. I have attempted to show that ethical proselytizing is indeed possible. I now want to shift my focus to a positive defence of proselytizing as an ethical enterprise. What arguments can be made to show that proselytizing is in general a good thing? This should not be interpreted as suggesting that proselytizing is always moral. Sometimes proselytizing is carried out in ways that are immoral. Indeed, chapters 7 and 8 will try to develop criteria to distinguish between ethical and unethical proselytizing. Before I do this, however, I want to look at some arguments in support of proselytizing generally.

A generalized defence of the morality of proselytizing as an institution can proceed only if we can agree on standards of morality. In chapter 2, I outlined the ethical framework being assumed in this analysis of the ethics of proselytizing. I am assuming the dignity and value of persons. This basic presupposition also underlies the positive defence of proselytizing being undertaken in this chapter. This presupposition may be derived from a religious worldview – persons are created in the image of God. Or, if one prefers a secular interpretation, one can hardly do better than Kant's passionate plea for treating persons as ends in themselves. Either way, whatever is said about the morality of proselytizing, it must uphold the dignity and worth of the human being. This belief in the dignity and worth of the human being is at the heart of liberalism, and so I begin with some liberal arguments for proselytizing. Later in the chapter I will examine some arguments focusing specifically on the dignity of the proselytizer and the proselytizee.

John Stuart Mill's argument

I begin with John Stuart Mill and his classic defence of liberty. I realize Mill's defence of liberty is concerned primarily with the political problem of government interference with individual liberty. But Mill moves easily from political to moral concerns. His advocacy of utilitarianism extends both to political and moral realms. Indeed, in a footnote on the first page of the chapter dealing specifically with "the liberty of thought and discussion", Mill himself suggests that his arguments for "the fullest liberty of professing and discussing" are in fact "a matter of ethical conviction" (1978, 15). So I believe it is fair to apply Mill's classic defence of liberty also to the morality of proselytizing.

Mill's defence includes the liberty of conscience and thought, as well as the liberty of expressing and publishing opinions, a liberty which Mill considers to be "practically inseparable" from the principle of liberty of thought (1978, 12). Although Mill is primarily concerned about protecting individual and minority groups from "the tyranny of the majority" (4), especially the tyranny of prevailing opinion and feeling, his arguments for the liberty of thought and discussion can be extrapolated so as to justify the institution of proselytizing. In fact, Mill does, from time to time, introduce the topic of religious proselytizing, and he specifically objects to attempts to restrict the propagation and diffusion of religious beliefs.[1]

There are both deontological and utilitarian dimensions to Mill's defence of proselytizing. The institution of proselytizing is of benefit to humankind, says Mill, because without such proselytizing, human beings may be deprived of the opportunity of exchanging error for truth (1978, 16). To silence the proselytizer because he or she may be in error is to make the very questionable assumption of infallibility, according to Mill. Even if the proselytizer is propagating false beliefs, society as a whole still has much to gain by allowing such propagation, because the propagation of error stimulates thought and discussion, without which individuals and society as a whole are in danger of falling into "the deep slumber of a decided opinion" (41). Truth held without opposition runs the risk of degenerating into superstition and dead dogma, according to Mill.

Here we see Mill at his best, but the implication of his argument is that we must view proselytizing as a healthy phenomenon because it encourages controversy and discussion on "subjects which are large

---

[1] See, for example, Mill (1978, 7–8, 22–23, 28, 31).

and important enough to kindle enthusiasm", and which therefore enable even ordinary persons to rise "to something of the dignity of thinking beings" (1978, 33). Mill even provides us with an example. He describes the condition of Europe during the times immediately following the Reformation as a period of history when the benefits of such intellectual stimulation were especially apparent. This example provides a corrective to the widespread view that the Reformation period was a time when intolerance prevailed. Clearly, the religious persecution occurring at the time calls for moral outrage, but we must not lose sight of the positive dimensions of the religious fervor and extensive proselytizing of that time – dimensions which Mill in fact defends.

Contemporary liberalism

The argument of the previous section dealt with a classic statement of liberalism. There have been significant developments in liberalism, and so it is helpful also to examine some contemporary versions of liberalism to see if they have anything more to say by way of a defence of proselytizing. The late John Rawls, arguably one of the most important political philosophers of the twentieth century, in his first major work, *A Theory of Justice* (1971), maintained that a genuinely just society would give free reign to a variety of notions about the meaning and purpose of life. In his more recent writings, Rawls gave more explicit attention to the fact of pluralism, and was even more concerned to acknowledge the deep divisions between opposing and incommensurable conceptions of the good existing in a society (1987; 1993). In both the earlier and later works, Rawls expressed the heart of liberalism – attempting to find a way to accommodate the differing conceptions of the meaning, value, and purpose of human life existing within a pluralistic society. In his more recent work, *Political Liberalism* (1993), Rawls tried to accomplish this end without relying on a comprehensive moral framework such as is found in Mill and in his own earlier work. Whether he succeeded in avoiding any moral and metaphysical assumptions is debatable, but this issue need not concern us here.

In his earlier work, Rawls devoted a section to the "Equal Liberty of Conscience" (1971, 205–11). He maintained that in the "original position" where contracting parties do not know the religious convictions of themselves or other persons, they would choose equal liberty of conscience for all as a fundamental starting point. Liberty of conscience is therefore based solely on a conception of justice, for Rawls. He was further very careful to point out that his case for liberty does not rest on scepticism or an indifference to religion. Also, his advocacy of toleration "is not derived from practical necessities or reasons of state" (219). "Moral and religious freedom follows from the principle of equal liberty; and assuming the priority of this principle, the only ground for denying the equal liberties is to avoid an even greater injustice, an even greater loss of liberty," Rawls maintained (214). He went on to consider some cases where such liberty of conscience might be limited by the common interest in public order and security. Interestingly, Rawls specifically objects to Rousseau who advocated limited toleration for Catholics because for them there is no salvation outside of the church. Hence, Catholics must either torment or convert others, and this was seen by Rousseau to be a threat to public order and civic peace. Rawls objected to such psychological speculation, arguing that it was based on limited historical experience, and a limited knowledge of the possibilities of political life (216). So here we find Rawls defending proselytizing as an expression of liberty of conscience. Only if it is done in ways that undermine the security of other citizens, or if the institutions of liberty are themselves put in danger would any restrictions on the freedom to proselytize be justified, according to Rawls (220).

Jeff Spinner-Halev, in a more recent work, *Surviving Diversity: Religion and Democratic Citizenship* (2001), chastises liberals for not paying enough attention to religious identities. He himself takes up this challenge, and in so doing stretches liberal theory so as to accommodate religious conservatives and moderates, such as Conservative and many Orthodox Jews, evangelical and some fundamentalist Protestants, many practicing Mormons, and orthodox Catholics (10). Spinner-Halev is particularly worried about liberals becoming illiberal in their attitudes and treatment of religious conservatives. Indeed, he accuses liberals of hypocrisy in their failure to support religious freedom when they hold this as a cardinal virtue of liberalism. The failure to endorse proselytizing as a morally acceptable activity is one example of such liberal hypocrisy.

Although he only touches on the topic of proselytizing a couple of times, I believe Spinner-Halev would concur with me that liberalism should support the proselytizing activities of almost all conservative and moderate religious traditions. The acceptance of proselytizing activity is simply another expression of the tolerance advocated by genuine liberalism. To disallow proselytizing is to be illiberal. It is no accident that countries, which have laws or policies that either prohibit or discourage proselytizing, are generally considered to be illiberal, e.g. Islamic and Communist countries. Such laws or policies have as their implication a refusal to allow a religious tradition to express its faith in the way it deems right. Clearly there are limits to liberal tolerance. But proselytizing should be classified as being within the boundaries of liberal tolerance.

Spinner-Halev is well aware of the inherent tension between conservative religious traditions, and liberalism. Liberal religious traditions do not share these same tensions. They rarely insist that they have found the only way to salvation. They support the key liberal virtues of autonomy and diversity. And interestingly, many liberal religions "have either softened or given up on the injunction to proselytize, thinking that this will offend others, or that conversion is unimportant since there are several paths to God" (Spinner-Halev 2001, 215). Conservative religious traditions, by contrast, declare their way to heaven (or its equivalent) as the only way. They try to ensure that their children are raised within a particular communal vision of the good life. They are further bold in defining the rules of their moral community, rules which provide clear boundaries to mark who is a member and who is not. "These rules and the goods that conservative religions promise to people, like eternal salvation, give a very clear reason why people should join or remain a member of the religion" (217). All this is somewhat worrisome to contemporary liberals.

However, Spinner-Halev is concerned to make liberalism "more hospitable" to religious conservatives and other restrictive groups (2001, 204). Clearly liberals cannot give up some values – a minimal level of autonomy and education, tolerance, and liberal citizenship. Spinner-Halev goes farther than most liberals in only demanding a thin version of liberal values. While choice is important, there is such a thing as having too many choices, he argues (64). Liberals must also be careful not to make blanket condemnations of the internal restrictions inherent in cultures and communities (61). Restrictions not only create limitations, they also open up certain options and extend the range of meaningful choices. His overall project is "to defend the choice that people make to live an illiberal life", and to explore ways in which cultural and religious groups can protect their unique identities within the context of pluralistic liberal democracies (6–7).

What does this entail for proselytizing? Clearly proselytizing on the part of religious conservatives involves a concerted effort to place before people the choice to live an illiberal life. If, as Spinner-Halev argues, liberalism should allow people to choose to live an illiberal life, then by extension, liberalism should also allow for attempts to advertise these choices about the good life. Otherwise talk about choice becomes meaningless. Obviously such advertising should be done in an ethical manner. But there are no grounds for the liberal to object to religious advertising and proselytizing *per se*. Indeed, it should be welcomed as a means of broadening the choices individuals can make.

Spinner-Halev introduces several principles to help the liberal state navigate policy matters with regard to religious communities and institutions. One of these is the principle of inclusion – a liberal state should try to include religious conservatives in its institutions and in public debate, except when doing so harms citizenship (Spinner-Halev 2001, 20, 107). Of particular significance here is Spinner-Halev's objection to other liberals who maintain that any religious talk in the public square is illegitimate. This is to deny religious conservatives the rights of full liberal citizenship.[2] A genuine liberalism allows religious language to be used in the public square. A genuine liberalism will therefore also welcome religious proselytizing in the public square. Of course, restrictions can be introduced as soon as such proselytizing harms liberal citizenship. But this is surely the exception rather than the rule.

Etiquette vs. ethics

The heart of liberalism, as I have already suggested, is to find ways to accommodate differing conceptions of the good life found in pluralistic societies. Clearly, these differing conceptions of the good life vary in terms of their seriousness. Some divisions existing within a society concerning opposing conceptions of the good are not as serious as others. This brings me to another important point with regard to defending the ethics of proselytizing. We need to distinguish between matters of etiquette and matters of ethics. This book is about the ethics of proselytizing. Concerns about whether or not proselytizing involves good manners are really quite irrelevant.

John Stuart Mill gets at this distinction though he uses different terminology. Mill warns against a kind of social intolerance, which discourages people from making any effort for the diffusion of contrary

---

[2] Elsewhere I have argued that any attempt to limit the language used in the public square to a neutral public reasonableness rests on an antiquated epistemology (Thiessen 2001, 235–38). Stephen Carter has further suggested, such an approach requires religious believers to "split their public and private selves", treating their religion as a hobby – discrete, unimportant, and confined to the weekend (1993, 8, 56, 63).

opinions (1978, 31). Again I think it is fair to extrapolate. What Mill is cautioning us against here is the use of social sanctions to discourage or even prohibit proselytizing. This kind of social intolerance, Mill argues, is "a convenient plan for having peace in the intellectual world", but "the price paid for this sort of intellectual pacification is the sacrifice of the entire moral courage of the human mind" (31).

The social sanctions against proselytizing are very powerful in our time. A contemporary writer goes so far as to suggest that "evangelists are the heretics of our age" (Gaede 1993, 45). Although we are nice enough not to burn them at the stake, we like to silence them nonetheless, and we do it in the name of civility. Think, for a minute, about the prevailing attitudes towards proselytizing. Proselytizing is not "nice", we tend to feel. It is embarrassing, even uncivil. It is a betrayal of the liberal virtue of public decency. I sort of wish the Jehovah's Witnesses would stop coming to my door. I feel badly each time I make an effort to be civil to them and tell them I am not interested, as I close the door to preclude any further conversation. In chapter 2, I described my embarrassment over one of my students giving me the Book of Mormon. What I am suggesting here is that this sort of embarrassment may be at the root of a lot of contemporary opposition to proselytizing.

But all this has nothing to do with *ethics*, though it has everything to do with *etiquette*. I quite agree that in our secular and liberal society we have come to treat proselytizing as uncivil and not nice. It violates the norms of civil religion, as John Cuddihy has argued in his classic study, *No Offense: Civil Religion and Protestant Taste* (1978). Given the dominance of civil religion in Western cultures, Cuddihy maintains that to proselytize "is to commit a social impropriety that is at the same time a religious heresy" (27). Cults or new religious movements who often are actively engaged in proselytizing, sometimes in unusual ways, are said to be "incivil religions" (Robbins 1984, 242). We prefer "benign religious groups" who aren't preoccupied with recruitment (West 1990, 126). Charles Kimball, in his recent book, *When Religion Becomes Evil*, describes missionary campaigns informed by absolute truth as falling "somewhere on the spectrum between irritating and deeply offensive" (2002, 64). But just being irritating, or uncivil, or even deeply offensive, surely does not make proselytizing immoral. Maybe our standards of civility are in need of overhaul.

Our embarrassment over proselytizing is, in part at least, rooted in the very influential private/public distinction that is at the heart of liberalism. For Cuddihy, it is precisely the making of specific allusions "in public places" to the saving gospel of Jesus Christ, for example, which is seen to be committing a social impropriety (1978, 27). Novak, in explaining the contemporary Jewish response to Christian proselytizing, suggests that such proselytizing efforts seem to "violate the new atmosphere where religion in general could no longer claim to be the foundation of anything of public significance" (1999, 42). In other words, religion belongs to the private domain. And if we are nice and civil, we will keep religion private. The public domain is reserved for those items that are common to us all, that are open to discussion via a kind of public reasonableness.

Proselytizing is problematic because it crosses the boundaries of the public/private distinction. Religious proselytizing, because it is religious in nature, belongs to the private domain, according to traditional liberal thought. But you can't proselytize in private. Proselytizing, by its very nature occurs in the public square. And so, because proselytizing crosses the standard boundaries between the private and the public, we find it embarrassing and uncivil. This, according to Sawatsky, is also one of the key factors explaining why, in North America, large segments of the Christian church have raised questions about earlier church efforts at missionizing and proselytizing (1986, 84–87). To seek converts to one's own heretical religion "is uncivil and uncouth, and not something that properly civilized people would entertain", observes Sawatsky (86).

The problem here is that the private/public distinction of liberalism has itself been problematic from the very beginning. Mill gave us the classic formulation of this distinction but even he ran into problems with it.[3] Private actions and even attitudes invariably have public consequences. There simply is *no neat and tidy distinction between private and public domains.* And therefore the objection to proselytizing based on this distinction is likewise problematic.

I return to my earlier point: Being nice or civil, belongs to the domain of etiquette, not ethics.[4] This monograph is about the ethics of proselytizing. In the previous chapters I have argued that there are no

---

[3] For example, Mill is forced to admit that his so-called self-regarding faults are in fact other-regarding, and do have an effect on the public (1978, ch. 4).

[4] Here it should be noted that opinion is divided on making the distinction between tastefulness and ethics. Johannesen cites a writer who believes "tact (or politeness) to be of ethical importance because we have no right to injure the feelings of others unnecessarily" (1996, 137–38; cf. Keiner 2007, 107). I would suggest that this position simply fails to distinguish between levels of importance in matters that relate to human conduct and relationships. Indeed, sometimes it is necessary to injure the feelings of others.

legitimate moral objections that can be raised against proselytizing as a whole. In this chapter I am trying to defend proselytizing as a moral enterprise. In all this I am trying to appeal to standards all would agree on. The standards of proper etiquette are relative to time and place. So if we find proselytizing embarrassing, it is not really that serious an issue. And maybe we ourselves are the problem.

Here I would point out a strange inconsistency in our culture. We seem to have no problem with certain kinds of proselytizing. We seem to feel no embarrassment about the proselytizing going on in the commercial domain. We accept the proselytizing inherent in advertising. We are not embarrassed with the huge billboards cluttering our freeways, whose purpose is to convert us in matters ranging from brushing our teeth with Colgate to putting our investments in banks that make huge profits by exploiting the ordinary citizen, though it would seem they do keep shareholders very happy. The average citizen in the United States is exposed to more than 3,000 advertising messages per day according to a number of sources cited by Seiter/Gass (2004, 6). We seem to have no problem with panhandlers of various sorts on our streets. But surely, if we accept this kind of proselytizing, we should also accept religious proselytizing as civil and nice. Perhaps what we should really be discussing here are ways to create a more positive cultural environment in our society where we would all become a little more comfortable with the phenomenon of religious proselytizing, where we would accept the practice of religious proselytizing as we do commercial advertising.

Of course, both of these practices still need to conform to ethical standards. But this is to introduce another issue entirely – indeed, an issue which is the primary concern of this book. What I have highlighted in this section is that we must not rule out proselytizing on the lesser charge of violating standards of social etiquette. Proselytizing is quite compatible with politeness. And if we don't find it so, then perhaps our standards of politeness need to be questioned. Offensiveness is often merely in the eyes of the beholder. There are various countries where it is perfectly acceptable to broadcast religious services in public places. For example, Danny McCain, an ex-patriot teaching at a Nigerian university, reports on Christians and Muslims alike hooking up huge loud speakers and broadcasting their services over the whole community. He could often hear a church service in progress from at least a mile away. "Somehow Nigerians tolerate this. I don't think I have ever heard one complaint about people disturbing their sleep or disturbing their peace."[5] Of course, this would be seen as offensive in most parts of the Western world. But even here this might not always have been the case. It is only quite recently that making specific allusions to religion in public places has come to be seen as a social impropriety here.

Lawrence Uzzell, in an essay outlining some guidelines for American missionaries in Russia, begins by pointing out that in religion, as in other areas of life, bad manners usually should not be outlawed. "Advocates of religious freedom correctly argue that the state should tolerate even boorish exercises of that freedom – if politicians and bureaucrats are given the power to curb religious activities which seem overly aggressive or obnoxious, eventually they will use that power to ban expressions of unpopular religious views simply because they are unpopular," Uzzell points out (1999, 323). But, then he adds this poignant sentence: "Nevertheless, bad manners remain bad manners" (323). Yes, indeed! The central point of this section has been to argue that not only should the supposedly bad manners of proselytizing be tolerated, they should also not be identified as bad morals. Etiquette needs to be separated from ethics. If we live in a free society and if we value our freedom, then perhaps we have a responsibility to be relatively "thick-skinned," so that we don't take offence or call the state police or the moral police too quickly when someone offends us by proselytizing.[6]

Dignity of the proselytizer

Liberal arguments for proselytizing ultimately rest on certain assumptions concerning the nature of human beings, despite Rawls' claim that his political liberalism avoids all metaphysical and moral assumptions. I therefore want to consider two more arguments for proselytizing that rest explicitly on human nature. I have already hinted at the first such argument in the previous chapters. Proselytizing is good because it is essential to the dignity of the proselytizer. And *all* human beings are proselytizers.

Various suggestions have been made historically as to the essence of human nature. I want to propose a revised essentialist definition,

---

[5] From a CEO Briefing, for the IICS Vision Community, by Daryl McCarthy, Dec 16, 1994.

[6] Jonathan Rauch (1997), "Offices and Gentlemen", *The New Republic* (June 23, 1997), p. 28.

which I believe incorporates the classic statements. Some philosophers have described a human as a social or political animal. Others have suggested that a human is a rational animal. I would describe humans as proselytizing animals, though I would want to put the word animals in quotation marks. It is in the nature of a human being to proselytize. As John Haughey has put it, "it seems to be endemic to the way we are as human beings to promote with others what we ourselves have come to understand as true and good" (1998, 266). Henry Johnstone defines man as, "among other things, a persuading and persuaded animal" (1981, 306).[7] So, if Jane has found meaning and purpose in her life by accepting and committing herself to the Bahá'í faith, and her friend Joe is struggling with the emptiness of human existence, Jane will very naturally want to share with Joe what has brought her fulfillment and peace.

This description of the essential nature of the human being in fact incorporates the other two historical definitions of what it means to be human. We like to argue. We like to persuade others of our point of view. We like to proselytize. On issues very dear to our hearts, we want others to be like us, to share what has given us meaning and purpose in living. But arguing, persuading, and proselytizing involve more than one person. So proselytizing is in part an expression of our social/political nature. Proselytizing also involves the mind, and so it is also part of our rational nature. My definition of man and woman as proselytizing beings is therefore in line with some of the traditional views of human nature. Proselytizing is central to our make up. It is also central to our dignity as human beings. As such, it must be a good thing. Of course, we can abuse this good aspect of our being. But, properly understood, and properly put into practice, it is good.

Richard Weaver makes this same point by looking at the human use of language. Human beings are obviously symbol-creating animals. We talk and write. But our use of language is not neutral. The language we use inherently expresses the communicator's choices, attitudes, dispositions, and values, and thus channels the perceptions both of sender and receiver. "We have no sooner uttered words", says Weaver, "than we have given impulse to other people to look at the world, or some small part of it, in our way. Thus caught up in a great web of inter-communication and inter-influence, we speak as rhetoricians affecting one

---

[7] Harold Coward makes the same point in this way: "The inherent desire to conceptualize and share religious experience is too deeply engrained in human nature to render silence an acceptable answer" (2000, 152).

another for good or ill."[8] All intentional use of language between humans is sermonic, for Weaver. We are born rhetoricians. Of course, rhetoric and sermons have to do with persuasion. So an examination of language use by humans again shows that human beings are by their very nature persuading and proselytizing animals. And these aspects of our being are good and are part of human dignity.

There are other ways to make essentially the same point. Proselytizing on the part of human beings would seem to be inevitable. It is therefore no accident that the term "proselytizing" appears in many contexts. As illustrated in chapter 1, the term appears quite often in the commercial and political realms. In the United Kingdom, the words "evangelism" and its derivatives, including the term "evangelical" (meaning "someone zealous for converts") are common in the secular world. Richard Dawkins is often called an evangelical atheist. Not only religious persons, but businesses, politicians, educators, media moguls and even atheists are all engaged in proselytizing. Proselytizing is inevitable.

Jay Newman, despite his ambivalence concerning proselytizing makes another interesting point relating to the dignity of the proselytizer. He concedes that there might be some utilitarian value of proselytizing for the proselytizer. Newman chastises the critics of proselytizing missionaries for usually failing to appreciate the psychotherapeutic value that the proselytizer's activity has for the proselytizer herself (1982, 90). If the Jehovah's Witnesses and Mormons do not make him substantially unhappier by vainly trying to convert him, "since it obviously makes them happy to be doing the kind of proselytizing that they are doing, their proselytizing would seem, all other things being equal, to be conducive to an increase in the general happiness", Newman maintains (90–91). How does proselytizing make proselytizers happy? It may help them to enjoy peace of mind and to feel important, according to Newman. It may also serve to reinforce their own beliefs and overcome cognitive dissonance, as dealt with in the previous chapter. Of course, this argument is contingent on all other things being equal – on there being no additional negative consequences of proselytizing on others. I have already argued in the previous chapter that objections concerning the harmful effects of proselytizing on others are considerably weaker than is generally assumed by the critics. There are significant benefits for society as a whole in allowing the activity of religious

---

[8] This quotation is taken from an essay by Richard Weaver entitled, "Language is Sermonic", and is found in Johannesen (1996, 3–4).

proselytizing. Thus from a utilitarian ethical perspective, the happiness resulting from proselytizing for the proselytizer would in itself suggest that proselytizing is a good thing.

If we take into account our social nature, proselytizing is also essential to defining who we are in relation to other groups. Proselytizing, by its very nature, involves making a statement of identity, by way of contrast to the other person being proselytized, and as such is essential to a person's dignity and self-worth. Martin Marty identifies this as one of the side-effects of proselytizing alluded to by several writers of a work discussing Jewish–Christian relations in light of proselytizing efforts. "Christians who set out to win Jews make a theological statement about their identity that shapes them in a certain way, whether or not they ever convert a single Jew" (Marty 1988, 162). Proselytizing has a lot to do with group identity and even "group-binding", according to Marty. If group-identity is essential to an individual's sense of worth and dignity, as is stressed by communitarians, the advocates of multiculturalism, and the politics of recognition, then again proselytizing should be acknowledged as an important good.[9]

It might be thought that this argument plays into the hands of the critics who question the motivation behind proselytizing. As we have already seen in the previous chapter, the ego-centric motive is thought by some critics to undermine the possibility of a moral form of proselytizing. Clearly, I am here appealing to a degree of self-interest in defending the morality of proselytizing. But a degree of self-interest is essential to the dignity of persons, as I argued in the previous chapter. The Bible teaches that we are to love our neighbour as we love ourselves (Lev 19:18). And Kant taught us to treat persons, whether others or your own person, as ends in themselves. Of course, we can become too preoccupied with ourselves, and then self-interest degenerates into selfishness. Only when proselytizing is *more* concerned with the self than with the other has it degenerated into selfishness. There is therefore nothing wrong with defending proselytizing in terms of a legitimate degree of self-interest. However, the interests of the other must also be considered. We therefore need to go on to consider whether there are also other-regarding interests that lie behind proselytizing in order to complete our defence of proselytizing as an institution.

---

[9] See Charles Taylor (1989) on communitarianism, and Gutmann (1994) on multiculturalism and the politics of recognition.

Dignity of the proselytizee

Proselytizing is also good because it upholds the dignity of the person being proselytized. Here I am making some further assumptions about human beings that I hope will be generally accepted. We as human beings generally desire to know the truth. Indeed, I believe this is a basic human need. William James highlighted the desire for truth as belonging to our passional nature.[10] Of course, there is also a tendency towards self-deception, but this is a flaw, a flaw that is in fact recognizable in the face of the more predominant tendency to want to know the truth. The desire for truth can be explained either theistically or from an evolutionary perspective. We see the theistic view expressed in the traditional and orthodox view of rationality – our God-given cognitive faculties have been given to us to help us to discover truth.[11] Other philosophers prefer an evolutionary and more pragmatic approach to explaining the function of our cognitive faculties.[12]

William James is sometimes interpreted as adopting the position that pragmatic concerns predominate in our search for truth. While it is possible to take an extreme position, and see pragmatic concerns as overriding or even incompatible with truth, I prefer to see them as commensurable, and I believe this is also James' position. If I choose to run my head into a concrete wall, it will lead to painful results, such as a headache and a bump on my forehead, but this lack of utility is rooted in the truth about the nature of reality. This illustrates the point made by Lorraine Code that "knowing well" is a key to living well (1987, 70). Normally human beings want to know the truth and they do their best to avoid error. Given a realist account of epistemology, we need to achieve a truthful account of ourselves, and the world out there, and it is therefore in our interest to discover truth and avoid error.

---

[10] "Our belief in truth itself, for instance, that there is truth, and that our minds and it are made for each other – what is it but a passionate affirmation of desire, in which our social system backs us up? We want to have truth; we want to believe that our experiments and studies and discussions must put us in a continually better and better position towards it; and on this line we agree to fight out our thinking lives" (Wm. James, "The Will To Believe" [1968], p. 94, cf. p. 100).

[11] For a recent version of a theistic argument for the reliability of our cognitive faculties, see Plantinga (1993, esp. pp. 4–7).

[12] See Hilary Kornblith, "Introduction: What is Naturalistic Epistemology", in her anthology (1985, 1–13).

If therefore I want to respect the dignity of other persons, then I need to respect their natural desire to know the truth and to avoid error. It is further in their interest that I do so. However, I too want to know the truth and avoid error. Our mutual desire to know truth and avoid error therefore has some moral implications for human interaction. It will entail, for example, that I pay respect to the truth claims made by others – I listen to the conclusions they have come to in their search for truth. But it further requires that where possible, I will seek to enhance the other's search for truth. Thus with regard to proselytizing, if I feel I have found some religious truth, then honoring other persons entails that I will share this truth with them.

There is a second way in which proselytizing upholds and even contributes to the dignity of the person being proselytized. Though not entirely independent of the previous point, the focus here is on the freedom of the proselytee to respond to the person doing the proselytizing. This point can be brought out by looking at what happens when there is disagreement between two people with regard to religion. Let us assume that both persons care deeply about finding truth. Clearly, if you have divergent religious, or even anti-religious convictions, then I will want to expose the error of your thinking. Indeed, to argue with you, to try to persuade you of the error of your ways, is in fact a way to honor you. Indifference is in the end an insult to you. The proselytizer, in attempting to convert you, to change your beliefs, is in fact upholding your dignity as a person who wants to know the truth. Further, the fact that a proselytizer resorts to persuasion rather than blackmail, for example, or outright physical force, is again a sign of respect for you. The proselytizer is appealing to your freedom to make up your own mind. Lamin Sanneh makes the point so well: "Belief premised on persuasion fosters the spirit of freedom and tolerance, while suppression or imposition of belief suffocates the spirit" (2003, 46).[13] Proselytizing is therefore again a moral activity, provided of course that it is not distorted in some way.

Epistemologico-ethical considerations

The claims of the previous section can be extended so as to have even more ethical punch. Human beings not only generally desire to know

---

[13] Jaksa and Pritchard (1994, 77), in a treatment of communication ethics, quote from Kenneth Andersen: "Functioning at its best, it [persuasion] both affirms and contributes to the mutual respect and self-respect of those jointly participating in the persuasion process."

the truth – they *ought* to seek truth. Here we are dealing with the interesting link between epistemology and ethics, often dealt with under
the rubric of the ethics of belief. In introducing epistemologico-ethical
considerations we can do no better than to start with the classic statement of orthodox rational choice theory as propounded by W.K.
Clifford (1879), as well as William James' equally famous response.
Clifford argues that a person reneges on her epistemic duty if she
believes on insufficient evidence.

> Belief is desecrated when given to unproved and unquestioned state-
> ments for the solace and private pleasure of the believer . . . If [a] belief
> has been accepted on insufficient evidence the pleasure is a stolen one
> . . . It is sinful because it is stolen in defiance of our duty to mankind . . .
> It is wrong always, everywhere, and for every one, to believe anything
> upon insufficient evidence.[14]

Assumed here is the epistemic duty to search for truth. William James
criticizes Clifford for being too preoccupied with avoiding error, but it
is a mistake to interpret James as softening the demands of truth-seeking, as is all too often done. "*We must know the truth* and *we must avoid
error* – these are our first and greatest commandments as would be
knowers" (James 1968, 99 – emphasis in original). James, however,
argues that these two commandments are not equivalent, and he
places the priority on the first, contrary to Clifford who emphasizes the
second. But both commandments presume we have obligations to
search for and to believe the truth. Note here that we are dealing with
moral commandments, not merely with a desire to know. We have a
moral obligation to search for truth.

While both Clifford and James agree on our moral obligation to search
for truth, they come to very different conclusions when this is applied to
religion. Clifford argues there is insufficient evidence for religious beliefs,
and therefore it is wrong to believe them, while James argues for the right
to make a commitment even in the face of the uncertainty of religious
claims. In chapter 3, I have already dealt with the problem of the uncertainty of religious truth claims as providing a basis for objecting to
religious proselytizing, so I do not want to deal with that problem here
again, except to caution again against making too sharp a contrast
between testable scientific claims and untestable religious claims. Given
recent developments in epistemology, science cannot escape a degree of

---

[14] Quoted in James, "The Will to Believe" (1968, 92–93).

subjectivity, and religion can claim legitimate status as providing an explanation of some aspects of reality. And in both areas we can legitimately talk about evidence, testability, and the search for truth. So we have a moral obligation to search for the truth in the area of religion, to the best of our ability.

Here another important dimension of truth-seeking comes up. We can't do this alone. We are very much dependent on others. We therefore also have a moral obligation to help each other in the search for truth. If therefore I believe something to be true, then I have a moral obligation to try to persuade those around me to accept my position. Interestingly, in bio-medical ethics it is generally conceded that a physician has a moral obligation to try and persuade a patient to adopt a solution to his or her medical problem that the physician believes to be the best for the patient. A politician has a moral obligation to propose and persuade voters to adopt policies that he or she believes will contribute to the common good. Of course, another politician of different political persuasion might disagree and try to persuade voters of the opposite. And may the best argument win! Both politicians, if they are genuinely caring people, will (and should) try to persuade voters of their position.

Similarly with regard to religious proselytizing. If I sincerely believe I have in my possession some wonderful news that gives meaning and purpose to my life, and which could do the same for you, then surely I have some kind of an obligation to you to tell you about this at some appropriate time. Indeed, religious claims are such that to get someone to believe in them is to confer enormous benefit on that person, as Pascal put it, "an infinity of infinitely happy life", and so the obligation would seem to be very strong according to Battin (1990, 161).[15]

---

[15] Battin, though critical of proselytizing, concedes that a missionary can be compared to the professional caregiver, and as such a paternalistic argument can be made for proselytizing, perhaps even justifying coercion (1990, 151–75). However, in the end, she rejects this argument, essentially on the grounds that the end doesn't justify unethical means. Her objection rests on a methodological principle she uses for assessing the moral issues of institutional religion: "unprovable, off-scale, self-interest-gratifying theological claims are to be considered suspect when their central function is to excuse violations of moral norms" (172). But, as has been argued by Baber (2000), Battin's argument against proselytizing ultimately rests on the assumption that religious claims are probably not true, and thus she betrays her earlier liberal methodological principle, not to rule out proselytizing on grounds of the questionable status of religious beliefs. Further, she assumes that theological claims will be used to excuse violations of moral norms, i.e. aggressive, manipulative, and deceptive methods in the case of proselytizing. But I would suggest that most proselytizing religions do not excuse violations of moral norms by appealing

This raises another interesting question as to what kind of a moral obligation is involved in religious proselytizing. Philosophers distinguish between obligations that are supererogatory – a good thing to do, but not required – and those that involve duties of justice – something that one owes to another person. So, is the obligation to proselytize more like an act of charity, or is it owed to others? Beach goes so far as to talk of a right to be proselytized (1999, 68). Although this distinction is very commonly made in ethics, I am not sure it is as sharp a distinction as is commonly assumed, and difficulties arise when it comes to categorizing certain actions. For example, when there are people starving in the world, is the obligation to contribute to famine relief an act of charity or a duty of justice? Margaret Battin, in reviewing the paternalistic argument for proselytizing, maintains that "the distinction between optional, supererogatory, and morally obligatory action fades as well", especially given the infinite benefits being promised by religion (1990, 162). I tend to agree. Proselytizing is not merely something that is nice to do, but rather something that we *owe* to other persons.[16] Given the interdependence of human beings and the need to help one another meet our basic needs and obligations, it follows that religious adherents have a *moral duty* to proselytize.

Lorraine Code has introduced the notion of epistemic responsibility as providing a key to approaching the difficult problems encountered in traditional treatments of the theory of knowledge (1987). For her, "*knowing well* is essential to the achievement of human well-being, hence cognitive activity *should be* performed as responsibly as possible" (70). Code agrees with me that human beings naturally want to know well. "Human beings care about knowing well in so fundamental yet so implicit a fashion that its value is, paradoxically often imperceptible" (71). And it is precisely because it is of such crucial importance, that the responsibility attached to knowing well seems nearly to make epistemology a branch of ethics – hence the frequently discussed demands of the ethics of belief (ch. 4). While Code maintains

---

to self-interest-gratifying theological claims, or by appealing to the immoral principle that the end justifies any means. For example, immoral methods are explicitly ruled out by the apostle Paul (2 Cor 2:17; 4:2, 5).

[16] One of the reviewers of my manuscript objected to making proselytizing something that we owe to others, because this would be too demanding – "almost all of us would have a duty to proselytize all the time". But, I don't think this follows. There are obviously limits to fulfilling our obligations, especially given that we encounter many obligations in life, some of which conflict with each other. So my obligation to persuade you about what I believe to be true is limited, and this is what makes it seem more like an act of charity.

that there is still a need to keep epistemological demands separate from ethical demands, she nevertheless underscores the importance and responsibility of knowing well. She also underscores the social nature of human beings, and so she objects to the individualistic, self-sufficiency-oriented epistemology so common in the past (ch. 7). "Human beings are cognitively interdependent in a fundamental sense, and knowledge is, essentially a *commonable* commodity" (167). Code goes so far as to suggest that the "human epistemic community seems to be essentially altruistic" – we are aware of one another's existence and of the need to consider one another, and therefore also of the need to share our discoveries and to speak truthfully to one another (189). Although Code does not specifically deal with the issue of proselytizing, it would seem her argument clearly entails not only the moral rightness of proselytizing, but also the moral obligation to proselytize within a society where participants care for each other and want to help each other in the all-important task of knowing well.

Jay Newman, in his treatment of epistemologico-ethical considerations, would seem to agree with the argument I have outlined. For "most of us it is intuitively obvious that it is usually morally right to believe and also to *teach what is true*", Newman suggests (1982, 99). In this same context he talks about the proselytizer as having "a moral right or even a moral obligation" to try to convert another person (99). Unfortunately, Newman gets sidetracked into considering a host of practical and factual objections to this essentially theoretical argument. He worries about proselytizers concealing truths, of their failing to give reasons or at least good reasons for the beliefs they hold, and the dangers of religious teaching giving way to religious propaganda and persecution in the light of the evidential problems listed. I will not respond to these objections here as I have already done so in a previous chapter. Nor is it necessary to respond to these objections in order to defend the central argument of this section, because they are essentially irrelevant. Indeed, Newman recognizes this when he concedes by way of summary, "a limited amount of religious proselytizing is morally advisable" (103).[17]

Let me return here to a question that is often implicitly raised as a way of countering the impulse to proselytize: Shouldn't everybody just

---

[17] Unfortunately Newman contradicts himself when he suggests that none of the deontological and epistemologico-ethical considerations "suggest that proselytizing in general is morally right, and some of them suggest that it is actually morally wrong" (1982, 103). As I have already pointed out, Newman's position is not at all clear (see ch. 1, n. 33).

leave everybody else alone? One way to answer this question is to say that we simply cannot leave everyone else alone. We are social creatures by our very nature. A more important answer to this question is that we ought not to leave everyone else alone. We have a moral obligation to care for our neighbor, to love our neighbor as we love ourselves. Hence Richard Weaver's use of Plato's *Phaedrus* and the metaphor of love and courtship to develop an ethics of rhetoric.[18] It is the non-lover who refuses to persuade, preferring to remain detached and uninvolved. The genuine lover, on the other hand, cares more about the welfare of the other person than he does about his own ego, and therefore he will seek to persuade the other, but do so in a way that is both loving and just. Hence also the moral imperative to proselytize in any area where we feel we have found the truth.

Conclusion

Let me summarize what I hope has been accomplished thus far. Proselytizing is thought by many today to be immoral by its very nature. Other critics make the weaker claim that proselytizing is often, or even most often immoral. The central thrust of chapters 3–5 was a careful examination of a number of standard arguments often used to dismiss proselytizing generally as immoral. Upon closer scrutiny, each of these arguments was found to be unsound. I concluded that proselytizing cannot be shown to be immoral by its very nature. We cannot simply condemn proselytizing as an institution. The arguments of these chapters also served to weaken softer claims to the effect that much or most proselytizing is immoral. These weaker claims rest on many of the same misconceptions that are used to condemn proselytizing generally.

In this chapter I have gone further and defended proselytizing as essential to human dignity, both for the proselytizer and the proselytizee. Indeed, we have a moral obligation to proselytize if we feel we have discovered truth that is important to the other. Drawing on Mill, I have also pointed to the beneficial effects of proselytizing on society as a whole. Liberalism too supports the freedom to proselytize. I conclude that proselytizing is a good thing, and that it is morally right to engage in proselytizing.

Clearly, like many other things that are in themselves good, proselytizing can become bad if it is abused. And, as is well known, the

---

[18] See Weaver (1965, ch. 1); cf. Griffin (1976, ch. 3) and Johannesen (1996, 103–4).

higher the good, the greater the danger of abuse. For example, eating is a good thing, a pleasant experience. The pleasures of eating can be enhanced with the addition of wine and other spirits. Yet, we all know the dangers of overindulgence and abuse. But this does not lead us, at least most of us, to conclude that we should prohibit all or even most alcoholic consumption. Yet, this is precisely the sort of thing that those who object to all proselytizing want to do.

What we need to focus on instead is to distinguish between proper and improper forms of proselytizing. Surprisingly, very little attention has been paid to this question, both in religious circles, as well as in the academic fields of religious studies and philosophy. In my arguments thus far I have from time to time touched on this distinction between moral and immoral forms of proselytizing. There is, however, a need to focus specifically on providing criteria that will help us to make this distinction. That is the remaining task of this monograph and the focus of the next two chapters.

Part IV:

Distinguishing Between Ethical and Unethical Proselytizing

Chapter 7

Criteria to Evaluate Proselytizing: Part I

The critical evaluation of the arguments often used to condemn prose-lytizing, as attempted in chapters 3 through 5, was a relatively easy task, while the constructive work of providing positive arguments in defence of proselytizing in chapter 6 was more difficult. But even there we could remain in the realm of generalities. Now I want to move on to the most challenging objective of this book, namely distinguishing carefully between ethical and unethical forms of evangelism or prose-lytizing. The operative word here is "carefully". What we need are clear and definitive criteria for making the required distinction. This is what I will address in this chapter and the next. But we want criteria that have some teeth, and hence these chapters will be very practical in orientation.

Surprisingly, the existing literature on proselytizing pays little atten-tion to the important task of distinguishing between ethical and uneth-ical approaches to proselytizing. As noted in chapter 1, only a handful of articles and chapters of books offer a philosophical treatment of the ethics of proselytizing, and even these essays do little by way of dis-tinguishing between ethical and unethical approaches (see the litera-ture review in the Appendix 2, #D6). Further, mainstream religions engaged in proselytizing have so far paid slight attention to the ethics of what they are doing. For example, evangelical Christians, for whom evangelism is a defining characteristic, tend to skirt ethical questions, although there have been a few attempts to define standards for ethi-cal evangelism (see Appendix 2, #D5).

More has been written on this topic in relation to what are often identified as cults, or new religious movements. However, as I have already explained in chapters 1 and 4, we should not expect too much by way of help from this corner in distinguishing between ethical and unethical proselytizing (see also Appendix 2, #D4). Further, I want to avoid focusing on the proselytizing activity of the cults and giving the impression that the criteria we seek will apply only to them. So, instead of focusing on criteria that have been used to condemn the proselytizing activities of cults, we need to deal with this subject more broadly, seeking criteria that can be uniformly applied to a variety of contexts, including those that are culturally valued.

Will we find any help in our search for criteria in any of these other contexts? Perhaps criteria have been developed in related fields such as communications, journalism, public relations, advertising, marketing, or education. Unfortunately, a review of the literature shows discussions of the ethics of persuasion in these fields are also somewhat underdeveloped and weak (see Appendix 2, #A; B; C). Scant help will come from this quarter, though I will draw on any material that might assist us. All things considered, I am striking out into relatively new territory and can at best offer only tentative suggestions. My focus is very specific: the ethics of trying to convert people with regard to *religion*, where conversion is understood in terms of a change of belief, behavior, identity, and a sense of belonging. This specific topic has largely been neglected.

Why this neglect? One major reason is the extreme positions most often taken about proselytizing. Either the critics condemn proselytizing wholesale, or adherents to a particular religion simply assume it to be a good thing to share the good news. In either case there is no need to distinguish between moral and immoral forms of proselytizing. It is either all good, or it is all bad; nothing more needs to be said. This is why, both in religious circles and in the academic fields of philosophy and religion, very little has been done heretofore in dealing with a middle position, namely that some proselytizing is good and some is bad. Accordingly little has also been done to define criteria to help us distinguish between good and bad proselytizing.

A kind of parallel thinking exists in other fields such as advertising and public relations. Genevieve McBride, reviewing ethical thought in public relations history, relates how a leading practitioner in the field detected "a great deal of public unease about persuasion" in the 1960s (1989, 14). McBride also points to the publication in 1957 of *The Hidden Persuaders* in which Vance Packard excoriated public relations and advertising as inherently unethical. At the other extreme is the blind acceptance of advertising and PR as good, particularly in the business world. Acceptance of either of these extremes will of course negate the very project of distinguishing between ethical and unethical advertising or PR. A similar difficulty marks the subject of proselytizing.

Another reason why little attention has been paid to the task of distinguishing between proper and improper forms of proselytizing is no doubt that it is not easy to be specific and practical. I want to dare to take up this difficult challenge. I offer my analysis of the criteria in this chapter and the next somewhat tentatively, hoping other scholars will further refine what I do here. (A summary of the criteria is found in Appendix 1, for those readers who would like a preview of the more detailed analysis that follows.)

While my aim is to be quite specific in the criteria I am proposing, some cautions are in order. The first concerns an inescapable vagueness inherent in some of the criteria. This will become particularly apparent in trying to define what coercion means with regard to proselytizing. Some methods of persuasion are obviously non-coercive, while others are obviously coercive. But, what of the gray area in between? The difficulties in providing precise criteria to differentiate acceptable and non-acceptable persuasion have led some scholars to propose a continuum of persuasion. For example, Richard Perloff, after pointing out that the relationship between coercion and persuasion has long been of interest to philosophers and communication scholars, seems to suggest that there may not be a sharp difference between these two terms (1993, 11). He then refers to another writer who places various modes of social influence on a continuum ranging from relatively noncoercive to highly coercive.[1] One problem with this approach is that it assumes that persuasion is still somewhat (relatively) coercive. This problem of treating persuasion as already on the morally problematic segment of a continuum is also found in other writers who talk about a continuum of influence.[2] I want a scale

---

[1] Other writers, who introduce the notion of a continuum of persuasion, include Margaret Battin (1990, ch. 3) and Michael Langone (1985, 378–80; 1989). Steven Hassan also introduces the notion a continuum of influence, with some methods being classified as positive, some benign, while others are hurtful. He locates cult mind control on the destructive extreme of such a continuum (2000, 113–14).

[2] For example, Battin (1990, ch. 3). I provide a more careful analysis of Battin's continuum in chapter 1, p. 18, n. 34; chapter 6, n. 15. Langone identifies four methods of influence and places them on a continuum (educative, advisory, persuasive, and coercive) (1985, 378–80). The first two methods are classified as choice-respecting, while the latter two fall under a compliance-gaining mode, and hence are seen as being increasingly unacceptable. My problem with this continuum is again that persuasion is seen as partially coercive. I would also argue that degrees of persuasion already exist in the first two methods – education and giving advice.

to begin with an unqualified notion of non-coercive and hence moral persuasion.

Clearly it will be easier to identify certain activities of proselytizing as being located on either extreme of a continuum of coercion, and therefore as being obviously either ethical or unethical. But caution will be in order about any activities located in between these extremes. This notion of a continuum also needs to be kept in mind as I try to identify various criteria to distinguish between ethical and unethical proselytizing. The criteria might not be as precise as we might wish, but should still be helpful in identifying where on this continuum, a certain approach to proselytizing lies.

My second caution relates to the nature of ethical principles. Ethics cannot be exhaustively defined in terms of principles or specific criteria.[3] Ethical theory has therefore more recently focused on virtue or character. Hence the focus would now be on ethical persuaders who, if they are good persons, will engage in ethical persuasion. However, I believe attempting to define ethical criteria still has a place. Indeed, there would seem to be a necessary connection between ethical principles and character – ethical persons follow ethical principles. So there is still some point to defining criteria to distinguish between ethical and unethical proselytizing.

It should be noted further that while I want to be as specific and practical as possible, my proposed criteria will vary with regard to their degree of generality. One problem with rule-oriented ethics is its tendency to assume that moral principles occur at the same level of generality or specificity. This is a simplistic view of morality. In order to solve complex moral problems we need a gradation of moral principles, ranging from the very broad and abstract to the more specific and concrete. We must be careful, not to carry the twin demands of specificity and practicality too far. It is impossible to take into account all the unique and detailed features of concrete situations in everyday life. There will always be a need for judgment in applying the proposed ethical criteria. At the same time, we must avoid staying at a level of generality that will be of little help to the individual decision-maker. Defining moral criteria for proselytizing is not a precise science. We need to heed Aristotle's wise counsel to seek only as much precision as

---

Interestingly, in a later treatment of this subject, Langone adds a third persuasive category to the choice-respecting methods (1989, 18–19). Here he seems to admit that some forms of persuasion are acceptable.

[3] Hence, the resistance to defining a code of communication ethics (Johannesen 1996, ch. 10).

the subject matter allows (*Ethics* Bk.1, Ch. 3). The criteria I am proposing to help us to distinguish between moral and immoral proselytizing will therefore appear in varying degrees of generality or specificity. All, I hope, will be of some aid in making the required distinction. Clearly, any classification of criteria is somewhat arbitrary, and overlap is unavoidable. I begin with a broad criterion.

Dignity criterion

Ethical proselytizing is always done in such a way as to protect the dignity and worth of the person or persons being proselytized. Proselytizing becomes unethical when it reduces the proselytizee to the status of an object or a pawn in the proselytizing program of any religious organization.

The principle of dignity is a broad principle and as such might be thought to be unhelpful in distinguishing between moral and immoral proselytizing.[4] But I want to treat it separately because of its importance as the foundation of some of the specific principles that follow. Furthermore, despite its generality, I believe it does have some teeth to it. All of us, I am sure, can testify to times when we have felt that our dignity was somehow violated. We want to be valued as persons. We want to be loved as persons.

The principle of dignity has already been highlighted in chapter 2 as being central to the ethical foundations being appealed to in my treatment of the ethics of proselytizing. I also suggested that this principle can be treated from two very different perspectives. It can be seen as growing out of a religious framework. Because people are created in the image of God, they need to be treated as persons having infinite value. The modern and secular version of this principle is best articulated for us by the German philosopher, Immanuel Kant. Persons are not things, Kant maintained. Instead, we must always treat people as ends in themselves, never simply as a means to an end.

---

[4] The principle of dignity in fact appears quite often in literature dealing with the ethics of communication, persuasion, and proselytizing. See, for example, Greenway (1993), Johnstone (1981), Langone (1985; 1989), and Lewis (1985). The Pontifical Council, in dealing with the ethics of advertising, identifies the dignity of the human person as one of three moral principles that are particularly relevant to advertising (1997). Brenkert correctly points to some vagueness inherent in this criterion, but I believe this problem does not undermine entirely the usefulness of this criterion in defining ethical advertising or proselytizing (1998, 329–30).

Kant himself worked out some of the practical implications of this principle. For example, he argued that it was wrong to make a false promise because this would make it impossible for the other person to give free and informed consent to the promise being made. Safeguarding the freedom of the individual was a sacred responsibility for Kant. Obviously this has a direct bearing on the ethics of proselytizing, and I will consider several implications of this principle of freedom in later sections of this chapter. For now I want to deal more generally with the idea of treating persons as ends in themselves and the implications this might have for proselytizing.

Anthropologist and long-time Christian missionary, Jacob Loewen, in reflecting on his life's work, draws attention to one way in which there can be a violation of the principle of treating persons as ends in themselves when proselytizing. He refers to what is often called "friendship evangelism" in Christian evangelical circles, an approach to evangelism where church members befriend non-churchgoing individuals with the goal of bringing them to church and/or leading them to conversion. While he acknowledges that establishing friendship with people is a positive way to develop a Christian witness, Loewen worries about this being subverted to become a "bated hook" approach to evangelism (2000, 90). The question needing to be addressed here is whether the friendship is a genuine one. If the friendship is merely a way of luring the unsuspecting into the Christian fold – hence the label, bated hook – then the person being befriended is not being treated as an end in himself or herself. Loewen gives a personal example.

> Some months ago I visited a recent acquaintance. I did not know much about him except that his health was not good and that someone had said he was not a Christian. During my visit I discovered that he was a serious thinker. We had a meaningful exchange about some research I was doing, and he showed me some beautiful artwork of which he was very proud. All in all, we had a very pleasant visit together.
>
> As I was about to leave, the host suddenly stopped me and asked if he could pose a serious personal question. When I responded affirmatively, he said, "There are several Christians who frequently come to visit me. They ask me to go out for coffee with them, but I am afraid of them, because I feel that the reason for their friendliness is that they want to convert me. I know that you are a Christian too, but I have never felt any kind of pressure from you, so I hope you don't mind if I ask you some religious questions . . ."

> The conversation that followed was serious and to the point . . . As we bared our inner lives to each other, we discovered that we had a lot in common; in fact, we discovered we were friends (Loewen 2000, 91–92).

Here we have an example of friendship being valued for its own sake. Loewen goes on to describe the religious conversation that he had with his friend as not being propaganda because it was "a solicited witness", citing a biblical passage encouraging Christians to be prepared "to give an answer to everyone who asks you to give the reason for the hope that you have" (1 Pet 3:15). Clearly proselytizing that occurs in response to a request to engage in the same protects the dignity of the proselytizee. However, I believe it would be erroneous to assume that ethical proselytizing must always be solicited.[5] For example, surely it would be morally appropriate for a religious person to initiate witness in response to a deep need shared by a friend, even though the friend did not ask for the same. Or, an atheist might come to a Billy Graham Crusade and respond to an alter-call after a proselytizing sermon – again no solicitation on the part of the atheist was involved, though clearly permission for proselytizing was given by coming to the Crusade in the first place. Here I merely want to stress that a solicited witness clearly satisfies the dignity criterion, though it is not the only way to satisfy this criterion.

We move on to another implication of the principle under consideration. Kant, in justifying the principle of not using people as a means to an end, argues that people are not things. There is a danger, when proselytizing, that people are reduced to things – pawns in a proselytizing program, statistics in an evangelistic campaign, and projects in a feigned friendship. For example, early in the twentieth century, Billy Sunday introduced the concept of a price for a soul, in which he literally charged a set amount for every person converted at each of his evangelistic rallies.[6] Such calculation of the economic costs of a soul is

---

[5] Here we must be careful not to assume an unrealistic ideal of human autonomy and independence, which lies behind much of the hostility to any sort of persuasion, as was pointed out in chapter 3. Against my claim that it is a mistake to think that ethical proselytizing must always be solicited, one of my anonymous readers argued, "that the capacity on the part of the proselytizee to choose one's exposure to a religious proselytizer is essential to its being ethical." One error here is to confuse the capacity to choose, with actually choosing. In fact, in ordinary human relationships we are constantly being exposed to persuasive appeals without our asking for them. But, clearly we have a capacity to reject them, although even this is sometimes difficult, what with the dominance of media in our lives.

[6] This practice is described in Andrew Walker's foreword to *The Logic of Evangelism*, by Abraham (1989, iv).

a terrible violation of the dignity of persons, reducing them to things. Sadly, this kind of thinking is all too common in contemporary evangelical churches committed to marketing and success.[7]

Much of the Jewish opposition to Christian proselytizing is also based on concerns such as these, and in part these concerns are justified. David Novak, for example, in talking about Jewish/Christian dialogue, reports that fundamentalists have not been part of this dialogue – indeed, they have excluded themselves – because "they see Jews as nothing more than objects of proselytizing".[8] Another Jewish writer describes the problem in this way: "The Jewish people will no longer be singled out as a target group for Christian missionaries or as objects in some theological numbers game" (Rudin, 1984, 43).

Clearly it is wrong to see a person as nothing more than an object of proselytizing. It is also quite wrong for a person to be reduced to a mere statistic in an aggressive church growth program. But here a problem needs to be addressed. It is hard to assess exactly when a person is nothing more than an object of proselytizing, or when a person is reduced to a mere statistic in a missionary program. To make such assessments would require a correct reading of the minds of those who are doing the proselytizing. And this is difficult to do. Of course, there can be tell-tale signs of the inner-workings of someone's mind. For example, if a friendship is completely dropped after a failed attempt at proselytizing, then the proselytizee might be justified in deducing that the friendship was not genuine, and that he or she was merely an object in a proselytizing program. But, what if the friendship continues, even after the rejection of the proselytizing message? Then it is simply very hard for the proselytizee to draw any conclusions regarding being reduced to an object or a project.

My son, a former youth pastor, tells of a good high-school friend of his, who asked him this question after five years of arguing with him about Christianity: "Would you be my friend if I told you that I would never become a Christian and didn't want to hear about it anymore?" My son responded, "Of course. It is because I am your friend that I want you to become a Christian. I wouldn't be a genuine friend if I didn't tell you." This conversation prompted some further penetrating

---

[7] Greg Pritchard provides a careful analysis and critique of preoccupation with marketing strategies, at the very influential Willow Creek Community Church in Chicago (1996, ch. 18).

[8] From a talk given in a library series at the University of Toronto, Nov. 13, 2000, launching a new book co-edited by Novak & Frymer-Kensky, *Christianity in Jewish Terms* (2000).

questions regarding Christianity, but did not lead to a conversion. And the relationship is continuing, though distance has made contacts between these two friends rather sporadic.

We must also allow for the possibility of someone being treated as an end, *and at the same time,* as a means to an end. This is surely what Kant had in mind in his careful formulation of the categorical imperative. What he condemned was a person merely being used as a means to an end. In fact all relationships involve an element of using the other person. It is only when this is not reciprocated or when it is not balanced with an element of treating the other as an end that the relationship becomes corrupted and a person is being used. Thus we must be careful not to conclude too quickly that because someone is targeted as an object within a proselytizing program, that the person is *merely* an object. If such proselytizing is accompanied by a genuine concern for the person, then that person is not simply being used as a means to an end, and the proselytizing cannot be condemned on the grounds that the dignity of the person has been violated. Charity programs too involve the targeting of certain groups of people with specific needs. Does this violate their dignity? Surely not, if such activity is an outgrowth of genuine care for these needy people.

Care criterion

The example of charity programs brings to the fore another dimension of the dignity criterion needing to be underscored. Ethical proselytizing that respects and protects the dignity of persons must always be an expression of concern for the whole person and for all of his or her needs – physical, social, economic, intellectual, emotional, and spiritual. To care only for the salvation of the souls of persons is unethical. It involves an objectification of a part of the person, and as such violates that person's dignity.

Here it might be well, first of all, to note that I am appealing to a broader notion of human dignity in this and the previous criterion. All too often, the dignity of persons is simply defined in terms of having basic human rights. But surely, as even Kant recognized, the upholding of human dignity involves more than respecting the freedom of persons, keeping promises, telling the truth, and respecting their property. If we really believe in the dignity of persons, we must also care for persons. Thus Joan Tronto correctly maintains that "justice without a notion of care is incomplete", just as an ethic of care "is incomplete unless embedded in a theory of justice" (1993, 61–97, 151–69). As was noted in chapter 2, the foundation from which I am considering the ethics of proselytizing includes an ethic of care. Ethical proselytizing must therefore grow out of genuine care for persons.[9] And, it must grow out of genuine care for the whole person. To fail to do this is a violation of human dignity.

Failure to care for the whole person when proselytizing is similar to racism or sexism where individuals are identified primarily in terms of a part of who they are, their race or their sex. Racism or sexism is wrong because it fails to treat individuals as *whole* persons who have value regardless of their particular race or sex. Hence, the frequent condemnation of advertising where women are treated merely as sex objects. Similarly, proselytizing which concentrates on the spiritual welfare of individuals alone, quite apart from other apparent needs, fails to acknowledge the value of persons as a whole.

Here we must be careful, however, not to be too demanding. Often it is not possible to address all the needs of another person. For example, as a philosopher, I am more apt to address the intellectual needs of another person, and may in addition feel very much at a loss in addressing the social needs of that person. Does this mean that I have violated the dignity of the other person? Hardly. My own personhood, with all its quirks, limitations, and weaknesses must also be taken into account. We must therefore allow for differences in ability to meet needs, based on the uniqueness of each of us as persons. A person who is adept at socialization will, of course, be able to meet the social needs of another person much better than many a philosopher. But in either case, what is required in order to satisfy the dignity criterion is at least a concern for other's needs, especially when these are very apparent.

Similarly, with regard to proselytizing: it would be morally wrong, for example, to preach the gospel to people who are starving to death, without at the same time addressing their dire physical needs. Alan Nichols provides a telling example of an abuse of this principle (1994, 146). In the week after the October 1993 earthquake in Maharashtra state of India, one Indian Christian agency printed and distributed to survivors of the earthquake, 50,000 tracts urging conversion to Christ. Nichols observes that not only did the people reject the message as irrelevant to their condition, but this distribution of tracts violated the dignity of these survivors.

---

[9] I am therefore in agreement with Stephen Littlejohn's and David Jabusch's stress on the relational dimension of persuasion, and their including caring, along with openness, as an important criterion of ethical persuasion (1987, 15–18, 66–67).

On the other hand, when there are no other apparent needs, it is quite legitimate to focus more on the spiritual needs of persons, though always being sensitive to the possibility of other needs coming to the fore. Here let me issue a caution for those who are very critical of combining human aid and proselytizing. For example, Christian groups who combined relief efforts and evangelism in response to the tsunami disaster in Asia in December of 2004 came under severe criticism in the media. Some of this criticism was unfair. Genuine care for whole persons, will respond to *both* physical *and* spiritual needs. Of course, the danger of exploiting human need is always present. More on this later.

Physical coercion criterion

The freedom to make choices is central to the dignity of persons. Moral proselytizing will therefore allow persons to make a genuinely free and uncoerced choice with regard to conversion. Coercive proselytizing is immoral.

It is rather easy to articulate the essence of the coercion criterion as a basis for distinguishing between moral and immoral proselytizing. Difficulties quickly emerge when it comes to describing exactly what is *meant* by "uncoerced choice". I have already examined coercion as an objection to proselytizing generally in chapter 4. In attempting to answer this commonly made objection, I pointed to the danger of starting with a deterministic view of human nature. Obviously if human beings are incapable of making free choices, then all proselytizing is coercive and nothing more can be said. Indeed, coercion could not serve as a criterion to distinguish between ethical and unethical proselytizing.

As stated in chapter 4, I am assuming that human beings are free, at least to some extent. They are self-determining beings who are, to some degree, the cause of their own behavior. Perhaps it would be better to use a word other than cause – a word such as "agents". People as agents *initiate* actions or *perform* them (Taylor 1992, 51–52). But human beings are not *completely* free – as existentialism and liberalism seem to assume. There are degrees of freedom and coercion. I would refer the reader to the diagram I used earlier to illustrate the tension between freedom and the constraining forces impinging on the freedom of every human being (ch. 4, p. 82). Human beings have only limited free will. We therefore need a more realistic notion of human freedom or autonomy, which I have described elsewhere as normal autonomy.[10] While in nearly all cases involving voluntary behavior, the agent has a degree of independence and choice, freedom is limited to some degree by such constraints as heredity, psychology, environment, and social context.

It should be evident that given this conception of human freedom some degree of vagueness will be inescapable in discussing the freedom criterion of proselytizing. But we cannot leave the criterion completely vague. Nor can we simply talk about coercion generally without defining more carefully what it means. These approaches lead to extreme positions and exaggerations as to the extent of coercive proselytizing, which, as I have already pointed out, are all too common in discussions about proselytizing. We must therefore try to become more specific in defining the boundaries between coercive and non-coercive proselytizing, all the while recognizing that these boundaries need to be understood as somewhat fluid. As already mentioned in the beginning of this chapter, the distinction between coercion and non-coercion needs to be seen as on a continuum. So, while we might not be able to identify precisely when we have crossed the line between non-coercive and coercive proselytizing, we must nevertheless provide some guidelines to help us make the necessary distinction.

I begin with a mark of coercive proselytizing that is probably the easiest to identify – physical coercion or the threat of physical coercion. Clearly, if I hold a sword over you while you are in a supine position, and then tell you to convert, I am being coercive in my efforts at proselytizing, as a Punch cartoon illustrates so well (see Figure #1: Physical Coercion). But even here questions can be raised as to whether this is necessarily coercive. After all, there are many examples in history, of persons who refused to convert to whatever religion, even under such obvious conditions of physical coercion. What do we make of them? Heroes and martyrs of a particular faith! But, they are surely the exception rather than the rule. We need criteria of coercion that are applicable to *average* or *normal* human beings. Ordinary people typically find themselves incapable of resisting the pressures of physical coercion. Therefore we generally understand the application of physical force as coercive and as being immoral. It is a violation of the dignity of persons.

---

[10] See Thiessen (1993, ch. 5). In developing the notion of normal autonomy, I draw on Haworth (1986).

"Tell me more about this
Christianity of yours. I'm
terribly interested."

Figure #1: Physical Coercion
Reproduced with permission of Punch Ltd., www.punch.co.uk

Sadly, as I have already alluded to in chapter 2, history is littered with examples of the use of physical coercion in proselytizing on the part of various religions. Christianity and Islam have probably been the worst offenders in this regard, though they are by no means the only religions to do so. Charlemagne's forcing of the pagan Saxons to be baptized at the point of the sword was morally wrong. Equally wrong was the explicit command of Abu Bekr, the successor of Mohammed: "Compel the rest of mankind to become Moslems or pay us tribute . . . If they refuse these terms, slay them" (Durant 1950, 188). Further documentation is surely unnecessary. Conversions prompted by the threat of physical violence and even death, are all too common in the history of various religions, and they are terribly wrong. Unfortunately, they continue to this day.[11]

Psychological coercion criterion

We also need to consider psychological coercion. This is a much more difficult criterion to deal with. Stated as a general principle, ethical

---

[11] For some documentation of contemporary conversions elicited by physical coercion, see Marshall (2007).

proselytizing avoids excessive psychological manipulation. There are various ways in which proselytizing can be psychologically manipulative. (a) Proselytizers should avoid intense, repeated and extremely programmatic approaches to bringing about conversions. (b) Care must be taken to avoid exploiting vulnerability. This becomes especially important when dealing with children, young people, vulnerable adults, and individuals facing personal crises. (c) Excessive appeals to emotion and fear must also be avoided. Clearly there is an inherent vagueness in this principle and its applications. Caution is therefore in order when applying this principle. The best approach in dealing with the psychological coercion criterion is to do a case-by-case analysis.

As we have seen in chapter 4, the charge of psychological coercion is often applied to cults. Various models have been used to describe the coercive methods used by the cults – brainwashing, thought reform, mind control, and coercive persuasion. These models have themselves come under critical scrutiny. Indeed, there has been an intense debate between so-called anti-cultists and pro-cultists among social scientists (see Appendix 2, #D4). I believe there are some lessons to be learned from this debate.[12] We must be very careful with making generalizations about psychological coercion in proselytizing. We must avoid extreme positions. We need to concede that some proselytizing needs to be identified as psychologically coercive, and some as non-coercive.

Eileen Barker argues in a similar vein. She argues that when discussing psychological coercion in proselytizing, it is important to avoid two extreme assumptions – that we are all brainwashed, or that brainwashing is impossible (Barker 1984, 135). Instead, as I have already pointed out earlier in this chapter, we need to think of a continuum of influence. At the one extreme is the use of extensive psychological coercion that must be admitted as immoral. At the other end of this continuum, we need to acknowledge the existence of psychologically non-coercive and hence moral persuasion. It is precisely here where I think some proposals of a continuum of influence founder – they tend to assume that persuasion is in and of itself a little bit coercive. This position represents the one assumption Barker is urging us to avoid, namely that we are all brainwashed. We need a continuum that moves clearly from non-coercive persuasion to obvious psychological coercion or mind control. Of course, methods of psychological influence

---

[12] Michael Langone, in an article reviewing this polarization (2000), tries to find some common ground between the anti-cultists and pro-cultists, and draws some lessons from this debate.

and persuasion lying in between these two poles will be difficult to classify, and hence the need for caution in making moral judgments in this gray area. But there should be no hesitancy to declare non-coercive persuasion as morally acceptable, and extreme mind-control as morally unacceptable. I therefore propose *excessive* psychological manipulation as another criterion to distinguish between non-coercive and coercive, or moral and immoral forms of proselytizing.

As already mentioned, there are different ways in which psychological manipulation can become excessive when proselytizing. I turn to the first more specific principle mentioned above: Proselytizers should avoid intense, repeated, and extremely programmatic approaches to bringing about a conversion.

In chapter 4, I dealt with two different ways in which the notion of psychological manipulation has been applied to the recruitment activities of cults. The first concern often raised about these recruitment techniques is that they can be taken to an extreme and thus become coercive. Singer and Addis, for example, talk about "intense and frequent attempts" to undermine a person's confidence and to cause them to reevaluate themselves, their values and beliefs (1992, 171). Secondly, concerns are often expressed about "coordinated programs of coercive influence and behavior control" (Singer and Addis 1992, 171). What is significant here are the modifiers used – intense, frequent, and coordinated. Despite the inescapable vagueness inherent in describing these processes of psychological coercion, there surely comes a point where one must say that programs of influence and persuasion are too coordinated and too intense, thus resulting in psychological coercion. As I have already pointed out, extremes in intensity, frequency, and coordination when proselytizing must not be seen as limited to cults. I believe it is possible, for example, for evangelical churches to try too hard to make converts. I also believe that much of contemporary commercial advertising is often carried to an extreme with regard to intensity, frequency, and coordination, and hence should be condemned as immoral.[13]

The problem here, of course, is determining exactly when such extremes have been reached. We can be too quick in labeling an approach to proselytizing as too intense, frequent, or coordinated. I believe such hasty generalizations have been made with regard to the

---

[13] For example, attempts are now being made to apply brain imaging technology to advertising in order to achieve new levels of efficiency. See "The Brave New World of Neuromarketing", by Jill Mahoney, *The Globe and Mail* (Sept 10, 2005), p. A10.

cults, as I have indicated in chapter 4. But, sometimes such charges are legitimate. Indeed, as I have already suggested, the best way to approach the application of this principle is to consider one case at a time.

Here is an example of psychologically manipulative proselytizing which I hope all will agree is excessive and hence immoral. Margaret Battin describes the practice of flirty fishing introduced around the end of 1973 by the leader of the Children of God, David Berg, known as Moses David or Mo (1990, 135–36). Mo would send his second wife or mistress, Maria, out onto the dance floor at a London dancing school as bait. At Mo's urging, Maria struck up a relationship, which quickly became sexual, with an Englishman named Arthur. Once Arthur was firmly "hooked" he was passed on to one of Mo's other wives. Maria was then commissioned to catch another fish. This became a regular practice of this group, and "was developed and refined practically into an art form". In his annual statistical newsletter for 1979, Mo reported that "Our dear FF'ers (women engaged in flirty fishing) are still going strong, God bless'm, having now witnessed to over a quarter-of-a-million souls, loved over 25,000 of them and won nearly 19,000 to the Lord" (Battin 1990, 136). This is an obvious case of a terribly immoral form of psychologically coercive proselytizing.

A second more specific principle involving psychological manipulation when proselytizing involves the exploitation of vulnerability. In chapter 4, I have already dealt with some of the problems surrounding claims about exploiting vulnerability in proselytizing programs. Loaded language and hasty generalizations are all too common. For example, a 1987 statement approved by the Executive Board of the Interfaith Conference of Metropolitan Washington, states: "Deceptive proselytizing efforts are practiced on the most vulnerable of populations – residents of hospitals and old age homes, confused youth, college students away from home. These proselytizing techniques are tantamount to coerced conversions and should be condemned."[14] As I have already argued in chapter 4, such charges of exploiting the vulnerability of young persons is fraught with vagueness, inconsistency and hasty generalization.

What is needed here is more specificity and clarity in defining the extreme in exploiting vulnerability. Clearly, there is the danger of

---

[14] Interfaith Conference (1989, 224). See also the statement made by the Central Committee of the World Council of Churches where proselytizing in the narrow sense of sheep-stealing is criticized for exploiting people's loneliness, illness, distress or even disillusionment with their own church in order to convert them (1997, 468).

exploiting the loneliness and vulnerability of teenagers, the sick and the aged. But surely it is possible for religious people to reach out to these needy individuals in a genuinely caring way.[15] And if in the process some proselytizing occurs as part of this genuine caring, this can hardly be described as excessive psychological coercion and hence immoral. Of course, it is difficult to determine whether the care being offered is genuine. And hence we need to be very cautious in making general pronouncements concerning such proselytizing.

A case in Britain, described in chapter 1, is instructive in this regard. Caroline Petrie, an evangelical Christian and a community supply nurse employed by the North Somerset Primary Care Trust, made it a practice to ask patients who seemed particularly in distress if she could pray for them after giving them treatment. She was suspended after a repeat offence. The elderly patient, in this case, had politely declined the offer, and Caroline simply wished her well and left. The patient had however mentioned the odd request to another nurse the next day and this led to the disciplinary hearings. Caroline's recollections of her conversation with the disciplinary panel are significant. She admits that if patients are very anxious then it might not be appropriate to offer to pray for them. "I will never impose my beliefs on people, but I cannot divorce my faith from my job."

The public outcry against the disciplinary measures that were imposed on Caroline was entirely justified. Caroline's offer to pray for patients in distress should not be seen as in any way exploiting patients' vulnerability. Instead, this should be seen as an act of genuine caring. Caroline is satisfying the care criterion discussed earlier. In the end the North Somerset Primary Care Trust conceded that Caroline had been acting in the "best interests of her patients" and that nurses did not have to "set aside their faith" in the workplace and could "continue to offer high-quality care for patients while remaining committed to their beliefs." They also admitted that for some people prayer was an "integral part of health care and the healing process".[16]

---

[15] Eileen Barker, in discussing love-bombing, points out that most Moonies would "be genuinely shocked at the suggestion that they were being deceptive when they offer their guests affection. They would not only protest that they *ought* to love them as people (and many undoubtedly do develop a genuine affection for some of their guests), they would also be convinced that it is in the guest's own interest (as well as the interests of the world) for him to become a Moonie" (1984, 186–87).

[16] See chapter 1, n. 4 for details on sources used for the description of this incident. See also DiSilvestro (2007) and Salladay (2006) for arguments defending physicians' and nurses' rights to proselytize patients if done in an appropriate spirit of care and humility, without compromising the informed consent of their patients.

Thirdly, ethical proselytizing must avoid excessive appeals to emotion and fear to bring about conversions. To do so is again to manipulate persons, and thus to undermine their dignity and freedom.[17] This principle is again rather vague, and hence best dealt with on a case-by-case analysis. I begin with some examples that are less obviously psychologically coercive. The first involves the infamous fire-and-brimstone sermon delivered by American revivalist, Jonathan Edwards, in 1741. The very title, "Sinners in the Hands of an Angry God", is indicative of the language and the vivid imagery Edwards used to scare sinners into the Kingdom of God.[18]

A more contemporary multimedia version of this approach to evangelism is found in the mass-marketing of hell by various Christian evangelical churches in North America. The object is to confront young people with the choices they need to make now in order to determine their eternal destiny – heaven or hell. "Hell House", for example, premiered in Arvada, Colorado, a Denver suburb in 1995, and in just seven years hosted more than 33,000 paying customers, and had nearly 500 other churches purchase Hell House kits so as to put on the production themselves.[19] The production includes strobe lights, smoke

---

[17] Billy Graham provides a clear statement of this principle in some instructions he gave at an international conference of itinerant evangelists held in the Netherlands in 1983. After quoting 2 Cor 5:11, where a call is made to "persuade men", Graham issues this caution: "But we must be careful that coercion does not enter into that persuasion. The Bible's urgent call can be abused by some well-intentioned evangelists. Gifted personalities have the ability to excite emotions and manipulate people. Others can use dubious means, such as threats, scare tactics, and psychological pressure to make 'converts', or become so anxious for numbers that the invitation is broadened to include any person or problem" (Graham 1984, 60–61).

[18] Here is a part of what George Marsden calls "the infamous passage" from that sermon. "The God that holds you over the pit of hell, much as one holds a spider or some loath-some insect, over the fire, abhors you, and is dreadfully provoked; his wrath towards you burns like fire; he looks upon you as worthy of nothing else, but to be cast into the fire; he is of purer eyes than to bear to have you in his sight; you are ten thousand times so abominable in His eyes as the most hateful venomous serpent is in ours. You have offended him infinitely more than ever a stubborn rebel did his prince: and yet 'tis nothing but his hand that holds you from falling into the fire every moment: 'tis to be ascribed to nothing else, that you did not go to hell the last night . . . Oh sinner! Consider the fearful danger you are in" (Quoted in Marsden 2003, 223). For a careful analysis of Jonathan Edwards' appeals to fear in evangelistic sermons, see Jackson (2007).

[19] My description of "Hell House" draws on an article by Greg Hartman, "Welcome to Hell", http://www.family.org/pplace/youandteens/a0018086.cfm (retrieved on Nov 26, 2003). Roberts, the founder of Hell House, is now with New Destiny Christian Center in Thornton, Colorado. http://www.godestiny.org/hell_house

machines, bellowing demons, burning Limburger cheese, and the damned screaming in agony, all to portray hell. Then there are graphically depicted abortions, drug overdoses, school shootings, occult worship, and drunken-driving deaths, all of which are shown as life-style choices that will eventually bring you to hell. When questioned about the use of fear to motivate young people to make a decision to become a Christian, Rev. Keenan Roberts, the founder of Hell House, responded thus: "We are not communicating fear for fear's sake. We are communicating reality and truth. We're saying, 'You're living in a burning house, and it's about to crash down.'"[20]

Do these cases involve psychologically coercive proselytizing? Most readers, I'm sure, will answer Yes, and might find it reassuring to know that I too find these approaches offensive. But we must be careful not to be too hasty in our condemnation. After all, what is so wrong with appealing to emotions? As I pointed out in chapter 4, there is a tendency to be overly suspicious about any kind of emotional appeals. Indeed, appeals to emotion and fear are sometimes necessary in order to get dispassionate and disinterested people motivated to action. And this would suggest, according to Randal Marlin, that "appeals to emotions are not necessarily wrong, and may well be justified in a majority of cases" (2000, 165). If so, what is so wrong with the graphic portrayal of hell in productions of Hell House or in sermons? If hell is indeed the destiny of those who make wrong choices, are not Jonathan Edwards and Keenan Roberts right in suggesting this approach is merely communicating reality and truth, and there is nothing wrong with engaging the emotions in doing so? Appealing to fear is not in itself wrong, although here again I think this can be taken to an extreme. Some might argue that Hell House is taking the appeal to fear to an extreme, but I am not so sure.

What is for me the more troubling aspect of Hell House is that the appeal is to young people, often children. We need to be especially careful not to exploit the emotions of children. But even here we need to be careful in making hasty judgments about Hell House. It is surely

---

(accessed Aug. 13, 2009). Fletcher (2007) provides a careful analysis of Hell House, using the criteria of community-based theater. He also identifies some of the variations of the Hell House theme that have appeared since Roberts first introduced the prepackaged Hell House idea (314). For another academic analysis of Hell House with a focus on its appeal to fear, see Jackson (2007).

[20] Greg Hartman, "Welcome to Hell", retrieved on Nov 26, 2003, from http//www.family.org/pplace/youandteens/a0018086.cfm (p.3). Jonathan Edwards too justified his appeals to fear by arguing that he was simply speaking the truth (see Jackson 2007, 46–47).

safe to assume that in most cases young people come to these events voluntarily. The advertising for these events is quite up-front, so those who choose to attend have a rough idea of what they are getting into. They even pay a fee to get into the church to see the production. So even on this score, it is not obvious that moral principles have been violated. This case is therefore borderline in terms of satisfying the criteria for ethical proselytizing. It is not an obvious example of psychological coercion, though I certainly believe it lies closer to the immoral end of the continuum of psychological coercion.

In conclusion, the psychological coercion criterion is somewhat difficult to apply. We need to be very cautious in making generalizations when applying this criterion. However, on a case-by-case analysis, the criterion of excessive psychological manipulation can still serve some purpose in distinguishing between moral and immoral proselytizing.

By way of a more general application, religious groups need to relax a little in their efforts at gaining converts. As we are reminded in a recent statement of Ethical Guidelines for Christian and Muslim Witness in Britain: "We cannot convert people, only God can do that. In our language and methods we should recognize that people's choice of faith is primarily a matter between themselves and God."[21] Too much of an appeal to emotions is manipulative. Too much organization is a dangerous thing. Too much control of any person's environment is an affront to the dignity of that person. Too much emphasis on the effectiveness of the evangelistic program of a church can lead to extremes in the programmatic nature of these programs.

Social coercion criterion

At the heart of many of our concerns regarding psychological coercion is a concern about a power-imbalance. This is essentially a social phenomenon and thus I am treating this criterion separately under the heading of social coercion. Power-imbalances can arise in a number of situations: group-individual; employer-employee; majority-minority; or parent and child. Noam Chomsky has provided extensive documentation regarding power-imbalances with regard to the mass media (1988).

I want to draw on Sue Jansen's helpful exploration of the connection between power and knowledge in her study of censorship (1988).

---

[21] This statement is a result of work done by the Christian Muslim Forum in Britain, and is available at http://www.christianmuslimforum.org (accessed Aug 13, 2009).

Knowledge cannot be divorced entirely from passion, power, and the institutional arrangements that are an expression of power, according to Jansen. But she is quick to point out that power can be abused in securing knowledge. We can, and must, try to escape the abuses invariably accompanying power-knowledge. We therefore need to distinguish between a normal degree of association of knowledge and power, and an excessive use of power to support knowledge. It is only arbitrary and excessive censorship, or arbitrary and excessive use of power to control the consciousness industry that must be condemned, according to Jansen.

We have here a key to defining another dimension of coercion as applied to proselytizing. While acknowledging the inescapability of power and control in proselytizing, we must avoid excessive expressions of such power. For example, to force individuals who have come to a relief agency for shelter and food to first listen to an evangelistic message is simply an abuse of power.[22] A U.S. court case provides another example.[23] Jake and Helen Townley made a covenant with God to run their Florida-based mining-supply company as a Christian, faith-operated business. They expressed their faith in a variety of ways, including requiring employees to attend weekly, non-denominational devotional services. When employee Louis Pelvas sought to be excused because he was an atheist, the Townleys said he could sleep or read the newspaper during the services but he *had* to attend. The results of this court case, when Pelvas quit and filed a law-suit, need not concern us here. What is relevant to our purposes is the abuse of power of an employer in trying to convert an atheist via required attendance at devotional services.

The problem of power-imbalance surfaces again in a case described in chapter 1. In the spring of 2005, a task force arrived at the U.S. Air Force Academy in Colorado Springs, to investigate accusations that officers, staff members, and senior cadets inappropriately used their positions to push their evangelical Christian beliefs on cadets. The task

---

[22] In a statement responding to charges for allegedly proselytizing in El Salvador while using government funds to build shelters for victims of an earthquake, the relief organization of Franklin Graham carefully articulates its policy with regard to the abuse of power when connecting relief work and evangelism. "Samaritan's Purse makes its physical aid available to anyone on the basis of need and never requires participation in any religious programs as a condition for receiving relief" (quoted in an article entitled, "Graham relief agency said to proselytize", *Christian Century* 118.10 (2001), p.10 (no author given).

[23] *EBOC v. Townley Engineering and Manufacturing Co.* (1988). The description of this case is taken from *CQ Researcher* 12.28 (2002), pp. 660–61.

force eventually cleared the Air Force Academy of overt religious discrimination. But, the report went on to say that the Academy had failed
to provide full accommodation for the religious needs of non-Christian
and non-evangelical cadets, and that there were some cases where faculty members and officers were too aggressive in sharing their evangelical faith.

I do not want to deal with the supposed problem of officers being
too aggressive in sharing their evangelical faith, except to say that I
suspect this criticism rests on an assumption that all proselytizing is
wrong. More to the point here is the charge that officers, staff members,
and senior cadets inappropriately used their positions to push their
evangelical Christian beliefs on Air Force cadets. Here we are on to
something important, because an inappropriate use of power due to
position involves coercion, and coercive proselytizing is immoral.
Extra caution is in order whenever you have individuals in power who
are influencing others. What would need to be investigated in this
Academy case is whether the senior personnel did *abuse* their power. I
believe they did go too far. For example, when the head football coach,
Fisher DeBerry hung a "Team Jesus" banner in the locker room, he was
abusing his position as coach. When Johnny Weida, commandant of
cadets, encouraged attendance at National Day of Prayer activities, he
was abusing his power.

Having said this, we must be careful not to let the possibility of the
abuse of power make us suspicious of all uses of legitimate power.
And, we need to address the all-important question – can an officer
ever talk to a cadet about his or her religious faith? I would answer, yes,
though the officer needs to be very careful to ensure this is done in
such a way that the cadet feels he or she can disagree without any
recriminations whatsoever.

More generally, potential converts must be given the space to think,
to challenge, and to disagree. Proselytizers must always respect the
right of the proselytizee to say no. Allowance must further be made for
new converts to change their minds. They must be allowed to leave
their new faith-group if they so choose.[24] It is here where cults are often

---

[24] Spinner-Halev introduces as one principle to help the liberal state navigate policy matters with regard to religious communities and institutions, a noninter-
vention principle (2000, 20, 107–8): religious communities should be able to
treat their members as they wish as long as they provide a decent education
to their charges, do not physically harm their children, allow members the right
to exit, and are not completely cut off from other communities and mainstream
society.

seen to fail, though again evidence suggests this criticism is vastly exaggerated.[25]

This criterion concerning the abuse of power is particularly relevant to children. Hence the general recognition that children need special protection from exploitive advertising.[26] The same protections need to be in place with regard to religious proselytizing. A teenager at a youth camp sponsored by a religious group probably cannot escape. Great care needs to be taken, therefore, not to misuse power when engaged in proselytizing activities in this context. Of course, parental consent is another factor needing to be taken into account here.

The issue of parental consent raises another important example of proselytizing and the possible abuse of power that needs to be considered – parents proselytizing their own children. I think this is a unique case that deserves careful treatment, but will not be undertaken here as I have dealt with this issue at length in relation to the related problem of indoctrination and education (Thiessen 1993; 2001, ch. 8). However, some brief comments might be in place. While there is nothing inherently wrong with parents seeking to convert their children (atheistic parents, it should be remembered, do the same thing), parents must at the same time also free their children to eventually make up their own minds as to whether they want to follow the example of their parents. As Terry McLaughlin argues, "a coherent way of characterizing the intention of parents is that they are aiming at *autonomy via faith*" (1984, 79). Children are inescapably influenced by the religion (or irreligion) of their parents. What parents need to do in order to ensure that they are not abusing their power is to nurture their children towards autonomy, also in relation to their religious or irreligious upbringing.

Leighton Ford, a Christian evangelist, gives a sad example of an abuse of power in relation to children in the context of evangelistic crusades. Ford tells the story of a young Canadian pharmacist who attended one of his crusades and was eventually converted to the Christian faith. In processing this conversion, this young man shared how he and his wife had not attended church for years, mainly because of an unsettling experience when she was a child.

> A traveling evangelist had come to their town, and as a girl of twelve she was carefully coached to respond to the appeal as a sort of decoy. When

---

[25] See studies referred to in chapter 4, p. 86 and n. 14.

[26] See, for example, Leiser (1978, 178–79), and the Pontifical Council (1997, 27–28).

the evangelist gave the altar call, someone gave the girl a shove, and she started forward down the aisle while the preacher intoned, "A little child shall lead them" [quote from a prophetic passage in Isa 11:6]. She sensed that she was being used in a deceitful way, and the emotional scar left behind kept her from approaching God for years (Ford 1966, 4–5).

This is an example of a horrendous abuse of power in evangelism. It is coercive, it violates the dignity of the person, and it is also deceitful. But worst of all, it involves an exploitation of a child. As such, this case of proselytizing deserves the strongest moral condemnation.

Moving beyond children, to a consideration of broader social contexts, how do we avoid a power-imbalance when proselytizing? This is where Jansen, drawing on Habermas and his notion of an ideal speech situation, has some very helpful things to say, although she is talking more generally about the consciousness industry. Jansen underscores the need for "reflexive power talk" (1988, 8–10, 202–17). We need to empower critical discourse. People need to reclaim their voices. We need a pedagogy of the oppressed. We need to remove the epistemological privileges routinely invoked by experts and intellectuals. Alternate interpretations of reality must be provided so that people become aware of interpretations reinforced by the establishment. In all this Jansen stresses that she is not trying to eliminate all domination, but make it visible and legible.[27]

These insights can be applied to the implicit proselytising resulting from a majority religious culture. Here let me again refer to a specific example. Stephan Feldman, in a critical history of the separation of church and state in America, complains that "during the late eighteenth century, the de facto Protestant establishment exerted an enormous and persistent pressure to convert on the few Jews living in America" (1997, 169). American Jews, he argues, "often lost their distinctive religious identity as they 'were all but engulfed by their environment'. Some Jews drifted to Christianity because of 'the sheer weight of [the] majority culture', and many others were subject to intentional (and often unrelenting) proselytization" (169). A little later, Feldman complains, "American Jews always were implicitly pressured to convert by merely living in a Christian nation" (192).

Clearly a majority culture or a Protestant establishment represents a form of social coercion. But is Feldman right in complaining about the

---

[27] Jacques Ellul similarly calls for the free interplay of various propagandas, as a response to the inescapability of using propaganda, even in a democracy (1969, 232–36).

implicit pressure to convert? We need to be very careful here, because there is surely nothing wrong with a majority culture *per se*. We should not be made to feel guilty by virtue of sheer numbers, whether this be a majority of Muslims, Mennonites, or Mormons living in a certain area. Indeed, in most countries, there would seem to be a majority culture. Of course, what needs to be preserved here is the freedom of minority cultures, especially the freedom to disagree with majority opinion. And, as is emphasized by Jansen, in a majority culture, people need to be made aware of interpretations of reality reinforced by the establishment, and there must be freedom of expression of alternate interpretations of reality. But, we must be careful not to view the implicit pressure to conform or to convert as morally culpable. At the same time, a majority culture, of whatever religious (or anti-religious) persuasion, must be very sensitive to the power-imbalance created by being a majority culture.

Inducement criterion

The final form of coercion to be considered in this chapter involves the use of inducements to convert. We need to be careful here, because, as was noted in chapter 4, charges of inducement to convert are in fact quite slippery. Indeed, it is easier to provide examples of immoral inducements to convert than it is to define the inducement criterion. Clearly, giving a person $1,000 cash to induce her to convert to Christianity is immoral. The same would apply to a gift of equivalent monetary value. This is outright bribery and plainly immoral. Lest we forget, blatant cases of bribery also occur in the commercial realm, and they are equally wrong.[28]

Earlier in this chapter, we considered Jacob Loewen's concern about the bated hook approach to evangelism and mission (2000, 89). Loewen's bated hook obviously relates to the problem of providing inducements to convert. Loewen reflects on his own experience as a

---

[28] For example, Leiser reports that drug companies distribute expensive medical instruments engraved with their logos to medical students almost as soon as they enter medical school (1978, 179). This kind of bribery continues throughout a physician's career, with free samples of drugs and various other gifts clearly identifying the company from which they came. All this is meant to engrave the company logo on the minds of medical students and physicians and to encourage them to prescribe the company's drugs for future patients. This kind of advertising works. But it is immoral. It involves coercion.

missionary in the Chocó of Columbia. In order to lure people to the mission station, he opened a dispensary to deal with medical problems. At first he adopted the following rule: "if you want to receive the 'Lord's medicine', then you must be willing to first listen to the 'Lord's message'" (89). Loewen confesses it took him more than a decade to realize "that honest-to-goodness missionary witness and the bated hook just don't go together" (90).

But, what if Loewen had offered medical care without making it conditional on hearing the Lord's message? Would the offering of medical care still involve a culpable form of inducement to convert? It is here where critics of proselytizing tend to be too demanding. Clearly the meeting of basic needs will make people more open to implicit and even explicit proselytizing. It is therefore important for providers of care not to exploit the needs of those in their care. Medical help should be provided for its own sake, simply as an expression of love and care for those in need. Proselytizing in these situations is best done in response to patients' asking questions. And the person providing medical care must make it very clear that care is given without the requirement to convert or even listen to the Lord's message.

More generally, in situations where providing medical care, humanitarian aid, or education is in some way linked with proselytizing, the greater the need, the more sensitive the proselytizer must be to the danger of exploiting that need, and thus inducing to convert. In situations where physical needs are overwhelming, proselytizing should be kept entirely separate from the activity of responding to these physical needs. A further requirement is a high standard of transparency. "Proselytizers must make it clear that they are not trading medical or humanitarian aid for conversion. There is no *quid pro quo*."[29] The proselytizee must therefore be given a clear sense that it is perfectly acceptable for him or her to accept aid, or medical help, and yet refuse any persuasive appeals to convert.

I conclude my treatment of various expressions of the coercion criterion with the observation that, though they are important, they are perhaps not quite as clear and useful in distinguishing between moral and immoral proselytizing as is generally assumed. Except for obvious cases of physical coercion and bribery to convert, there would seem to

---

[29] See Jonathan Miles, "Human Rights and the Ethics of Christian Proselytizing in Foreign Contexts." www4.samford.edu/lilly/humanrights/papers/Miles_Human.pdf (accessed Sept. 22, 2009). For some recent treatments of an ethical relationship between humanitarian relief and proselytizing, see Jayasinghe (2007) and Thacker (2009).

be an inescapable vagueness inherent in any attempts to define extreme measures of psychological coercion or coercive persuasion. But we must not dismiss these criteria entirely because of this problem. Surely, at some point, the intensity of persuasive techniques must be seen as extreme and then condemned as coercive. Surely, at some point attempts made to co-ordinate systematic programs of influence must be seen as being taken to an extreme, and hence labeled coercive. Surely at some point we need to worry about a power-imbalance being taken to an extreme, thereby becoming coercive. And when these extremes are identified in particular cases of proselytizing, they should be condemned as coercive and immoral.

Chapter 8

Criteria to Evaluate Proselytizing: Part II

This chapter continues with an examination of criteria to distinguish between ethical and unethical proselytizing. Much of the last chapter involved an exploration of various criteria relating to coercive proselytizing. Because the issue of coercion is so complex, I have deliberately tried to develop more specific criteria dealing with various aspects of coercion. The first two criteria being considered in this chapter can be seen as still related to the problem of coercion. However, they can also be seen as criteria in their own right, and thus deserving of separate treatment.

Rationality criterion

Another approach to defining coercive proselytizing involves an appeal to the notion of informed consent or competent choice, which are at the heart of the modern liberal ideal of free decision-making. Young and Griffith suggest this as a better approach to take than an appeal to the notion of coercive persuasion (1992, 99–101). The theory for assessing competent choice has been well worked out by psychiatrists, they claim, and can be applied equally to the proselytizing activities of cults and established churches. Rather than thinking of this approach as giving us an alterative to defining the nature of coercive persuasion, I prefer to see it as adding another dimension to delineating the distinction between ethical and unethical proselytizing.

So far, we have looked at physical and psychological techniques that can be used to undermine free consent. Little has been said, however, about the epistemological aspects of coercion. Clearly, the presence or absence of truthful information when proselytizing is an essential criterion in distinguishing between coercive and non-coercive proselytizing.

Proselytizing involves persuasion to convert. Ethical persuasion includes the providing of information in order to make such a decision. It also includes giving reasons for the proposed change of heart and mind. Proselytizing that attempts to sidestep human reason entirely is unethical.

There are, of course, many ways in which to sidestep human reason. One way is to appeal directly to another person's emotions in such a way as to make rational evaluation difficult if not impossible. I have already touched on the problem of emotional appeals in the previous chapter as an aspect of psychological coercion. We looked at appeals to fear and guilt as possible marks of coercive proselytizing. Here I want to expand on the appeal to emotions when proselytizing, contrasting this with an appeal to reason.

I draw on Aristotle's classic treatment of rhetoric. Aristotle clearly emphasized the capacity for reason as a uniquely human attribute. But at the same time, he recognized the need to appeal to emotion in order to move ordinary human beings to decision and action.[1] We need balance here. We can make too much of the rationality criterion of persuasion and proselytizing.[2] At the same time, we must be careful not to dismiss the need to provide information and to give reasons when persuading. This entails that we need to avoid making exclusive or excessive appeals to emotions, which ultimately have the effect of undermining rational assessment of the decision being considered on the part of the other person being persuaded. Aristotle describes such appeals as having the effect of producing a condition similar to men being asleep, mad, or drunk. He was also very careful to warn about appealing to harmful emotions and also to one's vegetative appetites such as sex drives which are irrational (Rowland and Womack 1986, 18, 21). So, while there are dangers in appealing to emotions, we must not discount them entirely either. In effect, Aristotle envisioned ethical rhetoric as the mean between appealing to reason and appealing to emotions.

---

[1] "The origin of action – its efficient, not its final cause – is choice and that of choice is desire and reasoning with a view to an end . . . Intellect itself, however, moves nothing" (Aristotle, *Ethics* Bk. 6, Ch. 2, 1139a 32–36; see also Rowland & Womack 1985, 17).

[2] All too often an appeal to rational autonomy is given as the only criterion for evaluating persuasion. Brembeck and Howell describe the limiting of ethical rhetoric to providing evidence and reasoning as due to succumbing to the "cult of reason" (1967, 10). "The zeal of the person dedicated to reason is often as irrational as are many of the targets of his criticism", they maintain. Some of the essays in the Johannesen anthology (1967), from which this essay is taken, seem to rely on such a narrow appeal to rational autonomy as the only criterion for ethical persuasion.

A good illustration of sensitivity to the dangers of an excessive appeal to emotions is found in Greg Pritchard's evaluation of the influential Willow Creek Community Church in Chicago, and its use of seeker services to evangelize (1996). Careful attention is given to the use of humor, drama, and music in Willow Creek programming.[3] In doing so they are following Aristotle's advice on effective rhetoric, the need for "putting the audience into a certain frame of mind".[4] Interestingly, the staff expressed some befuddlement when asked what distinguishes Willow Creek's programming from manipulation of the emotions. Their answers to this question, however, revealed some deeper insights. One of the staff working with drama explained, "You become manipulative . . . when you make someone think they've arrived at a decision, but they really didn't . . . You become manipulative when you sneak around and you get people to feel something in an attempt to sort of supersede . . . their thinking faculties" (113). Evangelism director Mark Mittelberg remarked about the programming team, that they "probably see opportunities where they could pull people's emotions around, if that's what they wanted to do. [But] it's got to be based on truth and legitimate emotions" (114). He continued, "I have a hard time putting my finger on the exact word or phrase to use, but 'true', meaning what we're getting people to feel is based on truth. True teachings, true ideas" (114). Surely there can be nothing wrong with proselytizing that appeals to the emotions when the feelings being expressed are appropriate responses to truth.

It is only the *excessive* or *exclusive* appeal to emotions that I consider to be immoral. I am only condemning what Bill Hybels, of the Willowcreek Community Church, labels "emotional turbo-charging" (Pritchard 1996, 220). Appeal to emotions becomes problematic only when it makes the use of reason on the part of the potential convert very difficult or impossible. Artists clearly use aesthetic forms of persuasion, and there is nothing wrong with this. For example, we might find ourselves deeply moved by watching a certain movie that makes

---

[3] Programming director, Nancy Beach explains: "If you give them a musical experience or a dramatic experience, you can go through what we call the back door and you can somehow get them to emotionally and intellectually respond . . . to some things, and they hardly even know it's happening because their resistance is much, much lower" (Pritchard 1996, 111–12). In reflecting on this statement later, Beech admitted that this "sounded so manipulative", and then went on to stress that the programming team doesn't ever want to "take away a person's God-given freedom to choose" (302, n. 22).

[4] See Aristotle's *Rhetoric* (Bk.1, Ch. 1, 1356a 6; Bk.2, Ch.1, 1377b 23).

us reevaluate some assumptions that we hold, or even our entire worldview.[5] There is nothing wrong with such persuasion as long as it does not completely sidestep the possibility of reflection on the message being conveyed.

Indeed, it is probably difficult to separate emotion from reason completely. Aristotle himself thought of emotions as at least potentially rational (Rowland and Womack 1986, 18). More recently, Martha Nussbaum has defended the intelligence of emotions, maintaining that emotions are essential elements of human intelligence and therefore should be seen as part and parcel of any system of ethical reasoning. Indeed, according to Nussbaum, "without emotional development, a part of our reasoning capacity as political creatures will be missing" (2001, 3). We must therefore be careful not to assume that appeals to emotions when proselytizing are in themselves irrational and hence immoral.

There are other ways in which we can fail to satisfy the rationality criterion of proselytizing. We can simply fail to give the information necessary for the proselytizee to make an informed choice. We can fail to provide reasons for the choice being proposed. Again it is instructive that Aristotle balances putting the audience into a certain frame of mind (by stirring the emotions), with the need to have persuasion effected "through the speech itself when we have proved a truth or an apparent truth by means of the persuasive arguments suitable to the case in question".[6] One can also be deceptive, and thus again undermine the other's ability to make a rational decision. Thus Aristotle warns: "for we must not make people believe what is wrong".[7] So important is this matter of deception in evaluating proselytizing that I want to devote a separate section to this topic.

Critics might object to the rationality criterion by asking whether it is even possible to talk about providing information and giving reasons in the area of religion. I have already dealt with this question in an earlier chapter, so I will be brief here. Clearly, a narrow Enlightenment and scientistic notion of reason has led many people to conclude that it is impossible to give reasons for religious faith. But, given more recent developments in epistemology, there is now a growing call for a broader understanding of rationality that acknowledges both science and religion as rational. Both science and religion involve

---

[5] This example was suggested to me by Perry Glanzer.

[6] Aristotle's *Rhetoric* (Bk.1, Ch. 2, 1356a 1–35).

[7] Aristotle's *Rhetoric* (Bk.1, Ch.1, 1355a 33). See also Rowland & Womack (1986, 21).

attempts to find the best explanation to the small and the big questions of life and reality. Both science and religion move beyond experience in order to explain empirical reality. Differences of opinion are to be found in both areas. Some degree of subjectivity also seems to be inescapable. We need a looser concept of reasonableness that has the effect of equalizing our understanding of the epistemological strengths and weaknesses of both religion and science.

We also need to acknowledge that what is rational to one person may not be seen as rational to another person. Hence John Rawls call for liberals to accept the "burdens of judgment", allowing that reasonable persons may affirm differing reasonable doctrines (1993, 12–13). We need to give each other the benefit of the doubt. Proselytizers need to give reasons for the faith they hold, as they seek to convert another person. These reasons may not be deemed to be satisfactory to another person, but in a way this is beside the point. Reason-giving is not quite as objective as we think. But, proselytizing must involve the mind. Failure to do so involves unethical proselytizing.

A corollary follows from the rationality criterion considered in this section. If ethical proselytizing involves the mind, then we must make sure that we allow the potential convert time to process the information being given to him or her. We must be very cautious about pressing for quick and easy conversions. Normally, proselytizing that leads to a conversion should involve a longer process of decision-making.[8] Proselytizing that fails to respect the process of conversion may in fact be unethical. This is not to rule out the possibility of sudden conversions. A comparison can be made here to the decision to marry someone. Sometimes this decision is made rather quickly, but it is better to make the decision based on careful deliberation. Proselytizers too need to be very careful to ensure that the proselytizee is given the time to make a proper assessment of the information and reasons being conveyed in an attempt to convert him or her.

Truthfulness criterion

Ethical proselytizing is truthful. It seeks to tell the truth about the religion being advocated. It is truthful also with regard to what it says

---

[8] Interestingly, staff at the Willow Creek Community Church were very sensitive to the danger of quick and easy conversions, and they cautioned about the "event-oriented" approach to evangelism. Evangelism director Mittelberg asserted the following: "People go through a process in coming to Christ – a process. And I believe in, and respect, that process" (Pritchard 1996, 106).

about other religions. Integrity characterizes the ethical proselytizer. Proselytizing accompanied by hidden agendas, hidden identities, lying, deception, and failure to speak the truth should be condemned as immoral.

This criterion too is linked with the issue of coercion. Truthfulness is closely connected to the modern notion of informed consent. A potential convert cannot be said to have given free consent when the information given to him or her was distorted. Freedom and truthful information are both essential in protecting the autonomy of the proselytizee in proselytizing efforts. Truthfulness is also linked to the dignity criterion we have already dealt with in the previous chapter. This is brought to the fore in Sissela Bok's treatment of lying. A fundamental assumption underlying her treatment is that trust in some degree of truthfulness is a *"foundation* of relations among human beings; when this trust shatters or wears away, institutions collapse . . . *Whatever* matters to human beings, trust is the atmosphere in which it thrives" (Bok 1978, 31). Despite these connections to other criteria, I am treating the truthfulness criterion separately because of its importance.

But what does it mean to be truthful? Indeed, what is truth? Here we must be careful to avoid a narrow conception of truth and truthfulness that is concerned only with the content of what is said. Dietrich Bonhoeffer encouraged us also to look at the truthfulness of the relationship involved in a particular communication. It is possible to speak "flatteringly or presumptuously or hypocritically without uttering a material untruth", according to Bonhoeffer (1955, 365). More recently, Jürgen Habermas posits at least four different types of validity claims with regard to our speech acts: the utterance must be understandable; its propositional content must be true; the speaker must be sincere in uttering it; and it must be appropriate for the speaker to be performing the speech act.[9] We must therefore explore various dimensions of truthfulness when dealing with this criterion.

Before doing so, I want to refer back to chapter 3, where I examined Jay Newman's concerns with regard to truthfulness in his important critique of proselytizing. "Rarely are proselytizers committed to making known the *whole* truth," says Newman (1982, 100). He goes on, "most missionaries *methodically conceal* truths" (100). I have already criticized Newman for failing to provide empirical evidence for these generalizations. But there is something right about Newman's claims. Human beings are simply incapable of making known the whole truth

---

[9] As summarized in Marlin (2002, 163).

about anything. They are finite. And missionaries, by virtue of being missionaries, are advocates for their understanding of truth and will therefore be selective in what they say about their religion. We must be careful not to demand too much of the proselytizer.

An essay by Ralph Barney and Jay Black, entitled, "Ethics and Professional Persuasive Communications", is instructive here (1994). Barney and Black argue that the American public philosophy can be characterized as having, at its foundation, the acceptance of advocacy and adversarial relationships. The most visible and formal expression of these twin characteristics is found in the judicial system. More generally, the acceptance of the ideal of a free-market of ideas, which characterizes Western countries, also rests on the assumption that truth is best found in the context of advocacy and adversarial relationships.

According to Barney and Black, it is therefore to be expected that an advocate will be selective in telling the truth – he or she is after all an *advocate* for a client or a product. It is left to adversaries to expose what has not been said, and to tell the whole truth. Such adversaries are guaranteed in a court of law. In the realm of public opinion it is assumed that journalists or some other consumer advocates will serve in this capacity (Barney and Black 1994, 241). Barney and Black therefore defend the idea of selectivity in truth-telling for public relations practitioners and professional persuaders. It is simply unfair to impose the foreign ideals of objectivity and fairness that are assumed to be characteristic of science, journalism, or education. What is needed is a unique ethics of persuasion or advocacy. Now I'm not so sure that science, journalism, and education are as objective and fair as Barney and Black assume. Advocacy and adversarial relations are also present in these three areas.[10] But this analysis is nonetheless helpful in highlighting some unique features of the ethics of public relations and professional persuaders that can also be applied to the area of proselytizing.

Being truthful:

I start with the assumption that the proselytizer is trying to persuade a potential convert. And obviously, the persuader will try to put his or her position in its best light, and this will involve some selectivity in telling the truth. What is to be avoided, and what should be condemned as immoral, is the telling of a blatant *lie*. Barney and Black

---

[10] I have argued that advocacy is inescapable in the area of education (Thiessen, 1993). For a critique of the traditional ideal of objectivity in journalism, see Ward (2004).

point out that this is one of the boundaries of advocacy – trial lawyers, for example, are admonished to refrain from passing along information they know to be false (1994, 244). Proselytizers too should not tell lies. Ethical proselytizing seeks to be truthful.

Here I concur with Jewish scholar, Arnold Seth Stiebel, who says that it is simply wrong for missionaries to inflate the number of their converts so as to encourage others to convert (1982, 49). Let me cite a specific case of deception involving a Christian evangelical crusade, held in the fall of 2001, in my former city of residence, Medicine Hat, Alberta. The preacher, the notorious Jimmy Bakker, after delivering an evangelistic sermon, asked the people in the audience to close their eyes, and then suggested that people who wanted to be saved, indicate the same by raising their hands. Each time someone supposedly raised his or her hands, Bakker would acknowledge the same with an appropriate comment, "Yes", or "I see you." Unfortunately, there was one person in the audience, a fine but critical Christian, who did not close his eyes, and noticed that in fact there were very few hands raised, contrary to the impression that Bakker gave with his repeated acknowledgements. This is deceptive and wrong.[11]

Michael Langone provides an example of deceptive advertising used at Rice University in Houston to promote an evangelistic speaker (1985, 376). The flashy poster announced the following: "Does Josh know everything about sex? NO. But what he does know will keep you talking for days. MAXIMUM SEX. That's Josh!" Josh was in fact Josh McDowell, an evangelist, and Langone is careful to add that Josh might very well be a sincere and ethical Christian. This advertisement, however, was deceptive and hence deserves to be labeled morally problematic.[12]

We are also justified in expecting of the proselytizer truthfulness when describing other faiths. Unfair criticisms are unwarranted.

---

[11] Bakker's sermon that evening included a brief interlude of self-justification in light of his rather checkered career. He compared himself to the Apostle Paul who was persecuted for the faith. How distorting! There is surely all the difference in the world between being in prison for the criminal activity of embezzling funds, and being in prison for proclaiming the gospel!

[12] See chapter 2 (pp. 41–42) for the story of a failure to be entirely truthful in a major missionary/educational endeavor prompted by an invitation by the Russian Ministry of Education in the early 1990s, when they invited evangelicals from America to come and instruct Russian public school teachers on how to teach Christian ethics (Glanzer 2002). Pelkmans analyses a lack of transparency about recent proselytizing efforts in Kyrgyzstan, though he is perhaps not entirely transparent about the presuppositions underlying his own critical analysis (2009).

Criticisms of other religions and worldviews must be truthful. This of course also relates to the need for tolerance about which I will have more to say shortly.

Selective truth:

While proselytizers need to be truthful, we need to be realistic in making demands about telling the *whole* truth. Indeed, as Sisella Bok, among others, observes in her careful analysis of lying, "The whole truth is out of reach" (1978, 4).[13] Newman, I believe is too demanding in this regard. What does the impossibility of knowing or declaring the whole truth mean practically? We should not expect of a recent convert who is excited about the truth he or she has found, and who is sharing it with another, the theological expertise of a graduate student in religious studies. But we can expect that this person tells the truth about his or her new-found faith to the best of his or her ability. We are also surely justified in expecting openness to honest questions, and an admission that this recent convert does not have all the answers when critical questions are raised that stump this proselytizer. Concerns can also surely be raised against the spouting off of pat answers to questions – there needs to be an integrity to the proselytizer's faith – an honest probing and deepening of the faith in light of new questions that might be raised by seekers and critics alike.

Can we further expect of the proselytizer that he or she raise possible objections to the faith being advocated? George Brenkert, for example, in responding to the Pontifical Council's statement on the ethics of advertising, raises the following questions about religious advertising and the communication of religious messages. "Would such messages have to include disclaimers that some thinkers have found arguments for the existence of God to be neither sound nor valid? Should recipients of religious advertising be informed that millions have been killed in the name of religion or that there are some religions that make fewer demands on a person's daily life than others?" (Brenkert 1998, 328). My response to these questions is that it all depends on context. All advertising, indeed all communication, is selective in truth-telling. Therefore we cannot demand of each instance of proselytizing that the entire truth be told about the faith being advocated. However, if the proselytizee raises these questions, then, yes, these questions need to be given truthful answers.

---

[13] Quine and Ullian similarly encourage us to be aware of the fact "that we have less than the whole truth about even those matters we understand best. Such awareness can never be misplaced since 'the whole truth' about anything is but a fanciful ideal" (1978, 133).

Is the message true?

Here another important question arises. We have been talking about being truthful, and about refraining from passing along information known to be false. But, is it even possible to be truthful in the area of religion? What if the message itself is false? Clearly some of them must be false, because some of the claims made by religious and (anti-religious) proselytizers are mutually exclusive.

Here we must be careful to distinguish between Truth, with a capital T, and the human understanding of truth.[14] Clearly religious proselytizers *believe* their message to be true. They can sincerely claim they are not *knowingly* passing on that which is false. Here again we need to be realistic. Rawl's principle that we discussed earlier is also relevant here. Reasonable persons may affirm differing reasonable doctrines as true. Given the diversity of opinion with regard to the truth of religions or worldviews, the most that we can expect of proselytizers is that from time to time they admit the fact that there are differences of opinion with regard to the message being conveyed.

Honesty about intention to proselytize:

Another important dimension of truthfulness relates to honesty about any intention to proselytize. Proselytizers need to be up-front about any proselytizing agendas. Advertising about evangelistic events needs to be honest, as has already been noted. An illustration of dishonesty with regard to "friendship evangelism" was addressed in the previous chapter. It is an affront to the dignity of a person to be befriended when the primary object of such overtures is really evangelism. Genuine friendships are based on integrity, not hidden agendas. "People have a right to know when someone is trying to sell them something."[15]

---

[14] See figure #1: Ladder of Truth, chapter 3, p. 69. Deaver (1990) also makes the distinction between Truth and truth, but I'm not sure it is helpful to place these terms on a continuum of "degrees of truth".

[15] This principle is at the heart of concerns raised about stealth advertising, product placements in Hollywood movies, or plugs for prescription drugs on prime-time TV shows. Any time a persuader can pay to embed messages in the mass media without the public's full awareness, they violate the principle that people have a right to know when someone is trying to sell them something. N.E. Marsden draws attention to these concerns in an article entitled, "Are TV programs nothing more than ads?" (*Waterloo Region Record* [Oct 31, 2009], p. A13).

Religious organizations also need to be honest in portraying events intended to be evangelistic in nature. It is wrong for a religious organization to use a series of front organizations to hide its identity, as was skillfully done by the Reverend Moon after arriving in America in 1971.[16] The Unification Church has defended these practices by appealing to the doctrine of heavenly deception, claiming that it is legitimate to lie to individuals about the group's identity in order to provide them with the opportunity to hear about the church's teaching. Such deception when proselytizing is morally culpable, and further not very heavenly![17] Moral proselytizing needs to be scrupulously honest with regard to the intent to proselytize. Here I again concur with Jewish writer, Stiebel, that it is deceptive and coercive to invite youth to programs, meetings, movies, and camps while hiding the identity of the sponsoring body or the missionary aim of the same (1982, 92–99). To conduct a religious survey as a pretext for doing evangelism is also underhanded.

Margaret Battin gives a personal example of underhandedness in evangelism, which involves the use of the bait-and-switch technique, common also among merchandisers.

> A couple of summers ago, three bright young college students knocked at my door. They were on a scavenger hunt, they said. One wanted a paper clip; another needed a three-inch length of blue thread. There's a certain cooperative, contributory delight that occurs when you can find the silly things scavenger hunters want, and I also managed to find a turkey wishbone, a cigarette butt, and a European road map. However, by the time one of them asked for "a person who has been thinking about the meaning of life", I realized something was different. Sure enough, they were not on a scavenger hunt at all, at least not an ordinary one; they were missionaries from the Campus Crusade for Christ and they had come to talk about Jesus (Battin 1990, 129).

Battin goes on to provide a careful analysis of precisely what is ethically wrong in using such an opening-gambit strategy in evangelism. Starting with what seemed to be a scavenger hunt allowed the missionaries to

---

[16] See Barker (1984, 94–120, esp. 100–3, & 176–78), and Dawson (1998, 111).

[17] In the U.S.A. court case of *Molko and Leal v. Holy Spirit Association* (1988), the California Supreme Court dealt with the issue of whether the Unification Church had engaged in fraud when it deceived two prospective recruits about its identity (Young & Griffith 1992, 94–95).

establish contact with the target of the eventual evangelistic conversation in a way that would rarely be possible if the purposes of the contact were to be announced in advance. Here we see an important difference with door-to-door missionizing, where the intent is obvious from the very beginning. Of course, door-to-door convert-seeking is hard and inefficient work because missionaries often find doors closed in their faces. "The problem, as door-to-door salespeople all know, is to get a foot in the door," says Battin (1990, 130). Hence the strategy of deception for overcoming the primary obstacle. But, this strategy is deceptive, and therefore immoral.[18]

Another illustration of a lack of integrity in proselytizing again involves an evangelistic crusade in Medicine Hat, in April of 2002. Impact World Tour, a group of Christian performers from around the world put on four nights of free entertainment, featuring teams of athletes, skateboarders, dancers, bikers, and performers doing stunts, feats of strength, and cultural dances. The public advertising of these events focused nearly exclusively on the free and extreme entertainment being offered. The groups also did extensive advertising in the city schools, and visited a number of them where the message focused not on religion but on positive choices for teens, the local coordinator said. But it is surely very deceptive to bill yourself as entertainment when the *real* purpose is to present evangelistic testimonies and make long altar calls. I received several reports from students and friends who knew of and observed individuals who attended these evenings of entertainment and who were very upset when they discovered that the underlying intent was evangelism. A group of three young men were observed to be muttering to themselves when the very awkward transition was made from entertainment to evangelism. They were very annoyed, and eventually walked out.

---

[18] Battin goes on to show how some of the objects requested as part of the scavenger hunt, while they seemed trivial, thus satisfying the conventions of a trivial game, served distinct ulterior motives. They elicited valuable information that was used later in the conversation. "The turkey wishbone provided an occasion for the players to ask what wish I was planning to make with it; they interpreted the cigarette butt as evidence that I had undesirable sinful habits; and they viewed the European road map as both evidence of cosmopolitan experience and a desire for something beyond one's present life" (Battin 1990, 131). The seemingly innocent requests "for items that have informative value is invasive of privacy; and it exploits an ordinary human relationship to serve ulterior purposes" (132). This approach violates moral standards in quite a mild way, Battin maintains, but it is immoral nonetheless.

Personal integrity:

I conclude my treatment of the truthfulness criterion by examining briefly one other application having to do with personal integrity. Aristotle, in dealing with rhetoric, suggested that "persuasion is achieved by the speaker's personal character when the speech is so spoken as to make us think him credible". He goes on to say that "we believe good men more fully and more readily than others."[19] Aristotle seems here to be more concerned with an analysis of effectiveness in persuasion, although he would no doubt also argue for personal integrity from a moral point of view.[20] Ethical proselytizing requires coherence between the proselytizer's character and the message being conveyed. To proclaim a message of love and peace when the proselytizer's life is characterized by hate and an inability to get along with others is dishonest. There is a lack of personal integrity here, and proselytizing that fails in this regard should be condemned as immoral.

Humility criterion

Moral proselytizing is characterized by humility. Proselytizing becomes unethical when it becomes arrogant, condescending, and dogmatic in the claims being made. Indeed, when religious proselytizing is accompanied with pronouncements that make no allowance for any ambiguity it is in danger of sliding into an expression of religious fanaticism.

Proselytizers clearly claim to have the truth, and therefore feel bound to share the truth with others. As we have seen in chapter 3, this has led some critics of proselytizing to make the charge of arrogance against all proselytizing. In responding to this charge I argued that it is often rooted in certain assumptions about truth, namely that truth is relative or that there is no such a thing as universal and absolute truth.

---

[19] Aristotle's, *Rhetoric* (Bk.1, Ch. 1, 1356a 1–35).

[20] This same kind of ambiguity is found in a statement of "Guiding Principles for the Responsible Dissemination of Religion or Belief", which emerged from a Conference of the International Religious Liberty Association. Principle #3: "Religion, faith, or belief is best disseminated when the witness of a person's life is coherent with the message announced, and leads to free acceptance by those to whom it is addressed" (*Fides et Libertas: The Journal of the International Religious Liberty Association*, 2000, 97).

I also argued that this charge rests on some fundamental misconceptions about arrogance.

However, there is something right about these concerns regarding arrogance. While I disagree that proselytizing is inherently arrogant, there is a danger that it becomes so. And thus it is legitimate to require of ethical proselytizing that it be done in a humble manner. This requirement, however, must be carefully defined in order to avoid misconceptions. What does it mean for proselytizing to be done in a humble manner? What it does *not* mean is that the proselytizer must forfeit all claims to have the truth. As Harold Coward has correctly stressed, we need to acknowledge that "ego-attachment to one's own position" is a "universal human characteristic" (2000, 150). Further, we must recognize that all human beings have a need to share their deepest convictions with others, and that such sharing is most often based on a feeling of strong commitment. At the same time, we must acknowledge that human beings will always have an incomplete grasp of truth. I am assuming a fallibilist account of human knowledge. What we can demand, therefore, is that proselytizing be done in a humble manner.

Here Aristotle's doctrine of the golden mean is helpful. Aristotle would define proper humility as a mean between two extremes: arrogance and self-depreciation (*Ethics* Bk.2, ch.7). Lesslie Newbigin has more recently described "proper confidence" as a mean between dogmatism and uncertainty (1995). Humility is required precisely because there is all the difference in the world between Absolute Truth and the human understanding and grasp of this truth.

Humility should therefore also characterize efforts to convert the other. Religious proselytizers (and secular proselytizers as well) are sharing *their* understanding and grasp of the truth, and they should recognize that they may ultimately be mistaken. But this recognition need not slide into a relativistic, self-depreciating uncertainty, which refuses to share with others the convictions about truth that are currently held. Surely we must allow individuals to try to persuade others of their best understanding of the truth.[21]

---

[21] M.R. Wilson gives expression to this humility criterion in an essay dealing with the relation between evangelicals and Jews. "Christians who truly care about the feelings of others will hold to their own deepest commitments of faith with a spirit of humility without compromising the conviction of truth" (1984, 24). Clark Pinnock states the requirement this way: "There is nothing to boast of in ourselves. We are just human beings speaking to other human beings, testifying to what we have found. We do not assume we are completely right and infallible or have nothing left to learn" (cited in Wilson 1984, 24).

Tolerance criterion

Ethical proselytizing treats persons holding beliefs differing from those of the proselytizer *with love and respect*. While this does not preclude fair criticism of other religious or irreligious beliefs, it treats the same with respect, and avoids hostile attitudes or ridicule against other religions and worldviews. Proselytizing becomes unethical when it is accompanied by intolerant attitudes towards other persons, or when it involves hostile attitudes or uses insulting and abusive language when describing other religious or irreligious beliefs.

With this criterion in particular, we need to be very careful to define tolerance in a way that is philosophically and morally defensible. As has already been argued in chapter 5, it is a mistake to assume that tolerance precludes proselytizing. Tolerant proselytizing is possible. Neither does tolerance preclude criticism of other religions or worldviews. Such a requirement loads the notion of tolerance with a relativistic understanding of truth, which is itself indefensible. Indeed, a relativistic epistemology undermines the very need for tolerance. It is precisely because we believe in truth and have feelings of commitment and ego-attachment to our own positions, and because we realize that others feel the same way about their own convictions that we need to cultivate the virtue of tolerance, also when proselytizing. Tolerance is fundamentally concerned with having a positive attitude of respect for *people* who hold beliefs with which we differ (Heyd, 1996).

The distinction between beliefs and the holders of these beliefs is very important. A proselytizer will obviously disagree with the beliefs being held by the other person. What is required of tolerant proselytizing is that the proselytizer respect the *person* he or she is trying to convert, despite the differences in beliefs. Catholic scholar Richard John Neuhaus correctly suggests that people who are religiously serious cannot and should not tolerate error. Catholic teachers used to say, "Error has no rights." The difficulty here, Neuhaus reminds us, is that "errors are attached to persons and persons do have rights" (1996, 31). Because it is important to respect persons, we do not silence the other, or exclude the other, when we disagree with him or her, but instead we seek to persuade the other, doing so with cognitive humility, forbearance, and patience.

While the central focus of tolerance should be on persons rather than beliefs, we need to keep in mind that the beliefs that we hold are often intimately bound up with our own person. Tolerant proselytizing therefore also requires that we treat the beliefs of the other with some degree of respect. This would preclude inflammatory language, flippant name-calling, ridicule, hostile denigration, and of course, the misrepresentation of the other's beliefs. But what tolerant proselytizing cannot preclude is the careful, patient labeling of another person's beliefs as false. Indeed, exposure of error can be an expression of care and concern for the other person, or an expression of love, as I have argued in chapter 6.

Sadly, after the terrorist attacks of September 11, 2001, some Christian evangelical leaders have been at the forefront of inflammatory language against the Islamic faith. Franklin Graham is quoted as having said that Islam is "a very evil and wicked religion". Pat Robertson described Mohammed as "an absolute wild-eyed fanatic. He was a robber and a brigand. This man was a killer."[22] Such inflamatary language is uncalled for, and any proselytizing accompanied by this kind of intolerance is immoral.

Another response to 9/11, this time in the United Kingdom, was an attempt to introduce the Racial and Religious Hatred Bill by Tony Blair's government.[23] This bill to make incitement to religious hatred unlawful had a long and controversial history, and was only given Royal assent in February of 2006 after significant amendments to the original proposed bill were made. The original bill had targeted speech "likely to stir up religious hatred", but in the end this phrase was removed. Also removed was a vague ban on "abusive and insulting" speech. The bill now covers only threatening conduct. Most importantly, the bill includes an added protection of freedom of expression, defending the right to ridicule, insult, or abuse religions or the beliefs and practices of their adherents. It also specifically allows for evangelism and proselytizing.

The Racial and Religious Hatred Bill is of course centrally concerned with tolerance. The controversy surrounding it highlights the tension between tolerance and freedom of expression. Lord Hunt, in opening the debate during the bill's committee stage, said: "You cannot promote tolerance by limiting freedom of expression. Tolerance and freedom of expression buttress one another. They are inseparable siblings."

---

[22] From William F. Buckley, "Onward, Christian Missionaries," *National Review* (30 June 30 2003), p. 58; and Jeff Adair, "Robertson Appearance Sparks Ire," retrieved on Oct 31, 2005 from http://www.metrowestdailynews.com/news/local_regional/fram_robertson04102003.htm, April 10, 2003. For additional examples of inflammatory language see chapter 5, pp. 106–131.

[23] Articles consulted on this story include Greg Hurst, "Religious hatred Bill hits buffers after Lords defeat", *The Times* (Oct 26, 2005), p. 2; Rob James, "Praise for 'Hate' Bill Changes", *Christianity Today* (Dec, 2009), p. 22; and Goodall (2007).

I agree, and am in support of the added freedom of expression clause in the bill. But it is important here to distinguish between law and morality. We need to be very cautious about trying to reinforce tolerance via hate *laws*. However, assessing the *morality* of hate speech is quite another matter. This book is about the morality of proselytizing. In this section I am arguing that intolerant proselytizing is immoral. Proselytizing that uses abusive and insulting language when describing other religions is immoral. But, again, this does not preclude careful critique. Most importantly, ethical proselytizing shows respect for people of other religious and irreligious traditions.

Motivation criterion

The primary motivation for ethical proselytizing is love for humanity. For religious proselytizers who believe in God, love for humanity will obviously be coupled with a love for and obedience to God. With immoral proselytizing, the ego-centric motives that have already been considered in chapter 5 become dominant, e.g. motives of personal benefit and reward, personal reassurance resulting from being able to convert another person to one's own position, personal domination over another person, and personal satisfaction about growth of one's own church. Ethical proselytizing is, by contrast, other-centered. It grows out of genuine concern for the other person's well-being, and his or her assumed need to hear the truth as understood by the proselytizer.

We need to be careful, however, when dealing with motivation, because the analysis of motivation is unfortunately very tricky. The motivation behind any human action is invariably mixed. There are always hidden motivations underlying explicitly stated motivations. It was Immanuel Kant who quite justifiably highlighted the importance of evaluating motivation when doing ethics. But Kant was too demanding, as we have already seen in chapter 5. Our motivation is never absolutely pure. We never do duty *simply* for duty's sake. We need realism here.

We therefore cannot demand of the proselytizer that his or her motivation be absolutely pure, with no regard for self-interest or with no concern about the consequences of proselytizing. It is for this reason that I have defined this criterion in terms of *primary* motivations. There will always be subsidiary motivations underlying proselytizing efforts. But the *primary* motivation should be the good of the person being proselytized, and the need to share the truth, with appropriate humility, of course. And for the religious person who believes in God, there is an additional ultimate motivation – proselytizing out of love for, and obedience to God.

While the motivational criterion is essential to defining the distinction between ethical and unethical proselytizing, there are difficulties in applying it. I have already alluded to the problem of mixed motives. More importantly, motives are personal and to a large extent hidden. It is very difficult for one person to assess the motivations of the other. Thus the motivational criterion should be seen primarily as a tool for self-analysis. And it is important to realize that it is difficult to be honest about one's motivation. Eugene Peterson has wisely suggested that self-deception is nowhere more common than in religion (1992, 14). It therefore behooves proselytizers to examine their motives carefully. However, the motivational criterion will not be too useful for objective analysis of proselytizing efforts of others.

Identity criterion

So far, in my discussion of various criteria to be used to distinguish between ethical and unethical proselytizing, I have been focusing primarily on the individual. In the previous chapter, when discussing the dignity of persons, the focus again was on individual dignity. But no man or woman is an island. A person is always part of at least a minimal community. And for most individuals, their membership in a community is an essential part of their dignity – a point that contemporary liberalism is increasingly coming to recognize.[24] A focus on communal identity leads to another criterion for ethical proselytizing: Proselytizing which completely disregards the dignity of the individual as rooted in his or her social attachments is immoral. Ethical proselytizing will take into account and show some respect for the communal identity of the proselytizee.

This has some obvious implications for proselytizing understood in its narrow sense, as discussed in chapter 1. Here Christians, for example, seek to convert Christians from another church tradition to their own tradition. Is it not wrong for evangelical Christians to "steal sheep" from another Christian fold if the dignity of these sheep is already intimately bound up with their Orthodox Christian identity, for example?

---

[24] Kymlicka, for example, argues for cultural membership as a primary good because of its close relation to the individual's sense of self-respect (1989, 166). See also Taylor (1989) and Gutmann (1994).

The question raised, however, can be extended to proselytizing beyond Christian borders. Is it right for a Christian to try to convert someone who already belongs to a Jewish or a Hindu community? For that matter, even atheists belong to a community – a community of humanists. In each of these cases, the question can be raised as to whether it is morally right to steal sheep from another fold, given that the social self is important. This question needs to be taken seriously if we take into consideration the intimate relation between individual dignity and communal identity.

The central problem with the concern being raised here is that it rests on an overemphasis of the social self. While I agree that the dignity of persons rests in part on their identification with a particular community, we must never lose sight of the dignity that is based on individual identity. We need a balance between individualism and communitarianism, as I have argued elsewhere (Thiessen 2001, 216–17). The rights of the religious community to sustain itself should never be allowed to completely override the rights of the individual. Therefore proselytizing cannot be ruled out *carte blanche* because of its failure to respect cultural and communal identity. However, morally acceptable proselytizing must always be sensitive to the social self that is part of human dignity. It must include a proper respect for the communities to which proselytees already belong.[25]

James McGuire (1985) provides an example where this principle was not followed. An eighteen-year-old friend of his, despite her being a graduate of twelve years of traditional Roman Catholic education, chose a Baptist school in South Carolina to begin her college education. Kim suddenly found herself rooming with a Baptist student who witnessed to her constantly, reading from the Bible and questioning Kim's commitment to Christ almost daily. Kim called McGuire, her senior mentor, several times, deeply upset and agitated that the fundamental structure of her personal faith and confessional experience were constantly under attack. He advised her to make the statement, "Yes, I am saved. As a Roman Catholic, I have encountered Jesus as my personal Savior, and the Holy Spirit is in my life" (348). He gave this advice because he was convinced that Kim did and still does believe in Jesus as her Lord. Her vocational interests were evidence of this. Unfortunately for Kim, this suggestion had little impact on her roommate who now shifted her approach to questioning various Roman Catholic doctrines.

---

[25] John Witte (2001, 628) and An-Na'im (1999) also argue for a balance between group and individual identities.

McGuire, while admitting that this case is not absolutely paradigmatic, nevertheless suggests that such encounters are all too often experienced by Catholic, Jewish, and non-Christian young people. He goes on to question the direct and confrontational approach being used by some Christian proselytizers whose opening question to a stranger might be, "Have you accepted Jesus as your personal Savior?" delivered without regard for the other person's background or readiness to answer (1985, 348–49). McGuire asks: Shouldn't the question be a little more protracted in order to include the necessary nuances? How about the following as an alternative starting point for the above scenario? "Given your Roman Catholic background and my Baptist background, do you feel as I do that we have a common ground to discuss and share one another's understanding of and [commitment] to the person of Jesus Christ?" (349)

McGuire then goes on to provide the ethical context of this advice. Such a wording, he suggests, recognizes "that every Christian is the sum total of each person and experience that he or she has met along the way in his or her family, church, school, and community. In other words, a person's individual, family, and religious history and church experience – his or her Christian *anthropology* – must be acknowledged and respected from the start" (McGuire 1985, 349). I agree entirely, and would add that this principle is not limited to the narrow sense of proselytizing (sheep-stealing), but should be extended to include all attempts at proselytizing. People's background and community membership needs to be taken into account and respected when proselytizing.

The emotional turmoil experienced by Kim in the above example, brings to the fore a final point of application. When proselytizing, there should be sensitivity to the pain involved in questioning someone's belief system and in seeking to bring about a conversion. Here it should be remembered that conversion has been defined in terms of a change of belief, behavior, identity, and belonging. Such radical change is painful. There is pain surrounding the uncertainty and the insecurity involved in undergoing a shift in worldviews.[26] Proselytizing which protects the dignity of persons, and is sensitive both to the individual self and the social self, will therefore show empathy for the pain involved in conversion. Adequate time should also be given to allow the proselytizee to process this pain.

---

[26] In a psychological study of the antecedents of religious conversion, Chana Ullman reports that 80% of the converts reported emotional turmoil during the period immediately preceding the conversion (e.g. "I thought I was going crazy", or "I had suicidal thoughts") (1982, 189, 190).

Cultural sensitivity criterion

In chapter 4 I dealt with the charge of religious colonialism or cultural genocide, often leveled at missionary endeavors. Clearly history reveals all too many examples of Christian missionary activity too closely tied to Western expansionism, or proselytizing tied too closely to Western European culture, resulting in a ruthless imposition of Western culture on other cultures in the name of spreading the good news. Two issues need to be dealt with here, although both are topics in their own right and cannot be dealt with adequately in this book.

The first has to do with the hitching of missionary endeavors to political or economic expansionism. This is obviously another form of coercion, an expression of social coercion already dealt with in the previous chapter. Clearly the use of political or economic power in order to spread a religious faith is coercive and hence immoral. Thus, we need to condemn Christian missionary activity insofar as it was tied too closely to Western expansionism during the exploration and settling of the Americas. Similarly, we need to condemn the spread of the Islamic faith by the use of political and economic power, which, as was discussed in chapter 2, would seem to be condoned at times in the Qur'an. However, as I have argued in previous chapters, we must be careful not to exaggerate these claims. The notions of social, political, and economic coercion are complex, and it is not always easy to identify when such coercion in fact occurs. Again, extreme cases can be more easily identified, and it is probably best to deal with this criterion on a case-by-case analysis.

I move on to the second dimension of the problem introduced in this section – the frequently made charge of cultural genocide or the imposition of Western culture on other cultures in the name of Christian missionary activity. Here again it is easy to exaggerate this charge, and we must be careful not to assume that proselytizing necessarily entails cultural genocide. However, there is a need to distinguish between culturally sensitive and culturally insensitive proselytizing. Much has in fact been written on the need for culturally sensitivity when proselytizing.[27] I can only provide a brief outline of this very important criterion.

Ethical proselytizing is sensitive to the culture of the persons being proselytized. It values the uniqueness of each culture, and attempts to retain what is good or neutral within each culture, while at the same

---

[27] See, for example, Kraft (1991); Newbigin (1989); Nichols (1994); and Sanneh (2003).

time seeking to convey the good news that is part of any attempts at proselytizing. Religious proselytizing that fails to distinguish between a particular cultural expression of a religion and the religious truths being conveyed is unethical. To impose a particular cultural expression of a religion on another culture is similarly unethical.

In chapter 4, I examined in some detail Inga Clendinnen's description of the Franciscan missionary activity among the Maya Indians. Clendinnen describes how the missionary friars were determined to reshape the institutions of native life at the village level "root and branch" (1987, 44). Though the Franciscans were technically working outside of the secular authority's jurisdiction, they served the Crown as enforcers of law and order, and civilized behavior, however artificial it might seem. They even went so far as to enforce Spanish notions of propriety at meals – "the sitting around the table, the cleanliness of the table cloth, the folding of the hands, the saying of Grace, all being laid out in obsessive and wistful detail" (58). To link Christian proselytizing and the imposition of Western proper etiquette, on a culture that knows nothing of tables and chairs and tablecloths, is plainly unethical.

This is a rather obvious violation of the cultural sensitivity criterion. What complicates the application of this criterion is the fact that there cannot be a culture-free religion. As Lesslie Newbigin was fond of saying about the Christian religion, "[T]here is no such a thing as a pure gospel if by that is meant something which is not embodied in a culture" (1989, 144). Therefore, a Christian missionary cannot help but proselytize on the basis of his or her own cultural interpretation of Christianity. What is required, however, is an awareness of this problem, and a commitment of the Christian missionary to *recontextualize* the gospel so as to respect the uniqueness of the culture in which the proselytizing is occurring. Much more needs to be said by way of addressing this problem and clarifying the above distinction, but this is beyond the scope of this chapter and this book.

Results criterion

Proselytizing involves persuasion, its goal is to make converts. Thus, it is quite natural to think of results or success as one way of evaluating proselytizing efforts. Ultimately, when someone does not undergo a conversion as a result of a proselytizing effort, there is a sense in which the proselytizer has failed. But, is this a moral failure? I don't think so, but the answer to this question is not as obvious as it might at first seem.

On the one hand it is tempting to say that success is completely irrelevant to a moral evaluation of proselytizing. As we have already seen, it is of utmost importance to respect the freedom of the other person in responding to one's proselytizing efforts. Thus the success of proselytizing efforts is ultimately taken out of the proselytizer's hands, and therefore should not be an ingredient in a moral evaluation of proselytizing. It is precisely the focus on results and success that leads to manipulation and coercion in proselytizing. Further, most religious traditions engaging in proselytizing would maintain that ultimately, the conversion of an individual is a work of God. Thus, Thomas Thangaraj, for example, reminds Christians (and others) that we need to "see ourselves as partners with God, acknowledging that ultimate responsibility for this universe (and for success in proselytizing) rests with God" (1999, 343).[28] So, acknowledging the divine component in proselytizing would again suggest that success should not be part of the moral evaluation of human efforts at proselytizing.

This point needs to be stressed, I feel, because it is all too easy to become preoccupied with success and results when proselytizing. The late Richard John Neuhaus tells the story of a young priest, newly ordained, who had the chance to visit the legendary Archbishop Fulton J. Sheen, who lay in the hospital dying. Sheen was famed for, among other things, winning many converts to the Catholic Church. "Archbishop Sheen", Neuhaus's friend said, "I have come for your counsel. I want to be a convert-making priest like you. I've already won fifteen people to the faith. What is your advice?" Sheen painfully pushed himself up on his elbows from his reclining position and looked Neuhaus's friend in the eye. "The first thing to do", he said, "is to stop counting."[29]

Greg Pritchard provides a penetrating analysis of the predominance of the marketing emphasis at the very influential Willow Creek Community Church, which has become a model for much of the broader evangelical church (1996, ch. 18). "There is nothing that dispels doubt faster than success," says one leader at Willow Creek (246). Thus numbers are constantly referred to as a means to justify what is done at the church. But such a preoccupation with success and numbers

---

[28] See also the Qur'an: "You cannot guide any one you like: God guides whosoever He please" (Q.28:56).

[29] From "While We're At It", by Richard John Neuhaus, *First Things* 178 (Dec, 2007), p. 74.

leads to manipulation and the engineering of conversions. Such thinking can also lead to an acceptance of the principle that the end justifies the means. A preoccupation with marketing success also fails in upholding the dignity and worth of persons. Pritchard puts it very bluntly: "Put through the meat grinder of market analysis, the gospel becomes a 'product,' the unchurched become 'consumers,' Christians become 'salesmen,' and the 'needs' of the unchurched become a potential tool of manipulation" (244). Pritchard correctly maintains that "marketing is not a neutral set of ideas and methods" (244). Indeed, it is not only a betrayal of the Christian gospel, but also a betrayal of morality.[30] Thangaraj similarly points to the dangers of making church growth the goal and measuring rod of evangelism, suggesting instead that it should be seen as a byproduct of being faithful in the area of evangelism (1999, 344).

Here we should not forget that the marketing approach in religion has been shaped to a large extent by commercial marketing, which lies at the heart of unbridled capitalism. A market economy, which depersonalizes and manipulates individuals, also needs to be condemned in the strongest possible terms. Commercial marketing and advertising that is measured only in terms of success in getting consumers to buy a product is pitifully one-sided. This does not mean that capitalism is inherently immoral. But capitalism without any moral constraints is as immoral as religious marketing without any moral constraints.

But, can results and the achievement of results be entirely rejected in evaluating proselytizing from a moral point of view? We need to look at the other side of this argument. Consider, for example, a physician who needs to persuade a patient to accept a certain treatment for a particular serious malady. For the sake of argument, let us suppose that there are no questions about the diagnosis or about the suitability of the treatment being suggested. Does the physician have a moral responsibility not only to try to persuade her patient to accept her diagnosis and suggested treatment, but also to be successful in this attempt at persuasion? If the physician were to use highly technical jargon while giving a casual, uncaring, and hasty suggestion as to the recommended treatment, would this not be seen as involving a moral failure?

---

[30] It should be noted that Bill Hybels, does at times recognize the dangers of the marketing emphasis at Willow Creek, and at one point very clearly affirms that it is "God's job to do the conversion" (Pritchard 1996, 220). Unfortunately most everything that is done at Willow Creek would seem to suggest that conversions are brought about by human effort and effective marketing methods.

Aristotle, in talking about rhetoric, suggests "that its function is not simply to succeed in persuading, but rather to discover the means of coming as near such success as the circumstances of each particular case allow".[31] There would seem to be a moral imperative involved here for Aristotle. Rowland and Womack summarize Aristotle's approach to virtuous rhetoric by referring to his notion of *phronimos*, or practical wisdom. "The *phronimos* bears an ethical responsibility to choose the most effective ethical means to achieve good ends" (Rowland and Womack 1985, 21). Thus an ethical rhetorician will pay some attention to effectiveness, and be careful to adapt to his audience, use arguments that will be intelligible to the audience, and also put the audience into a proper frame of mind, so they will be receptive to his persuasive appeal.[32] Effectiveness therefore seems to have some place as a moral criterion for proselytizing, though such an application needs to be carefully nuanced.

There is a final way in which results criterion can be applied to proselytizing, though again I'm not sure this application is that useful as it is open to variable interpretation. The goal of proselytizing is to convert someone, and conversion involves a change of belief, behavior, identity, and a sense of belonging. Surely one way to assess a conversion, and the proselytizing leading to a conversion, is whether in fact the end result leads to good behavior, and a sense of well-being on the part of a convert. If, as a result of proselytizing, the converts all turn out to be child-molesters, to use an extreme example, then clearly such proselytizing would be viewed as immoral. Consequences do have a bearing in evaluating an action. But, apart from obvious evil results, it will be difficult to get agreement on what results from proselytizing would be viewed as favorable or not. In chapter 5, I dealt with the question of empirical evidence relating to the consequences of religious proselytizing. We saw there that generalizations are hard to come by. So, this dimension of the results criterion too is somewhat problematic in helping us to distinguish between ethical and unethical proselytizing.

Golden Rule

I conclude my treatment of criteria to distinguish between ethical and unethical proselytizing with a broader criterion. Ethical proselytizing

---

[31] Aristotle's *Rhetoric* (Bk.1, Ch. 1, 1355b 9–14).
[32] Aristotle's *Rhetoric* (Bk.2, Ch. 1, 1377b 23; Bk.3, Ch. 17, 1395b 30–1396a 2). See also Rowland & Womack (1985, 21).

operates under the assumption that the other has the right to proselytize as well. It is immoral to assume or to work towards a monopoly of the proselytizing enterprise.[33]

This criterion involves an application of the Golden Rule, or Kant's universalisation principle, both of which are generally very useful guides to making moral decisions. Proselytizers affirming the right to proselytize must at the same time affirm and uphold the right of others to do the same.

Freud illustrated this point so well in a humorous story about a minister who was summoned by anxious relatives to try and extract a deathbed conversion from an atheistic and unrepentant insurance salesman. The meeting did occur, indeed, the longer the minister and the salesman continued to converse behind the closed door of the hospital ward, the more the concerned family members took hope. When the door finally opened, however, the salesman "had not been converted", writes Freud, "but the pastor went away insured."[34] The humor in this story turns on the surprise realization that it is not only ministers who proselytize. Indeed, what occurred here was a proselytizing dialogue, and it is clear that the salesman was more successful at proselytizing than was the minister. But it is equally clear that the minister must have allowed the salesman to pitch his story. This kind of reciprocity should be characteristic of all ethical proselytizing.

Many historical examples can be given where this principle of reciprocity has been violated with regard to proselytizing. John Locke, for example, despite his prophetic call for tolerance, excluded Roman Catholics and atheists from the scope of tolerance, and hence from the right to proselytize. Protestant Reformers objected to the proselytizing activities of the Anabaptists. More contemporary examples also abound. Take, for example the attitude of many Christians towards cults or new religious movements. It is one thing to object to immoral proselytizing on the part of cults, but the rhetoric against the cults often betrays another undercurrent – the assumption that it is right for Christians to proselytize, but not for cults.[35] This is simply unfair and immoral.

---

[33] See Greenway (1993, 152) for a clear statement of this principle. Henry Johnstone provides another version of this criterion as applied to rhetoric: "So act in each instance as to encourage, rather than suppress, the capacity to persuade and be persuaded, whether the capacity in question is yours or another's" (1981, 310; also cited in Johannesen 1996, 52).

[34] Cited in Sorenson (1994, 320).

[35] Lorne Dawson, for example, points to the obvious Christian polemic behind many of the attempts to apply brainwashing theories to cults and NRMs (1998, 113).

This same failure to apply the Golden Rule is found in Catholic and Orthodox objections to evangelical proselytizing in territories thought to belong to them, although there are obviously other theological issues at stake here.[36] Lawrence Uzzell, in a recent issue of the International Religious Freedom Watch, acknowledges the contribution that Jehovah's Witnesses have made towards religious freedom in various countries of the world by defending their right to proselytize, but then goes on to suggest that they function too much like special-interest lobbies, looking out only for their own rights and essentially ignoring the rights of other minority religious groups. "I believe that your policy is directly contrary to the Golden Rule", says Uzzell in an interchange with the Chairman of the Administrative Centre of Jehovah's Witnesses in Russia.[37]

This same kind of ambivalence is also found among Muslims. In discussions regarding Article 18 of the Universal Declaration of the Human Rights, and prior to the adoption of this article, which affirms the freedom to change one's religion, some Muslim delegates voted against this article, regarding it as the result of "a common plot of some missionary religions".[38] The Qur'an does not allow Muslims to change their religion or belief. However, the representative of Pakistan voted in favor of this declaration. "Islam is a missionary religion", he argued. "It claims the right and the freedom to persuade any man to change his faith and accept Islam. Surely and obviously, it must equally yield to other faiths the free right of conversion. It would be most unreasonable to claim (for oneself) the right of conversion and deny it to others."[39]

Thomas Robbins points to the "heresy factor" as a way of explaining the hostility of many Christians, including evangelicals, against the cults (1985, 363–64). Implicit in these explanations of opposition to the cults is the suggestion that Christians and evangelicals object to proselytizing activities on the part of cults, while of course reserving this right for themselves. Elsewhere Robbins points to the self-serving motivation behind clerical opposition to the cults, when clerics invoke accusations of mind-control against cults in order "to avoid appearing to persecute religious competitors" (1984, 253).

[36] These examples of Catholic and Orthodox resistance to evangelical evangelism involve the narrow meaning of proselytizing understood as sheep-stealing and hence the additional theological issues at stake. For a more careful treatment of this narrow sense of proselytizing and some other examples of resistance to evangelical evangelism, see chapter 1. See Glanzer (2002, 197–200), for an example of Orthodox resistance to a major evangelical initiative in Russia in the 1990s.

[37] Retrieved on Aug 25, 2005, from www.internationalreligiousfreedomwatch.org/archives/2005-06-20.htm.

[38] Cited in Jongeneel (1995/1997, Part 1, 311).

[39] Cited in Jongeneel (1995/1997, Part 1, 311). Arnold Stiebel, writing as a Jewish critic of Christian proselytizing, cites a Christian statement that clearly recognizes

Conclusion

This completes my survey of criteria that can be used to distinguish between ethical and unethical proselytizing. No doubt there will be readers who would like one or the other criterion to be highlighted or subsumed under another category. I trust readers will move beyond the issue of classification to the essential points made under each criterion. I offer this list of criteria somewhat tentatively, as there may well be some criteria I have overlooked. As noted in the beginning of the previous chapter, there are limitations to any attempt to define criteria or codes of conduct for moral action. What I hope this exploration of criteria has done, at the very least, is to stimulate continued discussion and reflection leading to possible modification and revisions towards a more adequate ethics of proselytizing. I would also hope that these two chapters will have provided some added reason to reject wholesale condemnations of proselytizing as immoral. I trust I have shown that it is possible to distinguish between ethical and unethical proselytizing, even though there might be room for improvement in defining these criteria.

---

the reciprocity principle. "For evangelicals to refrain from sharing the Good News with all men, including Jews, would be inconsistent with their faith. Our Jewish friends must live with our conviction, even as we recognize their right to try to make converts from among Gentiles" (cited in Stiebel 1982, 32).

Part V:

Conclusion

Chapter 9

Some Concluding Considerations

In his 1990 encyclical *Redemptoris Missio* (The Mission of the Redeemer), Pope John Paul II, in looking ahead to the third millennium, spoke of it as a new and great springtime for Christian evangelization (Donders 1996, 170). Such optimism will no doubt be greeted with a good deal of skepticism and even derision on the part of critics of Christianity. What arrogance? How pretentious? How insensitive to those who might not want to be evangelized? Indeed, behind these rhetorical questions posed by the critics lies an even deeper question: Is there not something wrong with the very idea of evangelism, whether in the name of Christianity or any other religion?

One of the central purposes of this book has been to answer this question. I have argued that it is a mistake to assume that there is something inherently wrong with proselytizing. To issue any kind of generalized condemnation of all proselytizing is therefore also mistaken. Indeed, as I argued in chapter 6, proselytizing can be a good thing, a natural expression of human dignity and the human desire to communicate. Proselytizing can even be seen as an expression of care and concern for others. This does not mean all proselytizing is good. Like many good things, it too can become distorted and bad. My overall position is similar to Aristotle's treatment of the more general topic of rhetoric, or the art of persuasion:

> And if it be objected that one who uses such power of speech unjustly might do great harm, that is a charge which may be made in common against all good things except virtue, and above all against the things that are most useful as strength, health, wealth, and generalship. A man can confer the greatest of benefits by a right use of these, and inflict the greatest of injuries by using them wrongly.[1]

---

[1] Aristotle's *Rhetoric* (Bk.1, Ch.1, 1355b 1–8).

The challenge therefore is to decipher when persuasion is rightly or wrongly employed. What I have tried to do in the last two chapters is to define criteria that will help us to distinguish between moral and immoral proselytizing.

I conclude this book by addressing briefly some final practical questions. Is dialogue an ethical alternative to proselytizing? What can and should we do to encourage moral proselytizing? What should be done about immoral proselytizing? And, if proselytizing as a general practice (assuming, of course, that it is being done morally), is indeed a good thing, then what needs to be done to uphold the freedom to proselytize? What should be done about countries where proselytizing is prohibited? These are big questions, and they clearly take us beyond the central focus of this book. But I want to touch on them, though only briefly.

Religious dialogue vs. proselytizing

Dialogue is frequently proposed as a moral alternative to proselytizing. Harold Coward, for example, concludes his study of pluralism in world religions by suggesting that the future of religious harmony lies in dialogue, and it would seem that he is proposing this as an alternative to "missionary activity that occurs when the superimposition of one's own criteria on the other is followed by efforts to convert the other" (2000, 143–44, 152–8). Jay Newman too, in his critique of proselytizing, proposes dialogue as an alternative to religious proselytizing, as a way of avoiding the undesirable consequences that often flow from proselytizing, such as resentment and intolerance. "But religious dialogue tends to promote understanding. Understanding promotes tolerance, which in turn promotes civilization", according to Newman (1982, 110).[2]

Now I have no quarrel with dialogue as one possible means of communication. However, I'm not sure these two means of communication are quite as different as is generally assumed. Dialogue, if it is a genuine interchange between two people who care about what they believe, will involve a degree of persuasion, and hence also some

---

[2] Newman is not entirely clear in his position. At one point he is careful to reject the idea that "religious dialogue is the only wholesome form of religious communication" (1982, 109). But he goes right on to suggest that dialogue rests on "more profound motives", and that most religious proselytizing promotes intolerance (110).

elements of old-fashioned proselytizing.[3] As I have argued in chapter 6, persuasion and proselytizing seem to be an inescapable element in inter-personal communication. Hence the recurring suspicion about the motives underlying Christians advocating dialogue as a way of communication with non-Christians and other religious adherents.[4] The latter are afraid dialogue is merely a tactical maneuver, a trojan horse that Christians want to bring into the fortified cities of those who are not Christians in order to convert them (Langone 1985, 374).

Another problem with proposing dialogue as an alternative to proselytizing is that such a proposal often rests on a relativistic approach to truth, a position that I have rejected in this book. For example, Coward suggests we need to accept the plurality of religions because it "safeguards against claims of absolutism of a kind that would cause religious dialogue to self-destruct" (2000, 154). Peter Berger has correctly pointed out that inter-religious dialogue (between Jews and Christians, for example) rarely deals with the truth claims of the communities involved (1979, 39). But truth matters, especially for those who feel they have a moral obligation to proselytize.

The problems I have identified are not meant to rule out dialogue as a way of communicating between people of different religious or irreligious persuasions. I believe dialogue is one way for people to communicate, and it is an important aid to facilitating mutual understanding. I also believe it is possible to keep conversionist motives in dialogue to a minimal level. We must be careful, however, not to assume that dialogue is the only ethical alternative to proselytizing. The relationship between religious dialogue and religious proselytizing can be compared to two quite different forms of communication between spouses. Married couples, for example, sometimes desire just to be understood, and here some dialogue might be very beneficial. But, sometimes either partner wants to spar with the other, persuade the other, and even convert the other. Both forms of communication are important and legitimate forms of marital communication. Similarly, with regard to religious communication. Religious dialogue must not be seen as an ethical alternative to religious proselytizing. Religious proselytizing is an equally valid form

---

[3] In an article summarizing UNESCO's approach to proselytizing and interreligious dialogue, it is even suggested that proselytizing is a condition of dialogue (Diene 1999).

[4] See, for example, Newman on Aquinas (1982, 106), Bracken, quoted in Grounds (1984, 221), and Marty (1988, 161).

of communication and it can be done in such a way as to satisfy ethical norms.[5]

The tendency to treat religious dialogue as an ethical alternative to
religious proselytizing has no doubt been influenced by Martin Buber's
contrast between dialogue and monologue, which in turn are an expression of two primary human attitudes and relationships, I-Thou and I-It
(1958; 1965). However, I believe Buber's central intent was not to define
dialogue as a separate form of communication, but to highlight the
nature of ethical communication. Indeed, Buber realizes that pure dialogue seldom occurs (1965, 36, 97). Instead, Buber's notion of dialogue is
better seen as representing "more of a communication attitude, principle
or orientation, than a specific method, technique, or format. One may
speak of a spirit of dialogue" (Johannesen, 1971, 374). For Buber, even
dialogue and conversation can become inauthentic and essentially
monologue in orientation, or an I-It relation (Buber 1965, 19–20). The
ideal in all forms of communication should therefore always be a *spirit*
of dialogue, or authentic communication. Johannesen summarizes:

> In the I-Thou or dialogic relationship, the attitudes and behavior of each
> communication participant are characterized by such qualities as mutual-
> ity, open-heartedness, directness, honesty, spontaneity, frankness, lack of
> pretense, nonmanipulative intent, communion, intensity, and love in the
> sense of responsibility of one human for another (Johannesen 1996, 64).

This analysis of the spirit of dialogue is a good description of ethical
proselytizing. It is a mistake to interpret Buber as offering us an alternative to proselytizing and persuasion, as some of his interpreters have
done.[6] Buber has instead given us a helpful description of authentic

---

[5] Pope John Paul II, in his 1991 encyclical letter, *"Redemptoris Missio*: On the
Permanent Validity of the Church's Missionary Mandate", makes this same distinction. His central concern is with those who want to replace proselytizing with
dialogue. He acknowledges inter-religious dialogue as one part of the church's
evangelizing mission. Dialogue must not be seen as opposed to the church's mission but as one expression of it, he maintains. On the other hand, John Paul II suggests that we must be careful not to see dialogue as a substitute for proclaiming the
good news, as some critics of proselytizing would suggest. "There is no conflict
between proclaiming Jesus Christ and inter-religious dialogue. The two are distinct
and intimately connected; they should not be confused or regarded as identical"
(Donders 1996, 163).

[6] Johannesen points out that some subsequent writers on dialogue have equated
monologue and persuasion and have argued that all attempts at persuasion are
unethical (1996, 71). But this was not Buber's own position. Dialogue can include

communication, which retains the dignity of persons, and is equally applicable to proselytizing and dialogue.

Encouraging ethical proselytizing: Resources within proselytizing religions

So, what can be done to encourage moral proselytizing and to discourage immoral proselytizing? I believe it is most important to draw on the resources of the religions themselves in order to accomplish this goal. Here I agree with a suggestion made by sociologist Mark Juergensmeyer, in his exploration of "the global rise of religious violence", to use the subtitle of his book, *Terror in the Mind of God* (2000). Juergensmeyer addresses the problem of what to do about ridding the world of religious violence, and he objects to those who think that the cure for religious violence is to get rid of religion itself. Instead, he concludes his book with an intriguing suggestion – "[T]he cure for religious violence may ultimately lie in a renewed appreciation for religion itself" (243). I too believe that the cure for abuses in religious proselytizing might best be found within each of the religious traditions themselves.[7]

I have already occasionally drawn attention to some of the resources for ethical thinking about proselytizing within each of the three religious traditions referred to for illustrative purposes throughout this book. Judaism, Christianity, and Islam all give clear support for the principle of respecting the dignity of persons, for example. All three traditions generally reject coercion in proselytizing and stress freedom as essential to genuine conversion. The Qur'an is very clear in affirming the freedom of conscience. "There is no compulsion in matter of faith" (Q.2:256; cf. Q10:99).

We have already seen that there is some dispute among Jewish scholars as to whether Judaism engages in proselytizing. But insofar as it is

---

persuasion, for Buber. Dialogue also does not preclude the attempt to show the other the wrongness of his or her ways. But, such influence must be exerted in a non-coercive, non-manipulative manner that respects the free choice and individuality of the listener. Further, dialogue can degenerate into monologue for Buber. Even monologue (understood as one-way communication) is not always wrong according to Buber. Indeed, it is unavoidable, though we must always be careful not to overuse it and we must ensure that it does not take on unethical qualities.

[7] One limitation of this book is its assumption of a liberal/pragmatic ethical framework. What is further needed is a defense of ethical proselytizing from within the ethical stance of each religious tradition engaged in proselytizing. I intend to write a sequel to the present monograph in which I will deal with the ethics of evangelism from an explicitly Christian perspective.

acknowledged, there would be a clear emphasis on choice within the Jewish Scriptures. Joshua, before his death, assembled all the tribes of Israel at Shechem and then enacted a covenant-renewing-ceremony (Josh 24). He challenged the people to fear the Lord and serve him with all faithfulness (Josh 24:14). And then this appeal: "[C]hoose for yourselves this day whom you will serve, whether the gods your forefathers served beyond the River, or the gods of the Amorites, in whose land you are living. But as for me and my household, we will serve the Lord" (Josh 24:15). Here we have a clear application of the principle of freedom within the Jewish Scriptures.

This emphasis is also found within Christianity. Jesus, for example, in giving instructions to his disciples before they engaged in a missionary outreach program, clearly affirms the principle of freedom. Jesus told his disciples that if they were not welcomed in a town and their message was being rejected, they were to respect that choice and move on (Lk 9:5). When the disciples, facing an actual case of such rejection, wanted to call down fire from heaven to destroy the village, Jesus "rebuked them and they went to another village" (Lk 9:55). The apostle Paul addresses some other principles governing his approach to the proclamation of the gospel: "We have renounced secret and shameful ways; we do not use deception, nor do we distort the word of God. On the contrary, by setting forth the truth plainly we commend ourselves to every man's conscience in the sight of God" (2 Cor 4:2; cf. 1 Thess 2:1–6).

This is not to say that there are not also elements within each of these three traditions that would seem to militate against ethical proselytizing. Ambiguities are to be found within religious traditions, which are at times difficult to resolve. Thus despite explicit warnings in the Qur'an against compulsion in religion, other passages seem to condone the use of violence to spread the faith. "Fight those people of the Book who do not believe in God . . ." (Q.9:29). As we saw in chapter 2, Augustine and Pope Innocent III used Jesus' parable of the wedding feast, in which a king instructs his servants to compel the guests to come in, as justification for force against heretics (Matt 22:1–14). What do we do with such ambiguities? Each religious tradition must try somehow to resolve the ambiguities found within each of them. Obviously this challenge raises important hermeneutical issues that need to be faced within each tradition.[8] It is quite beyond the scope of this book to deal with these issues here.

---

[8] Within the Christian tradition, for example, Pierre Bayle (1647–1706), French Protestant philosopher and critic, wrote a commentary on the passage Augustine used to support coercion in evangelism: "Compel them to come in" (Lk 14:23). Bayle contends that the word "compel" cannot mean force, and his 500 page commentary constructs a doctrine of toleration based on the ideal of a free conscience (Bayle 2005).

Beyond the exploration of the scriptures of each proselytizing religion, it would be well for theologians, philosophers, and ethicists of each religious tradition to develop an explicit code of ethics for proselytizing. Given the differing schools of thought or denominations, within these religions, this assignment needs to be taken up by each of these divisions. Indeed, such a code of ethics should also be articulated and regularly discussed at the micro-level of each denomination or school of thought (churches, mosques, synagogues).[9]

There has in fact been some significant work done by way of developing such ethical codes in the area of religious proselytizing in the last number of years (see Appendix 2, #D5). Here I will draw attention to just two of these attempts. The first is a project of a small working group of the Christian-Muslim Forum in the UK, a bilateral network of Muslim and Christian leaders set up by the Archbishop of Canterbury. On June 24, 2009, the Forum launched a set of ten "Ethical Guidelines for Christian and Muslim Witness in Britain". The preface to these guidelines states:

> As members of the Christian Muslim Forum we are deeply committed to our own faiths (Christianity and Islam) and wish to bear faithful witness to them. As Christians and Muslims we are committed to working together for the common good. We recognize that both communities actively invite others to share their faith and acknowledge that all faiths have the same right to share their faith with others.[10]

Within the Islamic tradition, Abdullahi Ahmed An-Na'im, a committed Muslim and legal scholar highlights the historical context of interpretations of sacred Scriptures (1990a). An-Na'im argues that just as early Muslims exercised their right and responsibility to interpret the divine sources of Islam in the light of their own historical context in order to produce a coherent and practical system which achieved significant human rights improvements in their time, so contemporary Muslims must do the same in order to produce modern Islamic shari'a for the present radically transformed context. In his concluding remarks, An-Na'im expresses the hope "that a modern interpretation of Islam will produce a version of Shari'a which is capable of sustaining the full range of human rights and can accompany the further development of these rights" (1990a, 68; cf. 1990b). See also Martin (1999) and Arzt (1999) for similar arguments for the possibility of interpreting Islam so as to support liberal moral values.

9 Michael Langone supports the need for such an ethical code by comparing it to the ethical codes that exist in various professions that seek to change people – physicians, psychologists, social workers, and advertizers (1985, 384).

10 For more information and a copy of these guidelines, see (http://www.christian-muslimforum.org/downloads/Ethical_Guidelines_for_Witness_v9.pdf) (accessed Feb. 17, 2010).

The Forum felt it was important for Muslims and Christians to have some guidelines about faith-sharing, based on the Qur'an and the Bible, that reflect the principles of justice, of respect for the autonomy of our fellow humans, and of compassion and concern for them. The hope is that these guidelines will be a framework that is sufficiently robust to be useful, but also one that will generate further debate. The Forum is sending out the guidelines and an open letter to a whole range of organizations, in the hope that people will discuss and engage with the document so that it begins to shape the nature of relations between Christians and Muslims.

A second example is an ethical code of evangelism developed by a team of evangelicals led by Inter-Varsity Christian Fellowship, prompted by the publication of a special edition of *Cultic Studies Journal* on the theme, "Cults, Evangelicals, and the Ethics of Social Influence."[11] Dietrich Gruen, in a prologue to this code, is careful to highlight the built-in limitations of such a code. Speaking on behalf of the task force of some twelve members representing more than seventy Christian organizations and evangelical leaders, Gruen says, "[W]e wanted it to reflect the work of reasonable people of faith who are aware of the issues, sensitive to our critics, and eager to reach consensus, while voicing our disagreements with one another. Hence, the code is limited to what we could all agree on and to which we could all be held accountable" (1985, 302). Gruen also stresses the tentative nature of the code – it is a work in progress that needs to be further discussed, field-tested, and amended for consensus building. As with any code of ethics, there are imprecise generalizations and there is always the further work of applying principles to concrete cases, Gruen points out.

Codes of ethics are, however, still merely theoretical codes. They will only be useful if in fact religious groups adopting these codes follow them, and have in place some mechanism of holding adherents accountable. Thus it is significant that Gruen raises the issue of accountability in discussing the limitations of "A Code of Ethics for the Christian Evangelist" (1985, 302). Gruen goes on to propose an "Evangelical Council for Accountability in Ministry", which could serve as a court of appeal for both critics and defenders arguing the issues of ethics involved in any given communication practice (303).[12]

---

[11] See *Cultic Studies Journal*, 1985, 2(2): 299–305. This code of ethics underwent a further revision, which is found in Rudin (1996, 67–72).

[12] Langone speaks approvingly of these evangelical efforts at policing themselves (1985, 385). For two other proposals for holding intentional groups accountable, see Zablocki (1999), and Sandhill (1999).

Such accountability structures could go a long way towards ensuring ethical proselytizing. Lawrence Uzzell criticizes many Protestants for having been "insufficiently zealous about monitoring one another for fraudulent or otherwise improper methods" in evangelism (2004, 16). He further suggests that if Christians are serious about missions, they should work not only towards developing their own specialized codes of ethics but also "to name and shame its violators". This challenge needs to be taken up by all religious groups engaged in proselytizing.

Social reinforcement

So far I have been focusing on ways to reinforce ethical proselytizing within the context of religious bodies themselves. In the last few paragraphs, I defended the idea of accountability structures, which already involves a degree of social reinforcement, though still restricted to religious communities. Naming and shaming violators of ethical norms in proselytizing can and should also be done at a broader societal level. Langone describes such social reinforcement as a healthy and inevitable result of participating in a pluralistic democratic society. "Individuals and groups which violate or tend to violate society's ethical norm can be restrained by encouraging their participation in a pluralistic community, criticizing them (publicly and privately), educating influencees, and taking appropriate legal actions" (Langone 1985, 385).

While I agree with the idea of this kind of social reinforcement, I have two concerns. First, an appeal to "society's ethical norm", while obviously important, is simply inadequate. What if society's norms are themselves problematic? A society that accepts conversion by some form of coercion, needs to be condemned in the name of some higher ethical standard even though this practice is generally accepted. Society's ethical norms may be faulty.

Secondly, social reinforcement of ethical proselytizing will only be effective (and legitimate) if critics take a balanced and reasonable position with regard to proselytizing. A central thrust of this book is that wholesale condemnations of proselytizing are unreasonable and ultimately an expression of intolerance. Critics who condemn all proselytizing, forfeit their right to engage in the process of social reinforcement of ethical proselytizing. I have argued that the only position that is philosophically defensible with regard to proselytizing, is that some proselytizing is ethical and some isn't. I have also defended a set of criteria by which to make this distinction. It is only if there is a general acceptance of clear criteria on the basis of which we can make a distinction between ethical and unethical proselytizing that the enterprise of social reinforcement will be effective. Criticism is only blunted if it rests on wholesale condemnations or vague criteria. Indeed, public criticism can and should be ignored by proselytizing religions if such criticism rests on undiscriminating and wholesale condemnations of proselytizing. Hopefully, the work of this monograph will contribute to an informed social reinforcement of ethical proselytizing.

The same must be said for other related fields like journalism, advertising, marketing, propaganda, and public relations, where, as was noted in chapter 7, little progress has been made in making the very same necessary distinction between right and wrong ways of engaging in each of these activities (see also Appendix 2, #A and B). Here the opposite danger often occurs – wholesale acceptance of all methods of persuasion. Until we admit that there are right and wrong ways of persuading people, of influencing people, of using the media, of advertising, of selling products, and of creating a public image, we will not be able to make any moral progress in any of these areas.

One important means of social reinforcement is the dissemination of information on religious groups, which violate ethical norms when proselytizing. In North America, organizations like the International Cultic Studies Association and Info-Cult provide an invaluable service in this regard.[13] In the United Kingdom, the main, and recently re-established organization monitoring cults, is The Family Survival Trust.[14] Two European examples include Infosekta in Switzerland, and Action for Mental and Psychological Freedom in Germany.[15] One of the problems with these organizations is that they tend to focus only on cults and new religious movements. This is problematic because unethical proselytizing is not limited to cults, and it needs to be condemned wherever it is found. Some of these organizations are becoming aware of this problem, and have been broadening their focus in the last few years.

The dissemination of information concerning unethical proselytizing must obviously be based on adequate research. Open discussion

---

[13] See the following websites: www.icsahome.com, and http://infosect.freeshell.org/infocult/ic-home.html.

[14] See the following website: www.familysurvivaltrust.org/.

[15] See the following websites: http://infosekta.ch/, and www.agpf.de/english.htm. There are also government agencies monitoring cult activities. See for example, MIVILUDES, in France (Interministerial Mission for Monitoring and Combatting Cultic Deviances) www.miviludes.gouv.fr/.

with groups who seem to be violating ethical norms is essential to ensuring objective information. Here some excellent work is being done by sociologists of religion, as was noted in chapter 1 (see also Appendix 2, #D4). However, because sociology is descriptive in nature, sociologists are not well equipped to deal with ethical questions. They also tend to identify ethical violations in terms of society's understanding of ethical values. Thus we are back to the problem of finding an adequate foundation for making ethical judgments. But, the publication of descriptive case studies is nonetheless useful in furthering the development and application of criteria to distinguish between ethical and unethical proselytizing, and thereby ultimately helping the public to discern, and to engage in social reinforcement of ethical proselytizing (Langone 1985, 383).

Many ways can be found to disseminate information about religious groups which violate ethical norms in proselytizing – publication of books and journals, conferences, public awareness campaigns, and lectures at college and university campuses. While I have expressed some concerns about exaggerating the vulnerability of students at universities and colleges, and while I would also caution against hasty condemnations of student attempts at proselytizing which may be in need of refinement given their inexperience, I support the efforts of student services offices at these institutions in issuing warnings about unethical proselytizing. I do have concerns, however, with the tendency to indiscriminately condemn all proselytizing, or with the use of vague criteria in distinguishing between ethical and unethical proselytizing.[16] Wherever it occurs, and whatever the means, we do need public criticism of proselytizing that violates ethical norms, together with public affirmation of ethical proselytizing.

---

[16] I provide some examples of such indiscriminate criticisms of proselytizing groups in chapter 1. The website of Harvard Chaplains issues a warning about destructive religious groups, contrasting these groups with the approach of supposedly healthy religious groups affiliated with Harvard Chaplains who are "subject to a collaborative code of non-proselytizing and mutual respect" (Retrieved on Aug 26, 2009, from www.chaplains.harvard.edu/about_us.php). Clearly, all proselytizing is implicitly condemned in this statement. Condemnations of destructive religious groups that are guilty of harassment, manipulation, and a tendency to be "less than candid" about their identity, are all problematic in being rather vague. Perhaps this is unavoidable, but a qualifier could be added stressing that students will need to use their own judgment in applying these criteria.

Legal reinforcement

Legal reinforcement is another way to encourage moral proselytizing. There is an educative function to law. In addition to this positive role, law can also function as a constraint. Laws are introduced to discourage violations of norms thought to be important for a correct ordering of society. The question is, can and should the law be used to reinforce ethical proselytizing? This is a question that deserves more attention, but I can only touch on it briefly here.[17]

To answer this question, we must be clear as to the relation between morality and the law. This matter is itself not without controversy. Franklyn Haiman, scholar of the First Amendment and communication ethics, gives expression to three standard guidelines used with regard to legal reinforcement of moral principles (1993, 81–86). He maintains, first of all, that a moral standard concerning a particular behavior should be codified in legislation only when there is near-unanimous consensus in society that the conduct in question is immoral. Haiman argues secondly that laws must be enforceable. Indeed, they must embody credibility and fairness by not being subject to capricious or unequal enforcement. Finally, laws should only be introduced to reinforce important moral principles. Not every violation of a moral norm is covered by a law. Serious violations, however, which cause significant harm to others, are given added legal sanction. Haiman goes on to suggest that a free society "will leave to the operations of social pressure, education, and self-restraint the control of behaviors whose harm to others is less serious, less direct, less immediate, and less physical" (86).

What does this entail for proselytizing? These three principles would suggest that governments can and should initiate legislation with regard to proselytizing only where there is serious ethical misconduct, where there is near-unanimous consensus in society that the conduct in question is immoral, and where the laws are enforceable. Here several problems emerge with regard to introducing such legislation. First of all, we have seen that the issue of proselytizing is in fact quite controversial in most Western societies, and even more so in non-Western societies. It will therefore be difficult to find near-consensus on most of the criteria that I have outlined in chapters

---

[17] Lee Boothby says the following in an article dealing with the question of law and proselytizing: "Without question, proselytism is one of the most controversial and sensitive issues in the arena of religious human rights" (1999, 46). See Appendix 2, #E for a review of some of the literature on law and the ethics of proselytizing.

7 and 8.[18] Perhaps two exceptions are the use of physical coercion and the use of outright bribery in proselytizing. Secondly, we have seen that many of the moral criteria are quite vague, and therefore would be difficult to enact into law and enforce. This would apply particularly to such criteria as the use of psychological or social coercion. Some of the criteria are also quite general, and as such are again unenforceable (e.g., dignity criterion; care criterion). Some of the criteria have to do with attitudes and are therefore obviously not legally enforceable (e.g., motivation criterion; humility criterion). You also can't enforce rationality! Thirdly, only serious moral violations that result in significant harm to individuals should be covered by law. Clearly, physical coercion when proselytizing, qualifies. Psychological coercion might qualify, but we have already seen that there are problems with vagueness and enforceability.

It therefore seems that the issue of ethical proselytizing is nearly entirely beyond the scope of legal enforcement, except for the use of physical coercion and outright bribery to convert. The late Richard John Neuhaus sums up the problem: *"proselytizing* is a very slippery term and, as a general rule, beyond the competence of the state to regulate."[19]

A further problem with regard to legislating the ethics of proselytizing concerns the possibility of conflicting laws in free democratic countries. Proselytizing obviously is an expression of free speech, and hence any legislation concerning proselytizing is going to come into conflict with regulations governing the protection of free speech. This is well illustrated in the controversies surrounding attempts to introduce the Racial and Religious Hatred Bill in Britain. The bill clearly relates to the tolerance criterion of ethical proselytizing. The bill was only given Royal assent after revisions were made to the original proposed bill. These included a statement protecting freedom of expression, defending the right to ridicule, insult, or abuse religions or the beliefs and practices of their adherents, as well as a statement relating specifically to allowing evangelism and proselytizing. The bill also required proof of intent to stir up hatred. Kay Goodall, in an article in *Modern Law*

---

[18] David Smolin (2000–2001) helpfully distinguishes between core rights with regard to proselytizing which should be universal, and varying interpretations of these rights in specific cultural contexts. At most, we should insist that government regulations with regard to proselytizing not be so severe as to constitute infringements of the core rights themselves.

[19] "While We're At It", *First Things* 188 (Dec 2008), pp. 158. See also van der Vyver (1998) for some cautions about state regulation of proselytizing.

Review, answers the rhetorical question raised in her suggestive title, "Incitement to Religious Hatred: All Talk and No Substance?" with a resounding, yes. The legislation is without substance, according to Goodall, because there is a tension between protecting freedom of speech and protecting citizens from hate speech. Further, confining offences to those "requiring proof of intention simply will not work" (Goodall 2007, 90).

A final problem concerning attempts to reinforce ethical proselytizing via legal enforcement involves the danger of such attempts being a cover for outlawing proselytizing, period. Let me illustrate by looking briefly at Israeli law. Israel's Declaration of Independence states that the state of Israel "will guarantee freedom of religion and conscience". The Declaration's principles were incorporated into the more recent Basic Laws and are regarded as enjoying constitutional status (Hirsch 1998, 446). Every individual enjoys the right to change his or her religion, and missionary work and proselytizing are legal. However, some forms of proselytizing are illegal, as defined by the 1977 Penal Law Amendment:

> Whosoever gives or promises to a person money, money's worth, or some other material benefit in order to induce him to change his religion – or in order that he may induce another person to change his religion – is liable to imprisonment for five years or a fine of 50,000 pounds.[20]

Hirsch goes on to suggest that this limitation to freedom to proselytize is consistent with contemporary rules of international law regarding the same. For example, Article 18(2) of the 1966 International Covenant on Civil and Political Rights, expressly prohibits coercive acts which impair freedom to change a religion. Hirsch sees the provision or promise of material benefits as an inducement to change a religion and as a clear impairment of freedom of choice to have or change a religion. As such this amounts to coercion, which can then quite legitimately be governed by legal sanctions. I am not so sure the above legal provision is as clear as Hirsch assumes. For example, as John Montgomery has pointed out, giving a New Testament to an unbeliever can be strictly construed as a "material benefit" offered to "induce him to change his religion" (2001, 5). Yet surely, this should be seen as a legitimate form of proselytizing. Clearly the use of financial bribery to induce someone to convert is a serious ethical offence and as such could be governed by

---

[20] Cited in Hirsch (1998, 446).

legal sanctions. Thus the above Israeli law would be better defined if it limited itself to the giving or promising to a person money in order to induce him or her to convert, omitting the reference to "money's worth or some other material benefit".

Sadly, it would seem the 1977 Israeli Penal Law Amendment was meant to do more than to outlaw unethical proselytizing. It was in fact largely due to the influence and power of the ultraconservative, Orthodox community that the Israeli Knesset passed the above anti-proselytism law (Montgomery 2001, 5). Since then a private bill from two members of the Knesset was introduced in December of 1996, designed to restrict the freedom of proselytizing in Israel even more (Hirsch 1998, 446). The bill that was proposed provided for a one-year imprisonment for anyone who "holds, without a legal justifica-tion, or prints or copies or disseminates or distributes or imports pamphlets, or publishes materials which constitute solicitation to change a religion" (446). Hirsch reports that this bill aroused much criticism both within and outside Israel, and he expressed doubts as to whether this bill would be adopted by the Knesset.[21] Clearly such a bill would involve a gross violation of the freedom of religion. Unfortunately, it would seem that while many Christian churches, and other non-Jewish religious organizations, have long existed and continue to exist in the state of Israel, legally, they are more and more being quarantined, forced to operate as ghettoes, ironically reminiscent of Jewish ghettoes of medieval Europe (Montgomery 2001, 5–6).

I have considered just one example of possible legal responses to unethical proselytizing. I quite agree that violations of important ethi-cal criteria governing proselytizing should be punished. However, we must ensure the criteria are clearly defined. As Lee Boothby notes, the danger of vague statutory language is that it will "permit government officials to exercise broad discretion. Thus the officials choose to apply the statutes only against the most unpopular religious groups" (1999, 49). Boothby goes on to issue two warnings with regard to imposing severe legal sanctions against proselytizing. They will simply result in non-compliance on the part of religious groups, which are committed to sharing their faith with their neighbors. Further, "anti-proselytizing laws directed against religious groups and their members will only generate discord" (49).

---

[21] Natan Lerner, in a more recent article on "Proselytism and its Limitations in Israel", reports that this bill was in fact abandoned (2000, 33).

When legal sanctions are felt to be necessary, we must ensure that the violations of ethical criteria are of sufficient importance to a society that they deserve legal sanction. There are very practical reasons why it is inadvisable to try and police minor ethical infractions of those engaged in proselytizing. This does not, of course, rule out the application of social sanctions, as discussed in the previous section. Public condemnations of immoral proselytizing practices are quite appropriate. And hopefully, religious leaders themselves would join in such condemnation. In sum, legislation to proscribe improper proselytizing is a dangerous instrument, as Boothby correctly warns (1999, 49). One of the key dangers is that such legislation can be used by the majority religion in a society against minority religions (Durham 1999). The latter concerns raise the broader question of religious freedom, to which I now turn.

Religious Freedom

In the previous section, we have seen that there is a danger of overextending legal sanctions with regard to proselytizing. Such over-extension is in fact often simply an expression of a more general opposition to proselytizing that has been the concern of previous chapters in this book. Here it is significant that there are a growing number of anti-proselytizing laws and policies appearing in a variety of countries. John Witte draws attention to what would seem to be "a new war for souls" emerging in many East European, African, and Latin American countries where indigenous religious groups have persuaded political leaders to adopt regulations restricting the constitutional rights of their religious rivals (Witte and Martin 1999, xii). More generally, various reports reveal an alarming lack of religious freedom, including the freedom to proselytize or to change one's religion in various countries of the world.[22]

---

[22] See, for example, a series of reports from Special Rapporteurs appointed by the United Nations Sub-Commission on Prevention of Discrimination and Protection of Minorities, a summary of which is found in Lerner (1998); the International Religious Freedom Report 2009, which is submitted to the U.S. Congress annually by the Department of State in compliance with Section 102(b) of the International Religious Freedom Act (IRFA) of 1998. Available at http://www.state.gov/g/drl/rls/irf/2009/127215.htm (Accessed Nov 25, 2009); and the reports of the International Religious Liberty Association, e.g. "Religious Freedom World Report 2000", in FIDES ET LIBERTAS: *The Journal of the International Religious Liberty Association*, 2000, pp. 128–63. See also Paul Marshall (2007).

In December of 2009, the Pew Forum on Religion and Public Life released what it claims is the first quantitative worldwide study on how governments and societies infringe on the religious beliefs and practices of individuals.[23] The study covers 198 countries, representing 99.5% of the world's population, from 2006–2008. Measuring both government restrictions and social hostilities, the report finds that about one-third of the world's countries impose high restrictions on religion, but these 64 nations contain 70 percent of the world's 6.8 billion people.[24]

Increasing restrictions on religious freedom would also seem to be on the rise in Western democratic countries. Various European countries are formulating lists of religious sects and religious groups that are considered dangerous because their members seek to recruit or evangelize (Montgomery 2001; Fautre 2000, 28–34). France has assembled a list of more than 170 such dangerous religious organizations. In Austria, a religious registration act now places many of the newer Christian denominations, and all sectarian bodies, at a disadvantage as compared with the dominant Roman Catholic Church. An attempt has even been made in the European Parliament to draft what would amount to pan-European sect regulations (Montgomery 2001, 6). Legislation restricting the proselytizing activities of various new religious movements has also appeared in the United States and Canada.[25]

Surprisingly, these growing and world-wide restrictions on religious freedom and the right to proselytize are occurring at the same time that there would appear to be a growing acceptance of the importance of religious liberty, a seeming paradox highlighted by John Witte (Witte and Martin 1999, xi–xii). Around the globe more than 150 major new statutes and constitutional provisions on religious rights have been promulgated – guaranteeing liberty of conscience, religious pluralism and equality, free exercise of religion, nondiscrimination on religious grounds, and autonomy for religious groups, among other norms.

---

[23] The report is available at http://pewforum.org/docs/?DocID=491 (accessed Dec. 17, 2009).

[24] The Pew report goes on to say that nearly half of all countries either restrict the activities of foreign missionaries (41%) or prohibit them altogether (6%). In addition, national or local governments in 75 countries (38%) limit efforts by some or all religious groups to persuade people to join their faith.

[25] For some examples, see Mehra (1984) and Sawatsky (1986, 78–79). See Tyner (2001) and Hunter & Price (2001) for reviews of court cases and increasing regulations on proselytizing in the United States (2001). Sheffer, however, maintains that over the past two hundred years, court rulings have enlarged the scope of the free exercise clause in the First Amendment (1999, see esp. 109, 121, 125).

These national guarantees have been matched with a growing body of regional and international norms.[26] The provisions of these international statements on religious freedom are also reflected in various regional and national statements on religious freedom (Lerner 1998, 542–44).

A careful examination of these national and international documents and the discussions surrounding these statements of religious freedom will show, however, that not all is well. The formulation of these statements was invariably surrounded with controversy, and in the end, there would seem to be an increasing erosion of support for the right to proselytize.[27] Further, there is the inevitable discrepancy between reality and the ideals we hold. And so we have the strange paradox that despite growing recognition of the importance of religious freedom and seeming support for the right to proselytize, *the reality is quite different* – there is strong world-wide opposition to proselytizing and gross and widespread violations of religious freedom.

How do we respond to this opposition to proselytizing and to the broader lack of support for religious freedom in many parts of the world? What do we do with societies that fail to uphold religious freedom? These are, of course, big questions, and to provide a full answer to them is quite beyond the scope of this book. A brief response might nevertheless be in order, though I suspect my response will seem to be rather simplistic to many readers. We need to expose the lack of freedom where it exists. Here we must be careful not to let the niceties of political diplomacy stand in the way of speaking the truth. Truth must be spoken clearly, though always carefully, and with as much respect for the offending societies as possible.

---

[26] Moshe Hirsch (1998) has provided a useful overview of the primary initiatives in this regard. The Universal Declaration of Human Rights (1948) is, of course, foundational. Subsequent to this there has been the International Covenant on Civil and Political Rights (1966), and the Declaration on the Elimination of All Forms of Intolerance and of Discrimination Based on Religion or Belief (1981).

[27] For example, in the discussions prior to the adoption of the foundational U.N. Declaration of Human Rights, tensions were evident. The representative of Saudi Arabia, as well as other Muslim states, objected to the wording of Article 18, "this right includes freedom to change his religion or belief" (Hirsch 1998, 442). An attempt was made to delete the second part of the draft article as initially formulated. This amendment proposal was in the end rejected by the majority (27 states against, 5 Islamic states in favor, 12 abstentions) and so we have the final text of the Universal Declaration as stated above. In subsequent documents concerning religious freedom, it is rather clear that there has been an evolution – "the focus has shifted from an emphasis on the freedom to *change* a religion to an emphasis on the freedom to *retain* a religion" (Hirsch 1998, 444).

What else can be done about countries where there is little religious freedom? We need to have faith and hope that these illiberal countries will eventually come to understand the importance of religious freedom and then put it into practice. Liberal societies need to lead by example. As John Rawls has argued, there is a natural strength and stability inherent in free institutions, and I would add that the same applies to free societies (1971, 219). Rawls is more narrowly concerned with the problem of tolerating the intolerant within a free society (Section #35). Within this narrower context, he correctly observes that the liberties experienced by the intolerant will eventually persuade them to believe in freedom. "This persuasion works on the psychological principle that those whose liberties are protected by and who benefit from a just constitution will, other things equal, acquire an allegiance to it over a period of time" (219). I believe this principle can also be extended more broadly to intolerant societies. Treating them in a just and fair way, in the end, will persuade them to adopt the principles of freedom that those of us who live in free societies hold so dear. We should also not forget the persuasive power of those who have emigrated to free societies and who have come to experience the benefits of freedom. Their contacts with friends and relatives still living under illiberal regimes will surely have some positive transforming influence, over time.

What we need is faith and hope that others will eventually respond to ideals that are positive and good. We also need faith and hope that the good and the right are more powerful than evil and wrong, and that actions and attitudes flowing from goodwill will ultimately triumph. For some, such faith and hope are found within a religious tradition. For example, the writer of the book of Hebrews describes faith as "being sure of what we hope for", anchored in a belief and trust in God (Heb 11:1). For those who don't appreciate a religious source of faith, Annette Baier has proposed a "secular faith" in the eventual reciprocation of others to one's own moral actions (1980). A civilized world is not possible unless there is some faith.

Without goodwill inspired by faith and hope, liberal societies are impossible, as is progress towards a genuinely free world, and, as Thomas Hobbes saw so clearly, we will find ourselves increasingly in a state of nature where life is solitary, poor, nasty, brutish, and short. My hope and prayer is that such a state of nature will be avoided by a growing acceptance of genuine religious freedom throughout the world, and by allowing proselytizing religions to engage in ethical proselytizing.

Appendix 1

Summary of 15 Criteria to Distinguish Between Ethical and Unethical Proselytizing

1. Dignity criterion

Ethical proselytizing is always done in such a way as to protect the dignity and worth of the person or persons being proselytized. Proselytizing becomes unethical when it reduces the proselytizee to the status of an object or a pawn in the proselytizing program of any religious organization.

2. Care criterion

Ethical proselytizing is always an expression of concern for the whole person and all of his or her needs – physical, social, economic, intellectual, emotional, and spiritual. To care only for the salvation of the souls of persons is unethical. It involves an objectification of a part of the person and, as such, violates that person's dignity.

3. Physical coercion criterion

The freedom to make choices is central to the dignity of persons. Ethical proselytizing will therefore allow persons to make a genuinely free and uncoerced choice with regard to conversion. Proselytizing involving the use of physical force or threats is immoral.

4. Psychological coercion criterion

Ethical proselytizing avoids excessive psychological manipulation. There are various ways in which proselytizing can be psychologically manipulative. (a) Proselytizers should avoid intense, repeated, and extremely programmatic approaches to bringing about conversions. (b) Care must be taken to avoid exploiting vulnerability. This becomes especially important when dealing with children, young people, vulnerable adults, and individuals facing personal crises. (c) Excessive appeals to emotion and fear must also be avoided.

5. Social coercion criterion

While acknowledging that some degree of power and control is inescapable in proselytizing, excessive expressions of power, or the exploiting of power-imbalances when proselytizing is unethical.

6. Inducement criterion

Proselytizing accompanied by material enticement such as money, gifts, or privileges, is immoral. In situations where providing medical care, humanitarian aid, or education is in some way linked with proselytizing, the greater the need, the more sensitive the proselytizer must be to the danger of exploiting that need, and thus inducing to convert. In situations where physical needs are overwhelming, proselytizing should be kept entirely separate from the activity of responding to these physical needs. Proselytizers must also make it clear that they are not trading medical or humanitarian aid for conversion. The proselytizee must therefore be given a clear sense that it is perfectly acceptable for him or her to accept aid, or medical help, and yet refuse any persuasive appeals to convert.

7. Rationality criterion

Proselytizing involves persuasion to convert. Ethical persuasion includes the providing of information in order to make such a decision. It also includes giving reasons for the proposed change of heart and mind. Proselytizing that attempts to sidestep human reason entirely is unethical.

8. Truthfulness criterion

Ethical proselytizing is truthful. It seeks to tell the truth about the religion being advocated. It is truthful also with regard to what it says about other religions. Integrity characterizes the ethical proselytizer. Proselytizing accompanied by hidden agendas, hidden identities, lying, deception, and failure to speak the truth should be condemned as immoral.

9. Humility criterion

Ethical proselytizing is characterized by humility. Proselytizing becomes unethical when it becomes arrogant, condescending, and dogmatic in the claims being made.

10. Tolerance criterion

Ethical proselytizing treats persons holding beliefs differing from that of the proselytizer with love and respect. While it does not preclude fair criticism of other religious or irreligious beliefs, it treats the same with respect, and avoids hostile attitudes or the use of insulting and abusive language against other religions and worldviews.

11. Motivation criterion

The primary motivation for ethical proselytizing is love for humanity. For religious proselytizers who believe in God, love for humanity will obviously be coupled with a love for and obedience to God. Ethical proselytizing is other-centered. It grows out of genuine concern for the other person's well-being, and his or her assumed need to hear the truth as understood by the proselytizer. With immoral proselytizing, on the other hand, ego-centric motives such as personal benefit and reward, personal reassurance resulting from being able to convert another person to one's own position, personal domination over another person, and personal satisfaction about growth of one's own church, become dominant.

12. Identity criterion

Ethical proselytizing will take into account and show some respect for the communal identity of the proselytizee. Proselytizing which completely disregards the dignity of the individual as rooted in his or her social attachments is immoral.

13. Cultural sensitivity criterion

Ethical proselytizing is sensitive to the culture of the persons being proselytized. It values the uniqueness of each culture, and attempts to retain what is good or neutral within each culture, while at the same time seeking to convey the transformative message that is part of any attempt at proselytizing. Religious proselytizing that fails to distinguish between a particular cultural expression of a religion and the religious truths being conveyed is unethical. To impose a particular cultural expression of a religion on another culture is similarly unethical.

14. Results criterion

Results, success in persuasion, or church growth, should be seen as a by-product of ethical proselytizing. A pre-occupation with results, success, or church growth, when proselytizing, is unethical.

15. Golden Rule

Ethical proselytizing operates under the assumption that the other has the right to proselytize as well. It is immoral to assume, or to work towards a monopoly of the proselytizing enterprise.

Appendix 2

Literature Review on the Ethics of Proselytizing and Related Fields

This appendix is meant to guide the scholar wanting to pursue more seriously the topic of the ethics of evangelism/proselytizing or persuasion. Given my approach to referencing, the bibliography is rather large, and hence not that helpful in identifying essential reading. This appendix focuses on important references that will guide the serious reader who might wish to pursue the topic more carefully. It is meant to be both a literature review and a general evaluation of this literature. I start with the broader field of communication ethics, draw attention to some related and more specific fields, and end by treating sources that relate specifically to the ethics of proselytizing.

A. Ethics of Communication

1. General field of communication studies

Proselytizing is a form of communication. Hence the broadest way to look at the ethics of proselytizing is to examine the more general field of the ethics of communication. Indeed, considerable attention has been paid in the last few decades to the ethics of communication. This has not always been so, and, as noted in chapter 3, I trace this neglect to the general suspicion surrounding the very idea of persuasion. Hence, the recurring comment concerning the ethics of communication and persuasion as a field needing attention (see Brembeck and Howell 1967; Wallace 1967). Over a decade later, David Kale says this: "A review of current persuasion textbooks in search of substantive discussions of the ethics of persuasion would be almost futile" (1979, 16). For a book collecting much of this older literature, see an anthology edited by Richard L. Johannesen, *Ethics and Persuasion: Selected Readings* (1967).

Belonging to this same time period are some philosophical works that provide an analytical treatment of persuasion in relation to rationality and freedom (Garver, 1960; Benn 1967).

One exception to this seeming lack of concern about the ethics of communication in this earlier literature is Oliver (1957). See also Martin Buber's contrast between monologue and dialogue, as found in his classic, *I and Thou* (1958), and also in his *Between Man and Man* (1965). Buber's analysis has spawned a sizable literature: for example, Johannesen has developed a code of ethical dialogue based on Buber's work (1971, 376).

For some classic works on rhetoric and persuasion, see Aristotle's, *Rhetoric*, and Rowlan and Womack (1985) for a good summary of Aristotle's position. The title of Richard Weaver's classic, *The Ethics of Rhetoric* (1965) sounds promising, and Weaver's use of the metaphor of love to compare different speaker stances is interesting, but there is in fact little that is helpful in dealing with the rights and wrongs of rhetoric. For an alterative viewpoint on Weaver, which also examines his other writings on rhetoric, see Johannesen (1978).

For a helpful review and a bibliography of the literature from 1915 to 1985, see an essay by Ronald Arnett (1987). The ethics of communication seems to be getting increased attention in communication journals since the 1970's. Stanley Deetz evaluates this more recent literature – "much of the literature is filled with contradictions", and there is further "little unity of opinion" in the literature (1983, 263; cf. Deetz 1990). Henry Johnstone, commenting about his earlier experience as an editor of a journal, *Philosophy and Rhetoric*, admits that one of the themes of many of the manuscripts received by the journal was that of the relationship between rhetoric and ethics. But, after having read these papers, which arrived every three months or so, he was "usually ready to weep. Such unfulfilled promise!" (Johnstone 1981, 305).

Arnett identifies a book by Johannesen as now being "the major work on ethics in Speech Communication" (Arnett 1987, 45). Indeed, this book entitled *Ethics in Human Communication*, is now into its fourth edition (Johannesen 1996). For more recent works providing a good summary of the literature on persuasion, see Littlejohn and Jabusch (1987) and Perloff (1993), though here again only a few pages in each book are devoted to the ethics of persuasion. Foss and Griffin (1995) provide a feminist perspective on rhetoric. Deaver (1990) introduces a continuum of communication, based on "degrees of truth" with parallel ethical evaluations.

A title of a more recent work, *The Power of Ethical Persuasion* (1993), by a psychiatrist, Tom Rusk, sounds promising. While the book does appeal to the values of respect, understanding, caring, and fairness, as guiding the conduct of sensitive communications, what is being offered here is really just another technique that is more efficient than persuasion by argument. A more recent textbook on persuasion devotes one short paragraph in the introductory chapter to the ethics of persuasion (Seiter and Gass, 2004).

Of special note also are special issues of two journals devoted to the ethics of communication: *Communication* 12(3), 1991; and *Communication Quarterly* 38, #3 (Summer 1990).

I found the literature in this broad field of communications ethics to be disappointing. As one might expect from social scientists, much of the literature involves a systems analysis of the process of communication, and even ethics is treated from a social science perspective. There seems to be a preoccupation with analyzing differing approaches to communication ethics. Arnett thinks the more recent narrative approach holds some promise for advancing the discussion of the ethics of communication (1987). But given that ethical standards in this narrative approach are grounded in community, it is ultimately relativistic, and thus shares the overriding relativistic stance found in the literature on the ethics of communication. For an attempt to overcome this relativism by appealing to Habermas's ideal speech situation and Gadamer's genuine conversation, see Deetz (1983).

2. Ethics of journalism

Clifford Christians, in an essay reviewing fifty years of scholarship in media ethics, suggests that the scientific study of the morality of journalism emerged in the 1920s when journalists set standards for relations between organizations, and between newspapers and their publics (1977). After this brief focus on defining codes of ethics, interest in the ethics of journalism waned for nearly forty years, before there was a revival of interest in the subject in the 1970s. Genevieve McBride describes journalistic culture as having been dominated by the ideals of objectivity and neutrality, and hence its difficulty in dealing with ethics (1989, 9). Johannesen points to a commercial motive behind this ideal of objective reporting, namely, "the need to serve politically heterogeneous audiences without alienating any significant segment of the audience" (1996, 140).

For a recent challenge to this prevailing ideal based on new developments in epistemology and the philosophy of science, and a proposal to move forward by adopting a theory of pragmatic objectivity in journalism, see Ward (2004). In 2005, Stephen Ward launched a program devoted to encouraging international media values, sponsored by the Department of Journalism, University of British Columbia. The program is called "Journalism Ethics for the Global Citizen", and is now located at the University of Wisconsin-Madison where Ward is the Director of the Centre for Journalism Ethics. The website continues to be linked to UBC: www.journalismethics.ca. See also the very recent publications of Ward (2010), and Ward and Wasserman (2010), which I was unable to consult for the present work.

Aside from these more recent developments, and insofar as objectivity and neutrality still remain the prevailing ideals in an ethics of journalism, this field can be of little help in dealing with the ethics of proselytizing.

3. Ethics of public relations

McBride reviews the evolution of thinking in the field of public relations, which over time has tried to distance itself from its "putative parent profession" of journalism (1989, 6). Now there seems to be more willingness to be honest about the persuasive purpose of PR, some writers even describing the purpose of PR as propaganda. McBride, however, feels the development of a unique ethics of PR has been "stunted by a dysfunctional inheritance" (16). She quotes other writers who point to an absence of ethical guidelines in PR, and to the dominance of subjectivism and relativism among practitioners, some scholars even suggesting that writings on the subject range "from scarce to nonexistent" (8, 6).

Thomas Bivens, in a review article of texts used in university public relations programs shows that very little attention is paid to the ethics of public relations, and the little that exists is more anecdotal in nature, with little done by way of providing a conceptual framework for the treatment of this all-important topic (1989). More generally, Bivens suggests "there is a definite dearth of books on the subject of public relations ethics", although he does point to some emerging improvement in this area (47, 50). An entire issue of the journal, *Public Relations Review*, was devoted to the ethics of PR, and I have in fact drawn on some articles from this issue in chapter 8 (see Barney and Black 1994).

The Public Relations Society of America developed a new code of ethics in 2000, acknowledging, for the first time, *advocacy* as one of the core values of public relations. The code calls on professionals in PR to be responsible advocates, though the code does not define the theoretical or practical aspects of "responsible advocacy". A recent book edited by Fitzpatrick and Bronstein (2006) attempts to address this need by examining the ethical challenges in various domains of public relations advocacy.

4. Propaganda

Though the fields of PR and propaganda are interrelated, propaganda has become a separate field of study. Propaganda, according to one recent study, involves "the organized attempt through communication to affect belief or action or inculcate attitudes in a large audience in ways that circumvent or suppress an individual's adequately informed, rational, reflective judgment" (Marlin 2002, 22). Jacques Ellul, in his classic study of propaganda, gives a similar definition, though he focuses on psychological manipulation as the means to influence the masses (1969, 61).

Given its assumed manipulative nature, it would seem that there cannot be an ethical approach to propaganda. Further, it is primarily sociologists who have been studying the subject, and hence treatments of propaganda tend to be mainly descriptive in nature. Ellul barely touches on the ethical question when discussing the inevitability of the use of propaganda. Even democracies must use propaganda, Ellul argues, and then this advice – we need to democratize propaganda, to ensure a free interplay of various propagandas in order to avoid totalitarianism (1969, 232–36).

Another classic study written by Robert Merton in 1946 exposes the inherent tension between technique and morality in propaganda. A focus on the effectiveness of techniques of persuasion will of necessity conflict with morality because technique "expresses a manipulative attitude towards man and society" (cited in a reprint of part of the original study, "Mass Persuasion: A Technical Problem and a Moral Dilemma", found in an anthology edited by Robert Jackall (1995, 270)). Of note, the index of this anthology contains no subject heading, "ethics of propaganda".

A book with the suggestive title, *Age of Propaganda: The Everyday Use and Abuse of Persuasion*, concludes with a short section devoted to the subject of ethics (Pratkanis and Aronson 1992, 258–65). But this section deals very generally with the problem of evaluating means and ends, provides an analysis of some complex dilemmas in persuasion, and concludes with a suggestion that the current tendency to resort to simplistic persuasive techniques has dire consequences for democracy. There is only an occasional hint at making a distinction between ethical and unethical persuasion.

I was intrigued by the title of a more recent work by Randal Marlin, a philosopher. However, even though he has given his work the suggestive title *Propaganda and the Ethics of Persuasion*, his two chapters devoted to ethics *per se* do little by way of providing an analysis of criteria to distinguish between ethical and unethical forms of persuasion (Marlin 2002, chs. 4 and 5). These chapters are devoted to analyses of ethical theory and lying, examples, case studies, and a review of some works dealing generally with the ethics of persuasion.

Overall, the literature on propaganda is of little help in developing an ethics of proselytizing.

B. Marketing ethics

1. Advertising

The field of advertising is surely relevant to the ethics of proselytizing. As I point out in chapter 1, it can be argued that commercial advertising is not only trying to influence beliefs and behavior, but also a sense of identity and belonging. As such, the essential features of advertising are similar to the essential features of proselytizing which attempts to bring about religious conversion.

However, even though there is the occasional treatment of the ethics of advertising in the literature, many are hardly recognizable as ethical treatments of the subject. Perhaps we should not be too surprised about this. Once one accepts the basic premises of a market-driven economy, it is very difficult to introduce ethical constraints on advertising. Instead, efficiency is the norm. Hence, the dearth of materials seriously attempting to develop criteria to distinguish between ethical and unethical advertising.

Michael Phillips, in a more recent book, *Ethics and Manipulation in Advertising: Answering a Flawed Indictment* (1997), holds some promise in moving beyond merely utilitarian considerations, to applying Kantian ethics, virtue ethics, and the principle of autonomy to an ethical assessment of advertising. Unfortunately, his central argument is that advertising simply does not work in stimulating the propensity to consume, or in dictating the brand and product choices that consumers make. Hence, Phillips argues, most of the ethical arguments against advertising break down. There is, of course, another underlying theme behind his argument – he is strongly opposed to government controls in the area of business. A similar assumption underlies Jerry Kirkpatrick's treatment of consumer advertising (1994). Sadly one cannot expect too much help in developing criteria for ethical advertising in works so dismissive in tone.

The Journal of Advertising devoted a special issue on the topic, "Ethics in Advertising" (September, 1994). Two of the articles in this issue, survey the research done on advertising ethics, both concluding this topic is receiving a good deal of attention in advertising and marketing journals and texts (Hyman et. al., 1994; Zinkhan, 1994). However, these surveys and the conclusion reached are quite misleading because the orientation of the articles surveyed is primarily on social science research, including interviews at malls, surveys of consumers, surveys of experts, and a careful search of a computer database. Zinkan identifies another writer, who in a survey of 20 volumes of the *Journal of Advertising*, found only 5 articles of the 473 articles contained in these volumes that focused specifically on "Ethical Issues". Patrick Murphy, in a more recent assessment of the current status of corporate advertising ethics, points to "the lack of attention to advertising in ethics statements, as well as the generally low status of ethics in advertising" (1998, 318).

There are, however, some exceptions to this overall negative assessment of the literature on the ethics of advertising. For some positive contributions in this field, see Sandage and Fryburger (1967), Leiser (1978), and Pontifical Council (1997). For a careful critique of the Pontifical Council's booklet, *Ethics in Advertising*, see Brenkert (1998).

2. Sales

While advertising attempts to persuade someone to buy something indirectly, salespersons attempt to do this directly, and so the field of selling would seem to be even more closely related to proselytizing. However, here we encounter the same sort of weaknesses I have already identified in the field of advertising. For example, a book by Tom Lambert entitled, *The Power of Influence: Intensive Influencing Skills at Work* (1996), includes a chapter with the promising heading, "Ethical Sales Skills for Everyone" (ch. 3). Sadly, there is little to be found about ethics in this chapter, but a lot of practical advice on skills in selling. The same must be said, about a recent book with a seemingly religious title, *The Sales Bible* (2003), by Jeffrey Gitomer, a global authority on sales and customer service who leads more than 150 training programs and sales meetings annually. I hope this book doesn't get into the hands of religious proselytizers!

C. Ethics of teaching and education

Education is another domain where ethical questions arise with regard to teachers influencing students. In fact many attempts have been made to deal with this question in terms of making a distinction between indoctrination and a proper liberal education. I have reviewed this literature in my book entitled, *Teaching for Commitment: Liberal Education, Indoctrination, and Christian Nurture* (1993). In this work I argue that past attempts to make the distinction between ethical liberal education and unethical indoctrination are not very successful. Discussions of liberal education are also bedeviled with assumptions of neutrality. In this same work I try to provide a new paradigm of liberal education and also a more defensible and refined concept of indoctrination. These revised notions should then enable us to distinguish between ethical and unethical teaching. What I am attempting in the present work is to apply some of the insights from my previous work to the topic of proselytizing.

D. Ethics of Proselytizing

1. Missions

Proselytizing is one aspect of missionary activity. So one way to deal with the ethics of proselytizing would be to examine the broader topic of the ethics of missions. In chapter 4, I focus on this broader topic, but primarily in terms of answering the charge that mission activity is inherently immoral because it involves religious colonialism and cultural genocide. Lewis, in his book entitled, simply, *The Missionaries* (1988), implicates missionaries in all the evils of Western colonialism. I examine these charges as made by Inga Clendinnen (1987) in relation to the sixteenth century Spanish exploration and conquest of the Yucatan. For painful stories of European mission activity to the North

American Indians, see Cal (1997), Furniss (1995), Fournier and Crey (1997), and Glancy (2005).

Luis Rivera, in his book entitled, *A Violent Evangelism: The Political and Religious Conquest of the Americas* (1992), focuses on the theological discourse used to justify this violent evangelism. But Rivera also points out that within the sixteenth century Spanish empire, there were forceful theological critics of the coerced Christianization of the Americas (see also Cal 1997). Similarly, Kenelm Burridge, in an anthropological study of Christian missionary endeavors, reminds us that missionaries also stood "in the way" of exploiting the natives (1991). In chapter 4, I draw on Philip Sampson's careful analysis of charges and counter-charges concerning the Christian missionaries in relation to colonialism (2001, ch. 4).

The literature on Christian missions does not, I believe, pay enough attention to the ethics of missionary activity. Jongeneel, in his two volume bibliographical encyclopedia on the philosophy, science and theology of mission, concurs with my assessment, suggesting most philosophers of religion have neglected the study of mission as an item of philosophical scrutiny (1995/97). Another confirmation of this assessment is found in two review articles appearing in the *International Bulletin of Missionary Research*. The first, entitled, "Doctoral Dissertations on Missions: Ten-year Update, 1982–1991", is by W.A. Smalley (17.3 [1993]:97–125). The second, covering the years from 1992–2001, is written by S.H. Skreslet (27.3 [2003]:98–133). In these two reviews, only 21 entries were found under the subject heading "Ethics", but nearly all of these had to do with social ethics and the ethics of persons or tribes, with one possible exception, a Ph.D. dissertation at Duke University on "Gospel and Mission in Paul's Ethics".

There are a few exceptions to this neglect of the treatment of ethics in mission. For example, a book by Alan Sell includes a chapter on the integrity of mission (1990, ch. 5). See also Lawrence Uzzell's, "Guidelines for American Missionaries in Russia" (1999).

2. Proselytizing as sheep stealing

A very special use of the term proselytizing grows out of Christian ecumenical discussions. Here proselytizing is understood in the narrow sense of one branch of the Christian church seeking converts in another branch – what is often referred to as sheep stealing. For some treatments of proselytizing in the narrow sense that begin to touch on ethical questions, see Aagaard (1998) for a report on the Tantur Conference on Religious Freedom and Proselytism held in Israel in 1998. See also Central Committee of the WCC (1997), Cooney (1996), Guroian (1999), Haughey (1998), Hill (1997), Horner (1981), Joint Working Group (1996), Kärkkäinen (2000), Kerr (1996; 1999), Nicastro (1994), Robeck (1996), and Stalnaker (2002). As I point out in chapter 1, these discussions tend to involve a confusing mix of theological and ethical considerations. Given the interplay between theological and ethical considerations, these discussions are not that helpful for the purposes of this book.

The World Evangelical Alliance joined with the World Council of Churches and the Roman Catholic Pontifical Council for Inter-religious Dialogue, in a consultation entitled, "Towards an Ethical Approach to Conversion – Christian Witness in a Multi-religious World", held in Toulouse, France, Aug. 9–12, 2007. This was the second of three consultations whose aim is to produce a code of conduct on missionary and evangelism efforts, especially those aimed at other Christians. At the time of writing, I was unable to get any information on the third of these consultations to have been held in 2008. The aim was to approve a code by 2010. Hans Ucko, a Swedish theologian who heads the WCC program for inter-religious dialogue has written some of his personal reflections on this topic in an article entitled, "Towards an Ethical Code of Conduct for Religious Conversions", http://www.oikoumene.org/en/programmes/interreligiousdialogue/current-dialogue/no-50 (Accessed July 1, 2009).

3. Jewish/Christian dialogue

Discussions on the ethics of proselytizing can also be found in a number of conferences and books devoted to Jewish/Christian relations and the particularly contentious issue of evangelical Christian mission to Jews. For some treatments of Jewish/Christian dialogue that touch on ethical questions, see Cohen/Croner (1982), Croner/Kleniche (1979), and Tanenbaum/Wilson/Rudin (1978; 1984). The concerns here are, however, again mainly theological in nature, and thus not that useful for my purposes. An important article by David Novak raises ethical concerns about proselytizing, which grow out of "the aversion most Jews have to Christian efforts to proselytize them" (1999, 43). However, the discussion of the ethics of proselytizing in this article is very brief, as most of the article is descriptive and theological in nature – trying to explicate the Jewish attitude to proselytizing.

4. Cults and New Religious Movements (NRMs)

The extensive literature surrounding the so-called cults, or the more recent preferred term, NRMs, is obviously relevant to the topic of religious proselytizing. For some classic sociological and legal critiques of cults, and the brainwashing that is often linked to the cults, see Conway and Siegelman (1978), Delgado (1977; 1980), Lifton (1961), Lofland (1977) and Schein (1961). For some more recent books and articles that are critical of the cults, see Galanter (1989), Hassan (1988), Katchen (1992), Lalich (2004), Singer (1995), Tobias and Lalich (1994), and West (1990).

These standard critical treatments of the cults, which tend to associate the cults with brainwashing and mind control, have more recently come under increasing critical scrutiny by scholars. Indeed, as Michael Langone observes, during the 1980's scholars and professionals who studied cults and new religious movements divided into two camps, commonly labeled pro-cultists and anti-cultists (Langone 2000). For literature critical of the anti-cultists, see Barker (1984), Bromley/Richardson/Shupe (1981), Bromley and Richardson (1983), Dawson (1998), Robbins (1984; 1985), Robbins and Anthony (1982), Shupe and Bromley (1990), Wilson (1990) and Young/Griffith (1992).

Langone maintains that this polarization between academics in sociology and religious studies, who tend to be more sympathetic with the cults, and those more critical of the cults, who are in the main lay activists and mental health workers, has been diminishing in recent years. For example, Eileen Barker, in a presidential address given to the Society for the Scientific Study of Religion in 1995, suggested both camps have been guilty of unbalanced selectivity in reporting on the cults (Langone 2000, 85). Langone makes a plea for dialogue between these two camps, and in May of 2000, the American Family Foundation (now called the International Cultic Studies Association) of which he is Executive Director, hosted a meeting of critics and sympathizers who spent a day in candid discussions. Langone's article is in fact a follow-up on this discussion and includes a proposal concerning some acknowledgements he feels both sides can and should make (see also Zablocki and Robbins, 2001). Clearly, scholarly opinion still remains divided on identifying exactly what is objectionable in the cults (Young and Griffith 1992, 96). This is one reason why I have avoided getting too preoccupied with this cult literature and with this dispute concerning the cults.

There are other reasons for doing so. Much of the literature on the cults is not that useful for my purposes as it lacks the conceptual precision philosophers strive for, and that I am trying to achieve in this book. A question can also be raised as to whether sociologists, if they are doing sociology, are really qualified to do ethical evaluation. Sociology is, after all *de*scriptive in nature, not *pre*scriptive. Eileen Barker, herself a sociologist of religion, in her practical introduction to NRMs, is very explicit in recognizing the limits of the social sciences. "Social science cannot do everything. Like any other descriptive science, it is limited: it cannot decide between theological or ideological claims; it cannot pronounce moral judgments, telling people what is right or wrong; nor can it tell them what to do" (Barker 1989, xi). For all these reasons, I have found the literature on the cults not very helpful in dealing with the ethics of proselytizing.

Finally, as I point out in chapter 1, I have tried to avoid getting too preoccupied with the literature on the cults because I don't want to give the impression that unethical proselytizing is limited to the cults. There is a danger of making cults a scapegoat thereby hindering critical scrutiny of proselytizing in other so-called "benign religious groups" (West 1990, 126), or even more generally in other societal endeavors. My aim has been to examine religious proselytizing wherever it occurs, and to provide criteria to distinguish between ethical and unethical proselytizing that can be broadly applied.

5. *Christians and evangelicals on the ethics of proselytizing*

The comments and literature review of this section are focused primarily on evangelical Christianity, because this branch of Christianity defines itself in terms of a deep concern for evangelism or proselytizing. Sadly, evangelical Christians, have paid little attention to the topic of the ethics of proselytizing or evangelism. Other writers concur with this assessment. For example, Kendall Don Geis, in a report on a project dealing with the ethics of evangelism, submitted as part of a D.Min. degree at Hartford Seminary in New York (1993), introduces his study thus: "There is a void in the contemporary literature and practice pertaining to the addressing of this issue of ethics and evangelism." Adeyemo/Samuel/Sider similarly maintain that ethical assessments of evangelistic activity have been rare among evangelicals (1991, 1). Of the existing material, ethicist Stanley Hauerwas has this to say: "most of the work that is done in this area is terrible" (Geis 1993, 4). I believe this assessment is somewhat of an overstatement.

Some good initial work has been done on developing a code of ethics for evangelism. In chapter 9, I refer to two significant attempts:

one developed by the Christian-Muslim Forum in the UK (see http://www.christianmuslimforum.org/downloads/Ethical_Guideli nes_for_Witness_v9.pdf) (accessed Feb. 17, 2010), and the other developed by a team of evangelicals led by InterVarsity Christian Fellowship, reported in *Cultic Studies Journal*, 2.2 (1985): 299–305, and further revised and found in Rudin (1996, 67–72).

Some significant work has also been done by "The Oslo Coalition on Freedom of Religion or Belief", since its inception in 2006. After a series of seminars and conferences held with representatives from many countries and different religions, the Coalition released a statement in December 2009, entitled, "Missionary Activities and Human Rights: Recommended Ground Rules for Missionary Activities." It is hoped that this statement will stimulate further discussions, and also serve as a template for missionary organizations to produce their own codes of conduct. See http://www.oslocoalition.org/mhr.php (accessed Feb. 17, 2010).

For another statement on "The Issue of Proselytizing", see the website of the International Student Ministry of the Lutheran church: http://www.isminc.org/LinkClick.aspx?link=ContentRoot%2fDocs% 2fresources%2fproselytizing.pdf&tabid=631&mid=1585   (accessed Sept. 22, 2009).

Other recent projects in the same vein include Fuller Seminary's intent to produce an interfaith code of ethics. See http://www.chris- tianitytoday.com/ct/article?id=10547 (posted Jan. 12, 2003) (accessed July 10, 2009). See also comments in Appendix 2, #D2, on joint efforts of the World Evangelical Alliance and World Council of Churches in producing an ethical code for religious conversions, and comments in #E on the work of the International Religious Liberty Associations.

Beyond the development of ethical codes of evangelism, there are also some essays dealing with the subject. Greenway identifies some papers given at the Lausanne Consultations in 1985 and 1987 dealing with the question of ethics for missionaries and evangelists (1993, 153, 154). See also Beach (1999), Billy Graham (1984, 60–63), Greenway (1993), Griffin (1976, ch. 3), Griffiths and Elshtain (2002), Kelley (1992), Kraft (1991), Kusum- alayam (2004), Noyce (1979), Uzzell (1999), and Veenstra and Kooi (1979).

There are also a few essays focusing specifically on the problem of inducements to convert via material aid, and the exploiting of material, medical, and emotional needs. See DiSilvestro (2007), Jayasinghe (2007), Nichols (1994), Sallady (2006), Sherr/Singletary/Rogers (2009), Sider and Unruh (2001), Thacker (2009), and Wood (1999).

Although some of these evangelical treatments of the ethics of evangelism make some good contributions to the subject, most are rather brief. And some are quite disappointing. For example, I found the work of Geis (1993) weak, consisting mainly of a report on discussions of a Resource Team he had assembled in his Baptist church. Similarly, a recent book by Michael Zigarelli, with the promising subtitle, "15 Biblical Principles of Persuasion", is nothing more than a guidebook on "shrewd" and "effective" market-based persuasion (2008, 47, 95). Zigarelli makes the astounding claim that these principles are value-neutral (2, 42). He is forced, on several occasions, to admit that some of his shrewd principles raise some ethical concerns, but as long as the motivations are pure, the goal is sound, and Jesus used them, then they are still acceptable, according to Zigarelli (118, 134, 142). Other treatments I found disappointing include Fortner (1977) and Häring (1990, 25–41).

On the other hand, Pritchard (1996) makes an incisive careful ethical critique of the adoption of marketplace values at the influential Willow Creek Community Church in Chicago. For other more general critiques of the marketing of religion in a commercial and consumerist age, see Einstein (2007) and Stevenson (2007).

6. The ethics of proselytizing in philosophical and religious studies literature

I have uncovered only a handful of articles or chapters of books dealing with the ethics of proselytizing specifically, and in a rigorously philosophical manner. Jay Newman wrote a first essay on the topic entitled, "The Ethics of Proselytizing", in 1976. A revised version of part of this paper was incorporated in a chapter of his book, *Foundations of Religious Tolerance* (Newman 1982, ch. 5). I wrote a response to this later paper of Newman's (Thiessen 1985). I have also written a response to Novak's (1999) analysis of proselytizing in Judaism (Thiessen 2003). Margaret Battin provides another careful critique of proselytizing in her study of ethical issues arising from the practices of organized religion (1990). This has prompted a careful response and defence of proselytizing by H.E. Baber (2000). Antonio Pop Cal critiques proselytizing from an Indigenous perspective (1997), while Pelkmans (2009) exposes the lack of transparency in recent proselytizing efforts in Kyrgyzstan.

Two other noteworthy essays are available on the web. Jonathan Miles presented a paper at the Lilly Fellows Conference on Christianity and Human Rights, Nov. 11–14, 2004 – "Human Rights and the Ethics of Christian Proselytizing in Foreign Contexts". This paper is available

at: www4.samford.edu/lilly/humanrights/papers/Miles_Human.pdf
(accessed Sept. 22, 2009). Rajiv Malhotra presented a paper, "The Ethics
of Proselytizing", at the Cornell University Conference on Human
Rights and Religion, Nov. 8, 2000. This paper is available at: www.infin-
ityfoundation.com/ECITproselytizing.htm (accessed Sept. 22, 2009).

Special note should be taken of "The Religion and Human Rights
Series", undertaken by the Law and Religion Program at Emory
University, and Orbis Books. This series includes an anthology edited
by John Witte and Richard Martin, entitled *Sharing the Book: Religious
Perspectives on the Rights and Wrongs of Proselytism* (1999). This anthology includes descriptive and theological essays on the three major
religions, Islam, Judaism and Christianity, as well as some modern
mission movements. These essays occasionally touch on ethical questions. This series also includes studies of proselytizing in various
countries or continents – Russia, Africa, and Latin America. For the
anthology on Russia, see Witte and Bourdeaux (1999). Again, while
mainly descriptive in nature, there are occasional forays into ethical
considerations.

My review of the religious studies literature on the cults in section
#D4 could also have been placed in this section, but I felt it merited a
separate classification. A rich collection of essays on proselytizing is
found in a special edition of the *Cultic Studies Journal*, entitled, "Cults,
Evangelicals, and the Ethics of Social Influence", edited by Michael D.
Langone (Vol. 2, #2, 1985). Although more descriptive and sociological
in orientation, there is still much here that is helpful in dealing with the
ethics of proselytizing, including a code of ethics developed by
InterVarsity Christian Fellowship, a set of guidelines developed by the
European Parliament in 1985, as well as Langone's own essay (1985,
371–88; cf. Langone 1989). Another essay more sociological and theological in outlook, but nonetheless helpful in providing a defence of
proselytizing is an essay by Rodney Sawatsky (1986).

For essays specifically attempting to develop criteria to distinguish
between ethical and unethical proselytizing (though not necessarily
philosophical in orientation), see Jindal (1993), Kraft (1991), Lewis
(1985), Mecklenburger, who gives a Jewish perspective (1986), and
Uzzell (1999). Some of the essays listed above in section #D5 also deal
with this question. See also the codes of ethical communication as
found in Johannesen (1996 ch. 10; 287–88).

There is finally a Dutch thesis written by Van der Meiden (1972),
which compares the relation between ethics, and commercial, political,
and religious propaganda/evangelism. I'm not sure how helpful this

thesis is, as the English summary would suggest that this work at best comes up with some broad ethical principles derived in a rather eclectic fashion, trying to marry theology and the findings of the social sciences.

E. Law, human rights, and proselytizing

Increasing attention is being paid to the question of human rights and law in relation to religion and religious proselytizing. This literature does at times also touch on the ethics of religious proselytizing. See, for example, Hunter and Price (2001), Keiner (2007), Lerner (1998), van der Vyver (1998), and Witte and van der Vyver (1996).

A major study of proselytism and religious freedom was undertaken by the International Religious Liberty Association. A series of conferences sponsored by the IRLA, beginning in 1999, led to the issuing of a document entitled, "Guiding Principles for the Responsible Dissemination of Religion or Belief", *FIDES ET LIBERTAS: The Journal of the International Religious Liberty Association* (2000, 95–98). Some articles in the 1999, 2000, and 2001 issues of this journal deal with the ethics of proselytizing, though the focus tends to be on the narrow definition of proselytizing. See especially Beach (1999).

I have already mentioned "The Religion and Human Rights Series", in the previous section. Natan Lerner has written a book in this series entitled, *Religion, Beliefs and International Human Rights* (2002).

For books and articles dealing with legal perspectives on proselytizing from an international perspective, see An-Na'im (1999), Drinan (2004), Sabater (2000), Stahnke (1999), and Witte (2001). For a treatment of the legal dimensions of proselytizing in the US, see Garnett (2005), Hunter and Price (2001), Sheffer (1999), Smolin (2001), and Witte (2000).

Bibliography

Aagaard, A.M. (1998). "Proselytism and Privacy: Some Reflections on the Tantur Conference on Religious Freedom". *The Ecumenical Review*, 50(4): 464–71.

Abraham, W.J. (1985). *An Introduction to the Philosophy of Religion*. Englewood Cliffs, NJ: Prentice-Hall.

Abraham, W.J. (1989). *The Logic of Evangelism*. London: Hodder & Stoughton.

Adeyemo, T. and V. Samuel and R. Sider. (1991). "Evangelistic Ethics in the Context of Religious Pluralism". *Transformation: An International Dialogue on Evangelical Social Ethics* 8(1): 1–5.

Anderson, G.H. (1996). "To Evangelize or Proselytize?" *International Bulletin of Missionary Research* 20(1): 1.

An-Na'im, A.A. (1990a). "Quar'an, Shari'a and Human Rights: Foundations, Deficiencies and Prospects". In H. Küng and J. Moltmann (eds.), *The Ethics of World Religions and Human Rights*. London: SCM Press: 61–69.

An-Na'im, A.A. (1990b). *Towards an Islamic Reformation: Civil Liberties, Human Rights and International Law*. Syracuse, N.Y.: Syracuse University Press.

An-Na'im, A.A. (ed.) (1999). *Proselytization and Communal Self-Determination in Africa*. MaryKnoll, NY: Orbis Books.

Aquinas, T. (1945). *Basic Writings of St. Thomas Aquinas*, trans. Anton C. Pegis. New York: Random House.

Aristotle (1963). *Works*. Translated into English under the Editorship of W.D. Ross. Oxford: Clarendon Press.

Arnett, R. (1987). "The Status of Communication Ethics Scholarship in Speech Communication Journals from 1915 to 1985". *Central States Speech Journal* 38(1): 44–61.

Arnold, T.W. (1913). *The Preaching of Islam: A History of the Propagation of the Muslim Faith*, 2nd ed. London: Constable. (Original work published 1896)

Aronson, E. (1992). "The Return of the Repressed: Dissonance Theory makes a Comeback". *Psychological Inquiry* 3(4): 303–11.

Arzt, D.E. (1999). "Jihad for Hearts and Minds". In J. Witte and R. Martin (eds.), *Sharing the Book: Religious Perspectives on the Rights and Wrongs of Proselytism*. Maryknoll, NY: Orbis Books: 79–94.

Astley, J. (1994). *The Philosophy of Christian Religious Education*. Birmingham, Alabama: Religious Education Press.

Baber, H.E. (2000). "In Defence of Proselytizing". *Religious Studies* 36(3): 333–44.

Baier, A. (1980). "Secular Faith". *The Canadian Journal of Philosophy* 10: 131–48.

Barker, E. (1984). *The Making of a Moonie: Choice or Brainwashing?* Oxford: Basil Blackwell.

Barney, R.D. and J. Black. (1994). "Ethics and Professional Persuasive Communications". *Public Relations Review* 20(3): 233–48.

Battin, M.P. (1990). *Ethics in the Sanctuary: Examining the Practices of Organized Religion*. New Haven, CT: Yale University Press.

Bayle, P. (2005). *A Philosophical Commentary on These Words of the Gospel, Luke 14:23,"Compel Them to Come In, That My House May Be Full"*. Indianapolis, IN: Liberty Fund.

Beach, B.B. (1999). "Evangelism and Proselytism: A Religious Liberty and Ecumenical Challenge". *FIDES ET LIBERTAS: The Journal of the International Religious Liberty Association*. 64–72.

Benn, S.I. (1967). "Freedom and Persuasion". *The Australasian Journal of Philosophy* 45: 256–75.

Berger, P.L. (1967). *The Sacred Canopy: Elements of a Sociological Theory of Religion*. New York: Doubleday.

Berger, P.L (1979). "Converting the Gentiles?" *Commentary*. May: 35–39.

Berger, P.L and T. Luckmann. (1967). *The Social Construction of Reality: A Treatise in the Sociology of Knowledge*. New York: Doubleday.

Bird, M. (2004). "The Case of the Proselytizing Pharisees? Matthew 23:15". *Journal for the Study of the Historical Jesus* 2(2): 117–37.

Bivins, T.H. (1989). "Are Public Relations Texts Covering Ethics Adequately?" *Journal of Mass Media Ethics*. 4(1): 39–52.

Bok, S. (1978). *Lying: Moral Choice in Public and Private Life*. New York: Pantheon Books.

Bonhoefer, D. (1954). *Ethics*. Tr. Eberhard Bethge. New York: Macmillan.

Boothby L. (1999). "The Challenge of Proselytism: An American Perspective". *FIDES ET LIBERTAS: The Journal of the International Religious Liberty Association* 46–49.

Brembeck, W.L. and W.S. Howell. (1967). "The Ethics of Persuasion". In R.L. Johannesen (ed.), *Ethics and Persuasion: Selected Readings.* New York: Random House: 3–38.

Brenkert, G.G. (1998). "Ethics in Advertising: The Good, the Bad, and the Church". *Journal of Public Policy and Marketing.* 17(2): 325–31.

Bromley, D.G. and J.T. Richardson. (1983). *The Brainwashing/ Deprogramming Controversy: Sociological, Psychological, Legal and Historical Perspectives.* New York: Edwin Mellen.

Bromley, D.G. and J.T. Richardson and A. Shupe. (1981). *Strange Gods: The Great American Cult Scare.* Boston, MA: Beacon Press.

Broyde, M. (1999). "Proselytism and Jewish Law". In J. Witte and R. Martin (eds.), *Sharing the Book: Religious Perspectives on the Rights and Wrongs of Proselytism.* Maryknoll, NY: Orbis Books: 45–60.

Buber, M. (1958). *I and Thou.* Trans. Ronald Gregor Smith, 2nd ed. New York: Scribner.

Buber, M. (1965). *Between Man and Man.* Trans. Ronald Gregor Smith. New York: Scribner.

Budziszewski, J. (2003). *What We Can't Not Know: A Guide.* Dallas, TX: Spence.

Budziszewski, J. (2006). *Written on the Heart.* Downers Grove, IL: InterVarsity Press.

Burridge, K. (1991). *In the Way: A Study of Christian Missionary Endeavour.* Vancouver: UBC Press.

Cal, A.P. (1997). "The Old Face of the New Evangelization". In G. Cook (ed.), *Cross Currents in Indigenous Spirituality: Interface of Maya, Catholic and Protestant Worldview.* Leiden, Netherlands: E.J. Brill: ch. 13, 217–23.

Carter, S.L. (1993). *The Culture of Disbelief: How American Law and Politics Trivialize Religious Devotion.* New York: Doubleday.

Central Committee of the World Council of Churches. (1997). "Towards Common Witness: A Call to Adopt Responsible Relationships in Mission and to Renounce Proselytism". *International Review of Mission* 86(343): 463–73.

Charles, J.D. (2006). "Protestants and Natural Law". *First Things* 168: 33–38.

Chomsky, N. (1988). *Manufacturing Consent: The Political Economy of the Mass Media.* New York: Pantheon Books.

Christians, C.G. (1977). "Fifty Years of Scholarship in Media Ethics".

Journal of Communication 27: 19–29.

Cialdini, R.B. (1988). *Influence: Science and Practice*. 2nd ed. New York: HarperCollins.

Clendinnen, I. (1987). *Ambivalent Conquests: Maya and Spaniard in Yucatan, 1517–1570*. Cambridge: Cambridge University Press.

Code, L. (1987). *Epistemic Responsibility*. Hanover and London: University Press of New England.

Cohen, M.A. and H. Croner. (eds.) (1982). *Christian Mission-Jewish Mission*. New York: Paulist Press.

Conway, F. and J. Siegelman. (1978). *Snapping: America's Epidemic of Sudden Personality Change*. Philadelphia and New York: J.B. Lippencott.

Conway, F. and J. Siegelman (1982). *Holy Terror: The Fundamentalist War on America's Freedom in Religion: Politics and Our Private Lives*. New York: Doubleday.

Cooney, M. (1996). "Towards Common Witness: A Call to Adopt Responsible Relationships in Mission and to Avoid Proselytism". *International Review of Mission* 85(337): 283–89.

Coughlin, J.J. (2003). "Pope John Paul II and the Dignity of the Human Being". *Harvard Journal of Law and Public Policy* 27(1): 65–79.

Coward, H. (1989). "Can Religions Live Together in Today's World? Intolerance and Tolerance in Religious Pluralism". In M.D. Bryant (ed.), *Pluralism, Tolerance and Dialogue: Six Studies*. Waterloo: University of Waterloo Press: 1–18.

Coward, H. (2000). *Pluralism in the World Religions: A Short Introduction*. Oxford: Oneworld.

Cox, H. (1999). "The Market as God". *The Atlantic Monthly March* 283(3): 18–23.

Cromartie, M. (ed.) (1997). *A Preserving Grace: Protestants, Catholics, and Natural Law*. Grand Rapids, MI: Eerdmans.

Croner, H. and L. Klenicki (eds.) (1979). *Issues in the Jewish-Christian Dialogue: Jewish Perspectives on Covenant, Mission and Witness*. New York: Paulist Press.

Cuddihy, J.M. (1978). *No Offense: Civil Religion and Protestant Taste*. New York: The Seabury Press.

Daves, H.W.C. (1972). *Charlemagne (Charles the Great): The Hero of Two Nations*. Freeport, NY: Books for Libraries Press. (Original work published 1899)

Dawson, L. (1998). *Comprehending Cults: the Sociology of New Religious Movements*. Oxford University Press.

Deaver, F. (1990). "On Defining Truth". *Journal of Mass Media Ethics*

5(3): 168–77.

Deetz, S. (1983). "Keeping the Conversation Going: The Principle of Dialectic Ethics". *Communication* 7: 263–88.

Deetz, S. (1990). "Reclaiming the Subject Matter as a Guide to Mutual Understanding: Effectiveness and Ethics in Interpersonal Interaction". *Communication Quarterly* 38(3): 226–43.

Dein, S. (2001). "What Really Happens When Prophecy Fails: The Case of Lubavitch". *Sociology of Religion* 62(3): 383–401.

Delgado, R. (1977). "Religious Totalism: Gentle and Ungentle Persuasion Under the First Amendment". *Southern California Law Review* 51(1): 1–98.

Delgado, R. (1980). "Limits to proselytizing". *Society* 17(3): 25–33.

Diene, D. (1999). "Proselytism and/or Interreligious Dialogue". *FIDES ET LIBERTAS: The Journal of the International Religious Liberty Association* 28–30.

Digeser, E.D. (2000). *The Making of a Christian Empire: Lactantius and Rome*. Ithaca, NY: Cornell University Press.

DiSilvestro, R. (2007). "What's Wrong with Deliberately Proselytizing Patients?" *The American Journal of Bioethics* 7(7): 22–24.

Donders, J.G. (ed.) (1996). *John Paul II: The Encyclicals in Everyday Language*. Maryknoll, NY: Orbis Books.

Donovan, V.J. (1988). *Christianity Rediscovered*. Maryknoll, NY: Orbis Books.

Drake, H.A. (2000). *Constantine and the Bishops: The Politics of Intolerance*. Baltimore, MD: Johns Hopkins University Press.

Drinin, R.F. (2004). *Can God and Caesar Coexist? Balancing Religious Freedom and International Law*. Yale University Press.

Durant, W. (1950). *The Story of Civilization Vol. 4: The Age of Faith*. New York: Simon and Schuster.

Durham, W.C. (1999). "The Right to Engage in Religious Persuasion: Emerging and Minority Religions and Proselytism". *FIDES ET LIBERTAS: The Journal of the International Religious Liberty Association* 50–57.

Durham, W.C. (2001). "International Human Rights: The Protection of Religious Persuasion". *FIDES ET LIBERTAS: The Journal of the International Religious Liberty Association*: 17–31.

Einstein, M. (2007). *Brands of Faith: Marketing Religion in a Commercial Age*. New York, NY: Routledge.

Ellul, J. (1969). *Propaganda: The Formation of Men's Attitudes*. Tr. Konrad Kellen and Jean Lerner. New York: A.A. Knopf.

Epstein, L.J. (1991). "A Religious Argument for Welcoming Converts". *Judaism* 40(2): 218–24.

Fautre, W. (2000). "Western Europe: Trends in Religious Liberty". In P. Marshall (ed.), *Religious Freedom in the World*. Lanham, MD: Roman and Littlefield: 28–34.

Feldman, L.H. (1993). "Proselytism by Jews in the Third, Fourth and Fifth Centuries". *Journal for the Study of Judaism in the Persian, Hellenistic and Roman Period* 24(1): 1–58.

Feldman, S.M. (1997). *Please Don't Wish Me A Merry Christmas: A Critical History of the Separation of Church and State*. New York and London: New York University Press.

Ferre, F. (1973). "Self-determinism". *American Philosophical Quarterly* 10(3): 165–76.

Festinger, L. (1957). *A Theory of Cognitive Dissonance*. Stanford: Stanford University Press.

Festinger, L., H.W. Riecken and S. Schachter. (1956). *When Prophecy Fails*. New York: Harper and Row.

Fitzpatrick, K. and C. Bronstein. (2006). *Ethics in Public Relations: Responsible Advocacy*. Thousand Oaks, London: Sage Publishers.

Fletcher, J. (2007). "Tasteless as Hell: Community Performance, Distinction, and Countertaste in Hell House". *Theatre Survey* 48: 313–30.

Ford, L. (1966). *The Christian Persuader*. New York: Harper and Row.

Fortner, R.S. (1977). "Persuasion, Christianity and Ethics: A Cultural Perspective". *Christian Scholar's Review* 7(2): 153–64.

Foss, S.K. and C.I. Griffin. (1995). "Beyond Persuasion: A Proposal for an Invitational Rhetoric". *Communication Monographs* 62(March): 2–18.

Fournier, S. and E. Crey. (1997). *Stolen from our Embrace*. Vancouver/Toronto: Douglas and McIntyre.

Freedman, J.L. and D.O. Sears. (1965). "Selective Exposure". In L. Berkowitz (ed.), *Advances in Experimental Social Psychology*, Vol. 2, (58–97). New York: Academic Press.

Furniss, E. (1995). *Victims of Benevolence: The Dark Legacy of the Williams Lake Residential School*. Vancouver: Arsenal Pulp Press. (Original work published 1992)

Gaede, S.D. (1993). *When Tolerance is no Virtue*. Downers Grove, IL: InterVarsity Press.

Gager, J.G. (1988). "Proselytism and Exclusivity in Early Christianity". In M. Marty and F. Greenspahn (eds.), *Pushing the Faith: Proselytism and Civility in a Pluralistic World* (67–77). New York: Crossroads.

Galanter, M. (ed.) (1989). *Cults and New Religious Movements*. Washington, DC: American Psychiatric Association.

Gallup, G.H. and T. Jones. (1992). *The Saints Among Us*. Ridgefield, CT: Morehouse Pub.

Garnett, R.W. (2005). "Changing Minds: Proselytism, Freedom, and the First Amendment". *University of St. Thomas Law Journal* 2(2): 453–74.

Garver, J.N. (1960). "On the Rationality of Persuasion". *Mind* 69(274): 163–74.

Geis, K.D. (1993). "An Ethic for Christian Evangelism in the Marketplace: Developing a Code of Ethics that will Guide the Evangelistic Efforts of Calvary Baptist Church in New York City". Dissertation: D. Min. Hartford Seminary.

Gilligan, C. (1982). *In a Different Voice: Psychological Theory and Women's Development*. Cambridge: Harvard University Press.

Gitomer, J. (2003). *The Sales Bible: The Ultimate Sales Resource*. Hobeken, NJ: John Wiley and Sons.

Glancy, D. (2005). *The Dance Partner*. East Lansing, MI: Michigan State University Press.

Glanzer, P. (1999). "Teaching Christian Ethics in Russian Public Schools: The Testing of Russia's Church-State Boundaries". *Journal of Church and State* 41(2): 285–306.

Glanzer, P. (2002). *The Quest for Russia's Soul: Evangelicals and Moral Education in Post-Communist Russia*. Waco, TX: Baylor University Press.

Glassman, R.B. (1980). "An Evolutionary Hypothesis about Teaching and Proselytizing". *Zygon* 15(2): 133–54.

Gonsalves, M.A. (1985). *Right and Reason: Ethics in Theory and Practice*, 9th ed. Columbus, Ohio: Merrill Pub. Co.

Gooch, P.W. (1987). *Partial Knowledge: Philosophical Studies in Paul*. Notre Dame, IL: University of Notre Dame Press.

Goodall, K. (2007). "Incitement to Religious Hatred: All Talk and No Substance?" *Modern Law Review* 70(1): 89–113.

Goodman, M. (1994). *Mission and Conversion: Proselytizing in the Religious History of the Roman Empire*. New York: Clarendon Press.

Graham, B. (1984). *A Biblical Standard for Evangelists*. Minneapolis. MN: World Wide Publishers.

Greenway, R.S. (1993). "The Ethics of Evangelism". *Calvin Theological Journal* 28: 147–54.

Grice, P. (1989). "Logic and Conversation". In H.P. Grice (ed.), *Studies in the Way of Words*. Cambridge, MA: Harvard University Press: 22–40.

Griffin, E.A. (1976). *The Mind Changers: the Art of Christian Persuasion*. Wheaton, IL: Tyndale House.

Griffiths, P.J. and J.B. Elshtain. (2002). "Proselytzing for Tolerance". *First Things* (November) 127: 30–36.

Grounds, V.C. (1984). "The Problem of Proselytization: An Evangelical Perspective". In M.H. Tanenbaum, M.R. Wilson and A.J. Rudin (eds.), *Evangelicals and Jews in an Age of Pluralism* (199–225). Grand Rapids, MI: Baker Book House.

Gruen, D. (1985). "Prologue: The Evangelicals Set Forth Their Case". *Cultic Studies Journal* 2(2): 301–3.

Guastad, E.S. (1999). *Liberty of Conscience: Roger Williams in America.* Valley Forge, PA: Judson Press.

Guroian, V. (1999). "Evangelism and Mission in the Orthodox Tradition". In J. Witte and R. Martin (eds.), *Sharing the Book: Religious Perspectives on the Rights and Wrongs of Proselytism.* Maryknoll, NY: Orbis Books: 231–44.

Gutmann, A. ed. (1994). *Multiculturalism: Examining the Politics of Recognition.* Princeton, NJ: Princeton University Press.

Haiman, F.S. (1993). *"Speech Acts" and the First Amendment.* Carbondale, IL: Southern Illinois University Press.

Häring, B. (1990). *Evangelization Today.* (Revised edition) New York: Crossroad.

Harmon-Jones, E. and J. Mills (eds.) (1999). *Cognitive Dissonance: Progress on a Pivotal Theory in Social Psychology.* Washington, DC: American Psychological Association.

Hart, T. (1995). *Faith Thinking: The Dynamics of Christian Theology.* London: SPCK.

Hassan, S. (1988). *Combating Cult Mind Control.* Rochester, Vermont: Park Street Press.

Hassan, S. (2000). *Releasing the Bonds: Empowering People to Think for Themselves.* Somerville, MA: Freedom of Mind Press.

Haughey, J.C. (1998). "The Complex Accusation of Sheep-stealing: Proselytism and Ethics". *Journal of Ecumenical Studies* 35 (2): 257–68.

Haworth, L. (1986). *Autonomy: An Essay in Philosophical Psychology and Ethics.* Notre Dame, IL: University of Notre Dame Press.

Heyd, D. (ed.) (1996). *Toleration: An Elusive Virtue.* Princeton, NJ: Princeton University Press.

Hick, J. and P. Knitter. (1987). *The Myth of Christian Uniqueness: Toward a Pluralistic Theology of Religions.* Maryknoll, N.Y.: Orbis.

Hill, K.R. (1997). "Christian Mission, Proselytism and Religious Liberty: A Protestant Appeal for Christian Tolerance and Unity". *Religion, State and Society* 25(4): 307–32.

Hirsch, M. (1998). "Freedom of Proselytism: Reflections on International and Israeli Law". *The Ecumenical Review* 50(4): 441–48.

Hochschild, A. (1998). *King Leopold's Ghost: A Story of Greed, Terror and Heroism in Colonial Africa*. New York: Houghton Mifflan.

Horner, N.A. (1981). "The Problem of Intra-Christian Proselytism". *International Review of Mission* 70: 304–13.

How, W.G. and P. Brumley. (1999). "Human Rights, Evangelism, and Proselytism: A Perspective of Jehovah's Witnesses". In J. Witte and R. Martin (eds.), *Sharing the Book: Religious Perspectives on the Rights and Wrongs of Proselytism*. Maryknoll, NY: Orbis Books: 276–304.

Hunter, H.O. and P.J. Price (2001). "Regulation of Religious Proselytism in the United States". *Brigham Young University Law Review* 357(2): 537–74.

Huntington, S.P. (1996). *The Clash of Civilizations and the Remaking of World Order*. New York: Simon and Schuster.

Hyman M.R. and R. Tansey and J.W. Clark. (1994). "Research on Advertising Ethics: Past, Present, and Future". *Journal of Advertising* 23(3): 5–16.

Interfaith Conference of Metropolitan Washington. (1989). "Statement on Proselytism". *International Review of Mission* 78(310): 224–25.

Jackall, R. (ed.) (1995). *Propaganda*. Washington Square, New York: New York University Press.

Jackson, B. (2007). "Jonathan Edwards Goes to Hell (House): Fear Appeals in American Evangelism". *Rhetoric Review* 26(1): 42–59.

Jaksa, J.A. & M.S. Pritchard. (1994). *Communication Ethics: Methods of Analysis*. Belmont, CA: Wadsworth Publishers.

James, W. (1902). *The Varieties of Religious Experience: A Study in Human Nature*. New York: The Modern Library.

James, W. (1968). *Essays in Pragmatism*. New York: Hafner.

Jansen, S.C. (1988). *Censorship: The Knot that Binds Power and Knowledge*. Oxford University Press.

Jayasinghe, S. (2007). "Faith-based NGOs and Health Care in Poor Countries: A Preliminary Exploration of Ethical Issues". *Journal of Medical Ethics* 33(11): 623–26.

Jensen, J.V. (1992). "Ancient Eastern and Western Religions as Guides for Contemporary Communication Ethics". In J.A. Jaksa (ed.), *Proceedings of the Second National Communication Ethics Conference*, June 11–14. Annandale, VA: Speech Communication Association: 58–67.

Jhally, S. (1990). *The Codes of Advertising: Fetishism and the Political Economy of Meaning in the Consumer Society*. New York: Routledge.

Jindal, B. (1993). "Has Ecumenism Made Evangelism Irrelevant?" *America* 169(3): 8–13.

Johannesen, R.L. (ed.) (1967). *Ethics and Persuasion: Selected Readings.* New York: Random House.

Johannesen, R.L. (1971). "The Emerging Concept of Communication as Dialogue". *The Quarterly Journal of Speech* 57(4): 373–82.

Johannesen, R.L. (1978). "Richard M. Weaver on Standards for Ethical Rhetoric". *Central States Speech Journal* 29(Summer): 127–37.

Johannesen, R.L. (1996). *Ethics in Communication.* 4th ed. Prospect Heights, IL: Waveland Press Inc.

Johnstone, H.W. Jr. (1981). "Towards and Ethics of Rhetoric". *Communication* 6: 305–14.

Joint Working Group between the World Council of Churches and the Roman Catholic Church. (1996). "The Challenge of Proselytism and the Calling to Common Witness". *The Ecumenical Review* 48(2): 212–21.

Jongeneel, J.A.B. (1995/1997). *Philosophy, Science and Theology of Mission in the Nineteenth and Twentieth Centuries: A Missiological Encyclopedia. Part 1: The Philosophy and Science of Mission; Part 2: Missionary Theology.* Frankfurt and New York: Peter Lang.

Juergensmeyer, M. (2000). *Terror in the Mind of God: The Global Rise of Religious Violence.* Berkeley: University of California Press.

Kale, D. (1979). "An Ethic for Interpersonal Communication". *Religious Communication Today.* 2: 16–20.

Kant, I. (1981). *Grounding for the Metaphysics of Morals* Tr. James W.Ellington. Indianapolis, IN: Hackett Publishing Company.

Kärkkäinen, V.M. (2000). "Church Relations: Theological Issues Facing Older and Younger Churches". *The Ecumenical Review* 52(3): 379–90.

Katchen, M.H. (1992). "Brainwashing, Hypnosis, and the Cults". *Australian Journal of Clinical and Experimental Hypnosis* 20(2): 79–88.

Keiner, C. (2007). "Preaching from the State's Podium: What Speech is Proselytizing Prohibited by the Establishment Clause?" *BYU Journal of Public Law* 21(2): 83–107.

Kelley, C.S. (1992). "Ethical Issues in Evangelism". *The Theological Educator: A Journal of Theology and Ministry* 46: 33–40.

Kerr, D.A. (1996). "Mission and Proselytism: A Middle East Perspective". *International Bulletin of Missionary Research* 20(1): 12–16, 18–22.

Kerr, D.A. (1999). "Christian Understandings of Proselytism". *International Bulletin of Missionary Research* 23(1): 8–14.

Kimball, B.A. (1986). *Orators and Philosophers: A History of the Idea of Liberal Education.* New York: Teachers College Press.

Kimball, C. (2002). *When Religion Becomes Evil.* New York: Harper San Francisco.

King, E. (1991). *Proselytism and Evangelization: An Exploratory Study.* Washington, DC: Center for Applied Research in the Apostolate.

Kirkpatrick, J. (1994). *In Defense of Advertising: Arguments from Reason, Ethical Egoism, and Laissez-Faire Capitalism.* Westport, CT: Quorum Books.

Klein, N. (2000). *No Logo.* Toronto, ON: Alfred A. Knopf.

Kornblith, H. (ed.) (1985). *Naturalizing Epistemology.* Cambridge MA: MIT Press.

Kraft, C.H. (1991). "Receptor-Oriented Ethics in Cross-Cultural Intervention". *Transformation: An International Dialogue on Evangelical Social Ethics* 8(1): 20–25.

Kreider, A. (1999). *The Change of Conversion and the Origin of Christendom.* Harrisburg, Penn.: Trinity Press International.

Küng, H. (1977). *On Being a Christian.* Tr. Edward Quinn. London: Collins.

Küng, H. (1990). "Towards a World Ethic of World Religions". In H. Küng and J. Moltmann (eds.), *The Ethics of World Religions and Human Rights.* London: SCM Press: 102–19.

Küng, H. (1993). *Global Responsibility: In Search of a New World Ethic.* New York: Continuum International Publishing.

Küng, H. and K.J. Kuschel. (eds.) (1993). *A Global Ethic: The Declaration of the Parliament of World Religions.* New York: Continuum International.

Kuschel, K.J. (1990). "World Religions, Human Rights and the Humanum". In Hans Küng and Jurgen Moltmann (eds.), *The Ethics of World Religions and Human Rights.* London: SCM Press: 95–101.

Kusumalayam, J. (2004). "Ethics of Evangelism: Bartolomé de Las Casas". *Vidyajyoti Journal of Theological Reflection* 68(1): 43–55.

Kymlicka, W. (1989). *Liberalism, Community and Culture.* Oxford: Clarendon Press.

Lalich, J. (2004). *Bounded Choice: True Believers and Charismatic Cults.* Berkeley: University of California Press.

Lamb, C. and M.D. Bryant. (1999). *Religious Conversion: Contemporary Practices and Controversies.* London and New York: Cassell.

Lambert, T. (1996). *The Power of Influence: Intensive Influencing Skills at Work.* London: Nicholas Brealey.

Langone, M.D. (ed.) (1985). "Cults, Evangelicals, and the Ethics of Social Influence". *Special Edition of Cultic Studies Journal* 2(2): 231–403.

Langone, M.D. (1989). "Social Influence: Ethical Considerations". *Cultic Studies Journal* 6(1): 16–24.

Langone, M.D. (2000). "The Two 'Camps' of Cultic Studies: Time for Dialogue". *Cultic Studies Journal* 17: 79–100.

Latourette, K.S. (1937–45). *A History of the Expansion of Christianity.* 7 vols. New York and London: Harper.

Leiser, B.M. (1978). "The Ethics of Advertising". In R. DeGeorge and J. Pichler, (eds.), *Ethics, Free Enterprise, and Public Policy.* New York: Oxford University Press: 173–86.

Lerner, N. (1998). "Proselytism, Change of Religion, and International Human Rights". *Emory International Law Review* 12(1): 477–560.

Lerner, N. (2000). "Proselytism and its Limitations in Israel". *FIDES ET LIBERTAS: The Journal of the International Religious Liberty Association* 32–41.

Lerner, N. (2002). *Religion, Beliefs and International Human Rights.* Maryknoll, NY: Orbis Books.

Lewis, G. (1985). "Ethical evangelism, Unethical proselytizing". *Cultic Studies Journal.* 2(2): 306–07.

Lewis, N. (1988). *The Missionaries.* London: Secker and Warburg.

Lifton, R. (1961). *Thought Reform and the Psychology of Totalism: a Study of Brainwashing in China.* London: Gollancz.

Littlejohn, S.W. and D.M. Jabusch. (1987). *Persuasive Transactions.* Glenview, IL: Scott, Foresman and Co.

Loewen, J. (2000). *Educating Tiger.* Tabor College, Hillboro: Centre for M.B. Studies.

Lofland, J. (1977). *Doomsday Cult: a Study of Conversion, Proselytization, and Maintenance of Faith. Enlarged Edition.* New York: Irvington.

Lofland, J. and N. Skonovd. (1981). "Conversion Motifs". *Journal for the Scientific Study of Religion* 20(4): 373–85.

Loy, D.R. (1997). "The Religion of the Market". *Journal of the American Academy of Religion* 65(2): 275–90.

McBride. G. (1989). "Ethical Thought in Public Relations History: Seeking a Relevant Perspective". *Journal of Mass Media Ethics* 4: 5–20.

McGuire, J.E. (1985). "A Catholic Viewpoint on Christian Evangelizers". *Cultic Studies Journal* 2(2): 348–50.

McLaughlin, T.H. (1984). "Parental Rights and the Religious Upbringing of Children". *Journal of Philosophy of Religion* 18(1): 75–83.

Madden, T.F. (2005). *The New Concise History of the Crusades.* Lanham, ND: Roman and Littlefield.

Marlin, R. (2002). *Propaganda and the Ethics of Persuasion.* Peterborough, ON: Broadview Press.

Marsden, G. (2003). *Jonathan Edwards: A Life*. New Haven and London: Yale University Press.

Marshall, P. (2007). *Religious Freedom in the World*. Lanham, MD: Roman and Littlefield.

Martin, R.C. (1999). "Conversion to Islam by Invitation". In J. Witte and R. Martin (eds.), *Sharing the Book: Religious Perspectives on the Rights and Wrongs of Proselytism*. Maryknoll, NY: Orbis Books: 95–117.

Marty, M.E. (1988). "Conclusion: Proselytism in a Pluralistic World". In M. Marty and F. Greenspahn (eds.), *Pushing the Faith: Proselytism and Civility in a Pluralistic World*. New York: Crossroads: 155–63.

Marty, M.E. (1999). "Introduction: Proselytizers and Proselytizees on the Sharp Arete of Modernity". In J. Witte and R. Martin (eds.), *Sharing the Book: Religious Perspectives on the Rights and Wrongs of Proselytism*. Maryknoll, NY: Orbis Books: 1–14.

Marty, M.E. and F.E. Greenspahn (eds.) (1988). *Pushing the Faith: Proselytism and Civility in a Pluralistic World*. New York: Crossroads.

Mecklenburger, R.D. (1986). "Ethics in Proselytizing: A Jewish view". *Cultic Studies Journal*. 2(2): 351–52.

Megivern J.J. (1976). "A Phenomenology of Proselytism". *The Ecumenist: A Journal for Promoting Christian Unity* 14(5): 65–70.

Mehra, A. (1984). "ISKCON Court-Decisions – Setback for Proselytizing Rights". *Journalism Quarterly* 61(1): 109–16.

Middleton, J.R. and B.J. Walsh. (1995). *Truth Is Stranger Than it Used to Be*. Downers Grove, IL: InterVarsity Press.

Mill, J.S. (1978). *On Liberty*. Indianapolis: Hackett. (Original work published 1859)

Minnerath, R. (2000). "An Ethical/Catholic Perspective of Proselytism". *FIDES ET LIBERTAS: The Journal of the International Religious Liberty Association*: 42–51.

Montgomery, J.W. (2001). *The Repression of Evangelism in Greece: European Litigation vis-à-vis Closed Religious Establishment*. Lanham, Maryland: University Press of America.

Muldoon, J. (1999). "The Great Commission and Canon Law: The Catholic Law of Mission". In J. Witte and R. Martin (eds.), *Sharing the Book: Religious Perspectives on the Rights and Wrongs of Proselytism*. Maryknoll, NY: Orbis Books: 158–73.

Mumisa, M. (2002). "Islam and Proselytism in South Africa and Malawi". *Journal of Muslim Minority Affairs* 22(2): 275–98.

Murphy, P.E. (1998). "Ethics in Advertising: Review, Analysis, and Suggestions". *Journal of Public Policy and Marketing* 17(2): 316–19.

Nagel, T. (1986). *The View From Nowhere*. New York: Oxford University Press.

Nagel, T. (1997). *The Last Word*. New York and Oxford: Oxford University Press.

Nederman, C.J. (2000). *Worlds of Difference: European Discourses of Toleration*, c. 1000–c.1550. University Park, PA: Pennsylvania State University Press.

Neill, S. (1964). *A History of Christian Missions*. Harmondsworth, Middlesex: Penguin Books.

Nelson, R.H. (2001). *Economics as Religion: From Samuelson to Chicago and Beyond*. University Park, PA: Penn State Press.

Neuhaus, R.J. (1996). "Why We Can Get Along". *First Things* 60 (February): 27–34.

Newbigin, L. (1961). *A Faith for this One World?* London: SCM Press.

Newbigin, L. (1989). *The Gospel in a Pluralist Society*. Grand Rapids, MI: Eerdmans.

Newbigin, L. (1995). *Proper Confidence: Faith, Doubt and Certainty in Christian Discipleship*. Grand Rapids, MI: Eerdmans.

Newman, J. 1976. "The Ethics of Proselytizing". In J. King-Farlow (ed.), *The Challenge of Religion Today*. New York: Science History Pub: 6–25.

Newman, J. (1982). *Foundations of Religious Tolerance*. Toronto: University of Toronto Press.

Newman, J. (1986). *Fanatics and Hypocrites*. Buffalo, NY: Prometheus Books.

Nicastro Jr., R.V. (1994). "Mission Volga: A Case Study in the Tensions between Evangelizing and Proselytizing". *Journal of Ecumenical Studies* 31(3–4): 223–43.

Nichols, A. (1994). "Ethical Issues in Evangelism and Justice Among the Poor". *Evangelical Review of Theology* 18: 137–51.

Nichols, J.A. (1998). "Mission, Evangelism, and Proselytism in Christianity: Mainline Conceptions as Reflected in Church Documents". *Emory International Law Review* 12(1): 563–656.

Novak, D. (1995). *The Election of Israel: The Idea of the Chosen People*. Cambridge and New York: Cambridge University Press.

Novak, D. (1999). "Proselytism in Judaism". In J. Witte and R. Martin (eds.), *Sharing the Book: Religious Perspectives on the Rights and Wrongs of Proselytism*. Maryknoll, NY: Orbis Books: 17–44.

Novak, D. and T. Frymer-Kensky, et. al. (eds.) (2000). *Christianity in Jewish Terms*. Boulder, CO: Westview Press.

Noyce, G. (1979). "The Ethics of Evangelism". *The Christian Century* 96(32): 973–76.

Nussbaum, M. (2001). *Upheavals of Thought: The Intelligence of Emotions.* Cambridge University Press.

Ofshe, R. (1992). "Coercive Persuasion and Attitude Change". In E. Borgatta and M. Borgatta (eds.), *The Encyclopedia of Sociology*, Vol. 1. New York: Macmillan: 212–24.

Ofshe, R. and M. Singer. (1986). "Attacks on Peripheral versus Central Elements of Self and the Impact of Thought Reform Techniques". *Cultic Studies* 3(1): 3–24.

Oliver, R.T. (1957). *The Psychology of Persuasive Speech.* 2nd edition. New York: David McKay.

Packard, V. (1957). *The Hidden Persuaders.* New York: McKay.

Pelkmans, M. (2009). "The 'Transparency' of Proselytizing in Kyrgyzstan". *Anthropological Quarterly* 82(2): 423–46.

Perloff, R.M. (1993). *The Dynamics of Persuasion.* Hillsdale, NJ: Lawrence Erlbaum Associates.

Peterson, E.H. (1992). *Under the Unpredictable Plant: An Exploration in Vocational Holiness.* Grand Rapids, MI: Wm. B. Eerdmans.

Phillips, M.J. (1997). *Ethics and Manipulation in Advertising: Answering a Flawed Indictment.* Westport, CT: Quorom Books.

Plantinga, A. (1993). *Warrant and Proper Function.* New York and Oxford: Oxford University Press.

Plantinga, A. (2000). "A Defense of Religious Exclusivism". In P. Quinn and K. Meaker (eds.), *Philosophical Challenge of Religious Diversity.* New York: Oxford University Press: 172–92.

Polish, D.F. (1982). "Contemporary Jewish Attitudes to Mission and Conversion". In M. Cohen and H. Croner (eds.), *Christian Mission-Jewish Mission.* NewYork: Paulist Press: 147–69.

Pontifical Council for Social Communications. (1997). *Ethics in Advertising.* Vatican City: Liberia Editrice Vaticana.

Prager, D. and J. Telushkin (1983). *Why the Jews? The Reason for Anti-Semitism.* New York: Simon and Schuster.

Pratkanis, A. and E. Aronson. (1992). *Age of Propaganda: The Everyday Use and Abuse of Persuasion.* New York: W.H. Freeman and Company.

Pritchard, G.A. (1996). *Willow Creek Seeker Services: Evaluating a New Way of Doing Church.* Grand Rapids, MI: Baker.

Quine W.V. and J.S. Ullian. (1978). *Web of Belief*, 2nd edition. New York: Random House.

Rawls, J. (1971). *A Theory of Justice.* Cambridge, Mass.: Harvard University Press.

Rawls, J. (1987). "The Idea of an Overlapping Consensus". *Oxford Journal of Legal Studies* 7(1): 1–25.

Rawls, J. (1993). *Political Liberalism*. New York: Columbia University Press.

Richardson, J.T. (1988). "Proselytizing Processes of the New Religions". In M. Marty and F. Greenspahn (eds.), *Pushing the Faith: Proselytism and Civility in a Pluralistic World*. New York: Crossroads: 43–54.

Riley-Smith, J. (2008). *The Crusades, Christianity and Islam*. New York: Columbia University Press.

Riley-Smith, L. and J. (1981). *The Crusades: Idea and Reality, 1095–1274*. London: Edward Arnold.

Rivera, L.N. (1992). *A Violent Evangelism: The Political and Religious Conquest of the Americas*. Louisville, Kentucky: Westminster/John Knox Press.

Robbins, T. (1984). "Constructing Cultist 'Mind Control'". *Sociological Analysis* 45(3): 214–56.

Robbins, T. (1985). "Objectionable Aspects of 'Cults': Rhetoric and Reality". *Cultic Studies Journal* 2(2): 358–70.

Robbins, T. and D. Antony. (1982). "Deprogramming, Brainwashing: The Medicalization of Deviant Religious Groups". *Social Problems* 29: 283–97

Robeck, C.M. (1996). "Mission and the Issue of Proselytism". *International Bulletin of Missionary Research* 20(1): 2–9.

Rorty, R. 1982. *Consequences of Pragmatism*. Minneapolis: University of Minnesota Press.

Rorty, R. (1987). "Science as Solidarity". In J.S. Nelson and A. Megill and D.N. McClosky (eds.), *Rhetoric of the Human Sciences: Language and Argument in Scholarship and Public Affairs*. Madison: University of Wisconsin Press: 38–52.

Ross, W.D. (1930). *The Right and the Good*. Oxford: The Clarendon Press.

Rowland, R.C. and D.Womack. (1985). "Aristotle's View of Ethical Rhetoric". *Rhetoric Society Quarterly* 15: 13–31.

Rudin, J.A. (1984). "Current Evangelical–Jewish Relations: A Jewish View." In M.H. Tanenbaum, M.R. Wilson and A.J. Rudin (eds.), *Evangelicals and Jews in an Age of Pluralism*. Grand Rapids, MI: Baker Book House: 29–43.

Rudin, M.R. (ed.) (1996). *Cults on Campus: Continuing Challenge*. Bonita Springs, Florida: American Family Foundation.

Rusk, T. (1993). *The Power of Ethical Persuasion: Winning Through Understanding at Work and at Home*. New York: Penguin.

Sabater, J.M.H. (2000). "Constitutions and Proselytism". *FIDES ET LIB- ERTAS: The Journal of the International Religious Liberty Association*, 18–24.

Salladay, S.A. (2006). "Christian Ethics: Proselytizing or Spiritual Care". *Journal of Christian Nursing* 23(3): 37.

Sampson, P.J. (2001). *6 Modern Myths About Christianity and Western Civilization*. Downers Grove, IL: InterVarsity Press.

Sandage, C.H. and V. Fryburger. (1967). "Ethics and Truth in Advertizing". In R. Johannesen (ed.), *Ethics and Persuasion: Selected Readings*. New York: Random House: 192–204.

Sandhill, L. (1999). "How Should the Communities Movement Handle Questions of Abuse". *Cultic Studies Journal* 16(2): 193–96.

Sanneh, L. (2003). *Whose Religion is Christianity? The Gospel Beyond the West*. Grand Rapids, MI: Eerdmans.

Sawatsky, R. (1986). "In Defense of Proselytizing". In J.W. Miller (ed.), *Inter-Faith Dialogue: Four Approaches*. Waterloo: University of Waterloo Press: 75–96.

Schein, E.H. (1961). *A Socio-psychological Analysis of the 'Brainwashing' of American Civilian Prisoners by the Chinese Communists*. New York: W.W. Norton.

Scherer, J.A. and S.B. Bevans (eds.) (1992/1994). *New Directions in Mission and Evangelization: Vol. 1: Basic Statements (1974-91)*; Vol. 2: Theological Foundations. Maryknoll, N.Y.: Orbis Books.

Seiter, J.S. and R.H. Gass (eds.) (2004). *Perspectives on Persuasion, Social Influence and Compliance Gaining*. Boston, MA: Pearson Education.

Sell, A.P.F. (1990). *Aspects of Christian Integrity*. Calgary: University of Calgary Press.

Sharma, A. (2005). "Christian Proselytization: A Hindu Perspective". *Missiology: An International Review* 38(4): 425–34.

Sheffer, M.S. (1999). *God Versus Caesar: Belief, Worship, and Proselytizing under the First Amendment*. Albany, NY: State University Press of New York Press.

Sherr, M. and J. Singletary and R. Rogers. (2009) "Innovative Service or Proselytizing: Exploring When Services Delivery Becomes a Platform for Unwanted Religious Persuasion". *Social Work* 54(2): 157–65.

Shupe, A. and D.G. Bromley (eds.) (1990). *Anti-Cult Movements in Cross-Cultural Perspective*. New York and London: Garland Pub., Inc.

Sider, R.J. and H.R. Unruh. (2001). "Evangelism and Church-State Partnerships". *Journal of Church and State* 43(2): 267–95.

Singer, M.T. (with J. Lalich). (1995). *Cults in our Midst: The Hidden Menace in our Everyday Lives*. San Francisco: Jossey-Bass Pub.

Singer, M.T. and M.E. Addis. (1992). "Cults, Coercion and Contumely". *Cultic Studies Journal* 9(2): 163–89.

Smith, C. (2000). *Christian America: What Evangelicals Really Want.* Berkeley, CA: University of California Press.

Smith, C. (2003). *Moral, Believing Animals: Human Personhood and Culture.* Oxford: Oxford University Press.

Smith, D. (1996). "What Hope After Babel? Diversity and Community in Gen. 11:1–9, Exod. 1:1–14, Zeph. 3:1–13 and Acts 2:1–13". *Horizons in Biblical Theology.* 18(2): 169–91.

Smolin, D.M. (2001). "Exporting the First Amendment? Evangelism, Proselytism and the International Religious Freedom Act". *Cumberland Law Review* 30(3): 685–708.

Sorenson, R.L. (1994). "Sea Changes, Interesting Complements and Proselytizing in Psychoanalysis". *Journal of Psychology and Theology* 22: 319–21.

Spinner-Halev, J. (2000). *Surviving Diversity: Religion and Democratic Citizenship.* Baltimore and London: The Johns Hopkins University Press.

Stahnke, T. (1999). "Proselytizm and the Freedom to Change Religion in International Human Rights Law". *Brigham Young University Law Review* 1999(1): 251–350.

Stalnaker, C. (2002). "Proselytism or Evangelism?" *Evangelical Review of Theology* 26(4): 337–53.

Stevenson, T.W. (2007). *Brand Jesus: Christianity in a Consumerist Age.* New York: Seabury Books.

Stiebel, A.S. (1982). "The Marketing of Jesus: An Analysis of Propaganda Techniques Utilized by Christian Missionaries in their Attempt to Proselytize the American Jew". Thesis submitted in partial fulfillment of the requirements for Ordination. Hebrew Union College – Jewish Institute of Religion.

Stout, J. (1988). *Ethics After Babel: The Languages of Morals and Their Discourses.* Boston: Beacon Press.

Tanenbaum, M.H. and M.R. Wilson and A.J. Rudin (eds.) (1978). *Evangelicals and Jews in Conversation on Scripture, Theology, and History.* Grand Rapids, MI: Baker Book House.

Tanenbaum, M.H. and M.R. Wilson and A.J. Rudin. (eds.) (1984). *Evangelicals and Jews in an Age of Pluralism.* Grand Rapids, MI: Baker Book House.

Taylor, C. (1989). *Sources of the Self: The Taking of the Modern Identity.* Cambridge: Harvard University Press.

Taylor, R. (1992). *Metaphysics.* 4th edition. Engelwood Cliffs, NJ: Prentice Hall.

Thacker, J. (2009). "Holistic Gospel in a Developing Society: Some Biblical, Historical and Ethical Considerations". *Evangelical Review of Theology* 33(3): 213–20.

Thangaraj, M.T. (1999). "Evangelism sans Proselytism: A Possibility?" In J. Witte and R. Martin (eds.), *Sharing the Book: Religious Perspectives on the Rights and Wrongs of Proselytism.* Maryknoll, NY: Orbis Books: 335–52.

Thiessen, E.J. (1985). "Proselytizing Without Intolerance". *Studies in Religion* 14(3): 333–45.

Thiessen, E.J. (1993). *Teaching for Commitment: Liberal Education, Indoctrination and Christian Nurture.* Montreal and Kingston: McGill-Queen's University Press.

Thiessen, E.J. (2001). *In Defence of Religious Schools and Colleges.* Montreal and Kingston: McGill-Queen's University Press.

Thiessen, E.J. (2003). "Christians and Jews and Proselytizing: A Response to David Novak". *Religious Studies and Theology* 22(2): 55–63.

Tobias, M.L. and J. Lalich. (1994). *Captive Hearts; Captive Minds: Freedom and Recovery from Cults and Abusive Relationships.* Alameda, Calif.: Hunter House.

Toulmin, S. (1990). *Cosmopolis: The Hidden Agenda of Modernity.* New York: The Free Press.

Tronto, J.C. (1993). *Moral Boundaries: A Political Argument for an Ethics of Care.* New York: Routledge.

Tyner, M. (2001). "International Provisions for Proselytism: The United States". *FIDES ET LIBERTAS: The Journal of the International Religious Liberty Association:* 89–96.

Ullman, C. (1982). "Cognitive and Emotional Antecedents of Religious Conversion". *Journal of Personality and Social Psychology* 43(1): 183–92.

Uzzell, L.A. (1999). "Guidelines for American Missionaries in Russia". In J. Witte and M. Bourdeaux. (eds.), *Proselytism and Orthodoxy in Russia: the New War for Souls.* Maryknoll, NY: Orbis Books: 323–30.

Uzzell, L.A. (2004). "Don't Call it Proselytizing". *First Things* 146: 14–16.

Van der Meiden, A. (1972). "Mensen Winnen (Winning People: A Survey of the Relation between Ethics, Commercial, Political, and Religious Propaganda and Evangelism". Ph.D. thesis. Faculty of Theology, University of Utrecht.

Van der Vyver, J.D. (1998). "Religious Freedom and Proselytism: Ethical, Political and Legal Aspects". *Ecumenical Review* 50(4): 419–29.

Veenstra, C.D. and D. Vander Kooi. (1979). "Ethical Foundations for 'ReligiousPersuasion: A Biblical View". *Communication Today* 1: 43–48.

Wallace, K.R. (1967). "An Ethical Basis of Communication". In R.L. Johannesen (ed.), *Ethics and Persuasion: Selected Readings*. New York: Random House: 41–56.

Ward, S.J.A. (2004). *The Invention of Journalism Ethics: The Path to Objectivity and Beyond*. Montreal and Kingston: McGill-Queen's University Press.

Ward, S.J.A. (2010). *Global Journalism Ethics*. Montreal and Kingston: McGill-Queen's University Press.

Ward, S.J.A. and H. Wasserman. (eds.) (2010). *Media Ethics Beyond Borders: A Global Perspective*. New York: Routledge.

Weaver, R.M. (1965). *The Ethics of Rhetoric*. Chicago: Henry Regnery Co.

Weigel, G. (1999). *Witness to Hope: The Biography of Pope John Paul II*. New York: Cliff Street Books. Imprint of Harper Collins Publishers.

West, L.J. (1990). "Persuasive Techniques in Contemporary Cults: A Public Health Approach". *Cultic Studies Journal* 7(2): 126–49.

Wilson, B. (1990). *The Social Dimensions of Sectarianism: Sects and New Religious Movements in Contemporary Society*. Oxford: Clarendon Press.

Wilson, M.R. (1984). "Current Evangelical-Jewish Relations: An Evangelical View". In M. Tanenbaum, M. Wilson and A.J. Rudin (eds.), *Evangelicals and Jews in an Age of Pluralism*. Grand Rapids, MI: Baker Book House: 13–28.

Witte, J. (2000). "Human Rights and the Right to Proselytize: Inherent Contradictions?" *American Society of International Legal Proceedings* 94: 182–85.

Witte, J. (2001). "Primer on the Rights and Wrongs of Proselytism". *Cumberland Law Review* 31(3): 619–30.

Witte, J. and M. Bourdeaux. (1999). *Proselytism and Orthodoxy in Russia: The New War for Souls*. Maryknoll, N.Y: Orbis Books.

Witte, J. and R.C. Martin (eds.) (1999). *Sharing the Book: Religious Perspectives on the Rights and Wrongs of Proselytism*. Maryknoll, NY: Orbis Books.

Witte, J. and J.D. van der Vyver (eds.) (1996). *Religious Human Rights in Global Perspective: Religious Perspectives*. The Hague/Boston/London: Scholars Press.

Wojtyla, K. (1979). *The Acting Person: A Contribution to Phenomenological Anthropology*. Translated by Andrzej Potocki. Boston, MA: D. Reidel. (Original work published 1969)

Wojtyla, K (1981). *Love and Responsibility*. Translated by H.T. Willetts. New York: Farrar, Straus and Giroux, Inc. (Original work published 1960)

Wolfe, D.L. (1982). *Epistemology: The Justification of Belief.* Downers Grove, IL: InterVarsity Press.

Wood, D.K. (1999). "The Ethics of Evangelism in the Doctor-Patient Relationship". *Today's Christian Doctor* 30: 14–16.

Wuthnow, R. (1991). *Acts of Compassion.* Princeton University Press.

Young, J.L. and E.E. Griffith. (1992). "A Critical Evaluation of Coercive Persuasion as Used in the Assessment of Cults". *Behavioral Sciences and the Law* 10(1): 89–101.

Zablocki, B. (1999). "Proposing a 'Bill of Inalienable Rights' for Intentional Communities". *Cultic Studies Journal* 16(2): 185–94.

Zablocki, B. and T. Robbins. (eds.) (2001). *Misunderstanding Cults: Searching for Objectivity in a Controversial Field.* Toronto: University of Toronto Press.

Zigarreli, M. (2008). *Influencing Like Jesus: 15 Biblical Principles of Persuasion.* Nashville, Tennessee: B&H Publishing Group.

Zinkhan, G.M. 1994. "Advertising Ethics: Emerging Methods and Trends". *Journal of Advertising* 23(3): 1–4.

Author/Name Index

Stahnke, T. 253
Stalnaker, C. 9n19, 30n8, 247
Stevenson, T.W. 251
Stiebel, A.S. 87, 88, 94–5, 191, 194
Stout, J. 46
Sunday, B. 163–4
Swaggart, J. 112–13

Tanenbaum, M.H. & M.R. Wilson & A.J.
    Rudin 247
Taylor, C. 57n3, 145n9, 201n24
Taylor, R. 82n9, 167
Thacker, J. 182n29, 250
Thangaraj, M.T. 12n23, 62, 206, 207
Thiessen, E.J. 21n37, 22, 57n3, 73n14,
    74n16, 86n15, 113n14, 138n2, 168n10,
    190n10, 245, 251
Tobias, M.L. & J. Lalich 248
Toulmin, S. 56–7, 74n15, 75
Tronto, J.C. 44, 165–6
Tyner, M. 231n25

Ucko, H. 247
Ullman, C. 203n26
Uzzell, L.A. 8–9, 12n24, 25n40, 142, 210,
    223, 246, 250, 252

Van der Meiden, A. 252
Van der Vyver, J.D. 227n19, 253
Veenstra, C.D. & D. Vander Kooi 250
Vitoria, F. 102n34
Vivekananda, Swami 32n12

Wallace, K.R. 238
Ward, S.J.A. 190n10, 241
Ward, S.J.A. & H. Wasserman 241
Weaver, R.M. 143, 152, 239
Weigel, G. 44
West, L.J. 83, 139, 248, 249
Whately, R. 90
Wilberforce, W. 102
Williams, R. 62n7, 112
Wilson, B. 248
Wilson, M.R. 197n21
Witte, J. 202n25, 253
Witte, J. & M. Bourdeaux 13, 252
Witte, J. & R.C. Martin 28n1, 35, 230, 231,
    252

Witte, J. & J.D. van der Vyver 253
Wojtyla, K. 45n29
Wolfe, D.L. 75n17
Wood, D.K. 250
Wuthnow, R. 116

Young, J.L. & E.E. Griffith 87, 184,
    194n17, 248

Zablocki, B. 222n12
Zablocki, B. & T. Robbins 248
Zigarreli, M. 251
Zinkhan, G.M. 244

Subject Index

Printed in the USA
CPSIA information can be obtained
at www.ICGtesting.com
LVHW010508081223
766024LV00010B/484